IMAGES
of America

ALONG THE ADIRONDACK TRAIL

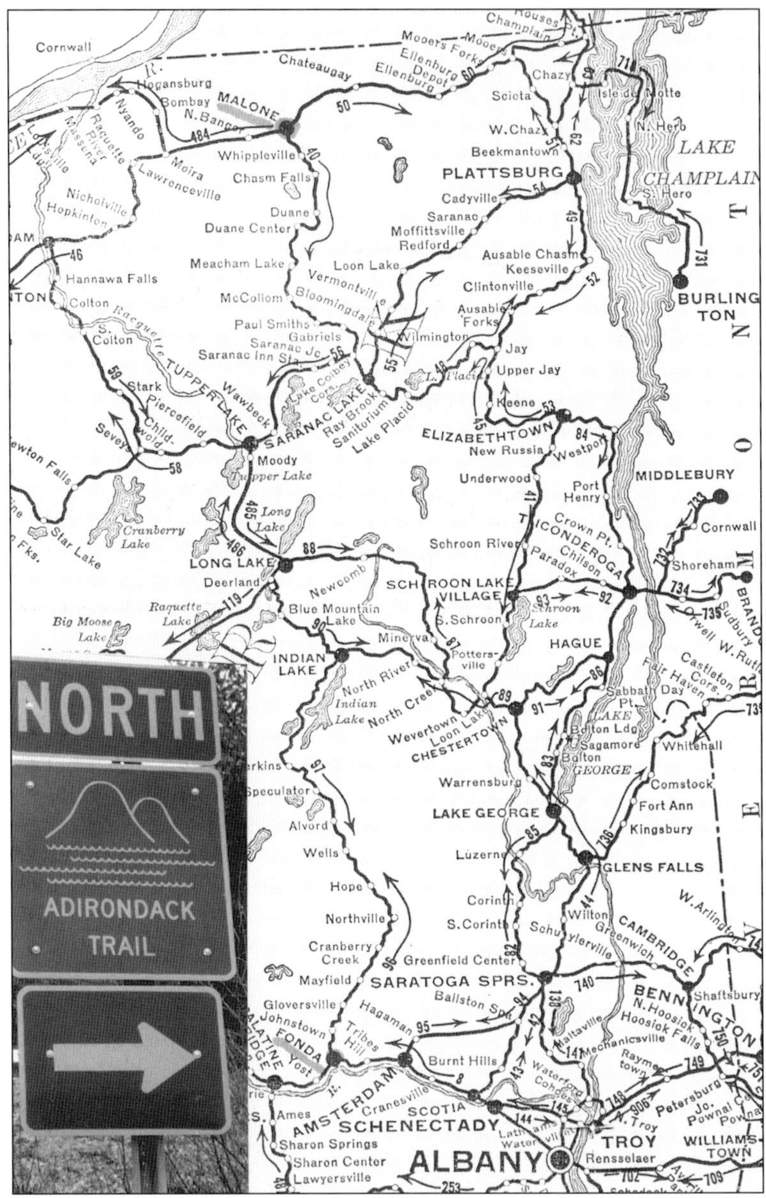

State Route 30A-30 was not always the Adirondack Trail. In its formative years, it was called the Sacandaga Trail. It was, at one time, Route 54. It did not go north to Malone; it went west at Speculator and ended in Utica. On the old touring maps, today's Route 30A from Fonda through the cities of Johnstown and Gloversville and on to Mayfield was Route 148. In the village of Mayfield, its path intersected with Route 30 from Amsterdam. When it reached Northville, it crossed the Northville Bridge over the Sacandaga River and passed through the village. A section of Route 30 between Sacandaga Park and Northville was Route 152 at that time. A 1932 map of the Adirondack Trail included several different route numbers: 30 to Wells, 8 to Speculator, 10 to Indian Lake, 28 to Blue Mountain Lake, 28N to Long Lake (where it became 10 again), 365 to Tupper Lake, and 10 to Paul Smiths and Malone. It is obvious that today's Route 30 all the way through the mountains to Malone was made up of many sections of roadway.

IMAGES
of America

ALONG THE ADIRONDACK TRAIL

Donald R. Williams

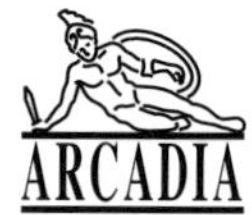

ISBN 0-7385-3648-2

First published 2004

Published by Arcadia Publishing,
Charleston SC, Chicago IL, Portsmouth NH, San Francisco CA

Printed in Great Britain

Library of Congress Catalog Card Number: 2004107303

For all general information, contact Arcadia Publishing:
Telephone 843-853-2070
Fax 843-853-0044
E-mail sales@arcadiapublishing.com
For customer service and orders:
Toll-free 1-888-313-2665

Visit us on the Internet at www.arcadiapublishing.com

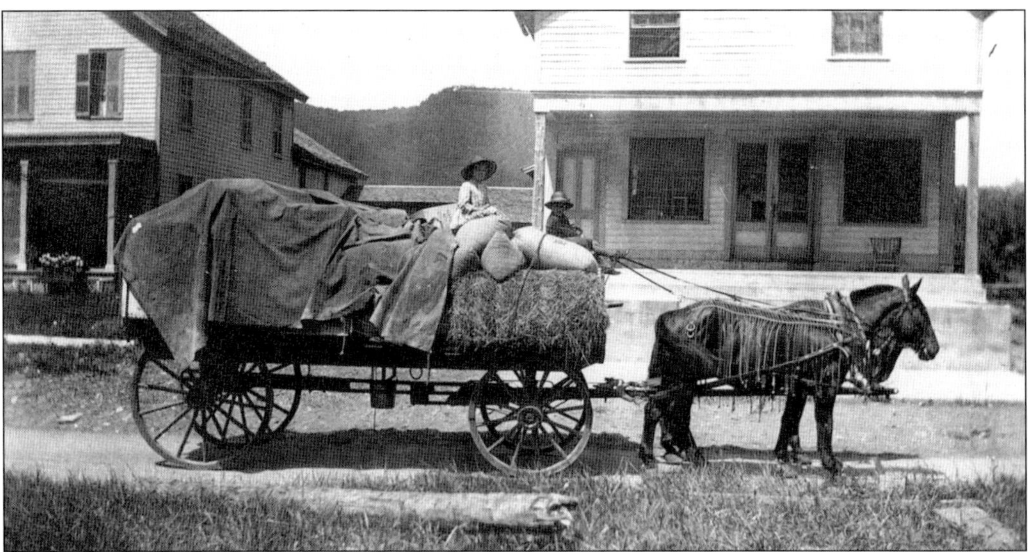

The Adirondack Trail had a varied history. It was much like a puzzle; many parts were constructed and put together to make the north–south route of today. One of the first recorded indications of the Adirondack Trail appeared on a 1780 map as Canada Island, in the Sacandaga River near Hope, a Native American trail to Canada. In 1850, a plank road was built from Fonda to Gloversville, and that road became a public highway in 1904. The road south from Malone to Tupper Lake was surveyed in the 1850s, and one from Lake Pleasant to Long Lake was authorized in 1855. The road from Northville to Lake Pleasant was constructed in 1858, and the entire route from Fonda to Speculator and west was designated Route 54, the Sacandaga Trail, in 1900. Macadam was added to the road from Gloversville to Northville in 1908 and added on to Wells in 1912. New sections, including Route 152 from Sacandaga Park to Northville, were built when the Sacandaga Valley was flooded in 1930. The new macadam road from Speculator to Indian Lake became a reality in 1955. The state legislature officially put all the routes together in 1962 and created the Adirondack Trail.

Contents

Acknowledgments		6
Introduction		7
1.	Mohawk and Johnstown	9
2.	Mayfield and Northampton	31
3.	Benson and Hope	47
4.	Wells and Lake Pleasant	53
5.	Indian Lake and Long Lake	69
6.	Tupper Lake and Santa Clara	83
7.	Brighton, Duane, and Malone	95
8.	Along the Trail	103

Acknowledgments

The collection of photographs and stories herein is part of my 50-year accumulation of Adirondackia. They add to that patchwork of Adirondack history and lore found in my other two Images of America books, *The Adirondacks: 1830–1930* and *The Adirondacks: 1931–1990*. My quest to seek out and record those many Adirondack stories is made possible only by those who willingly share the past with me. Thank you to each and every one who reads this and knows that your sharing brought this book to life.

—Donald R. Williams

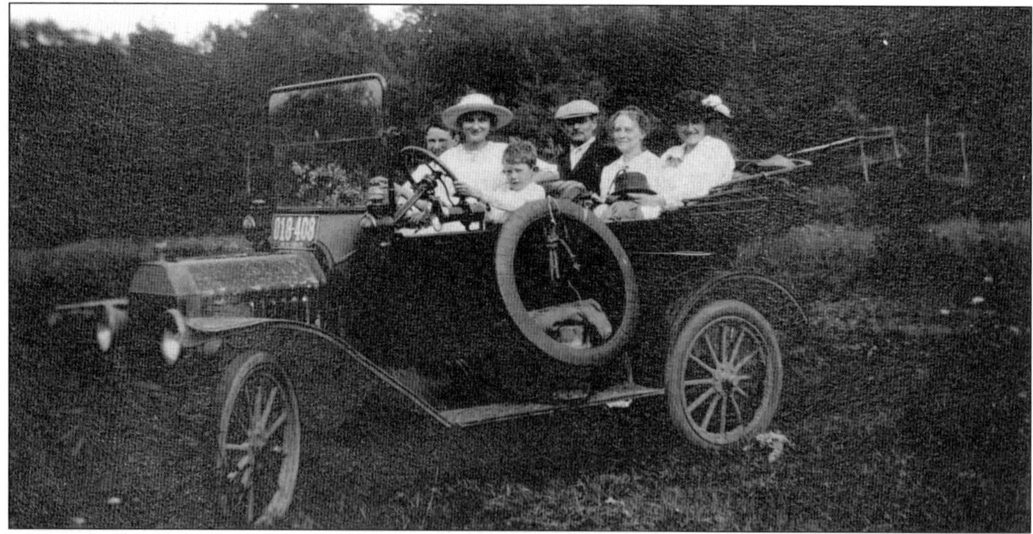

Once automobiles came on the Adirondack scene, the call for macadam roads became loud and clear. Section by section, the Adirondack Trail evolved from a dirt road to a hard-topped highway. Loading the family into the car and taking a tour along scenic byways became a national pastime. Old news clippings reported items such as "A gang of Italians were taken up to the neighborhood of Stony Creek [on Route 30] to begin work on the new macadam road at that place" in April 1910 and "An automobile party from Philadelphia passed through Northville on their way to Lake Pleasant" in June 1910. One Adirondack innkeeper lamented, "It means goodbye to our horses; I suppose we will have to put in cars now to meet the wants of our up-to-date guests." He was right.

INTRODUCTION

The Adirondack Trail, designated a New York State Scenic Byway in 1992, provides a north–south route through the heart of the Adirondack Mountain region. It begins at the Mohawk River at Fonda and ends at Malone, near the Canadian border. The New York State Scenic Advisory Board oversees the New York State Scenic Byways program, which is managed by the department of transportation's Landscape Architect Bureau.

Entering Route 30A, the Adirondack Trail, at New York State Thruway exit 28, Fonda-Fultonville, places the traveler in Caughnawaga country, original homeland of the Iroquois tribe of Mohawks. On Route 5, just west of Fonda, the Blessed Kateri Tekakwitha practiced Christianity among her tribe at the site of a Native American "castle" and today's Kateri Shrine and Mohawk-Caughnawaga Museum. The copper dome of the 1836 Greek Revival courthouse, which houses one of the best genealogical libraries in the country, can be seen in the center of Fonda Village.

Uphill from the Mohawk Valley at Fonda are the once fertile farmlands of the region's farmers. The Sammons farm, a short distance up the road, is designated by a state marker. The Sammons family typifies the Mohawk farm family who chose to join the patriots during the Revolution to protect their homes and farms. Sampson Sammons and his three sons served faithfully in the Revolution, and descendant Simeon Sammons became a colonel in the Civil War. The Sammons family cemetery is on the hill just off Route 30A on the Sammonsville Road.

At Johnstown, the first of the Route 30A cities, the Johnson Hall Historic Site with the restored 1763 baronial mansion of Sir William Johnson, is open to the public, as are other buildings constructed in the 1760s and 1770s: one of the few Colonial courthouses still in use, old Fort Johnstown, the homesite of suffragist Elizabeth Cady Stanton, and an early schoolhouse and tavern. The site of one of the last battles of the Revolution is marked with appropriate plaques, and a War of 1812 camping site borders Route 30A.

Johnstown and its twin city, Gloversville, were once known as the Glove and Leather Capital of the World. Those industries are well represented at the Fulton County Museum, as well as at glove and leather outlets in Gloversville. The city has a Colonial cemetery, and in the Kingsborough section, a New England common surrounded by early homes that are said to have included stops on the Underground Railroad. Gloversville also has an 1838 church, a World War II veterans monument, and the restored Glove Theater, flagship of the Schine movie enterprise.

Outside of Gloversville, the Adirondack Trail becomes Route 30 and enters the Adirondack foothills and Adirondack Park. It passes Riceville, Mayfield, Cranberry Creek, and Sacandaga Park—all Great Sacandaga Lake settlements. The 1790 Federalist-style Rice Homestead is open to visitors, and the old Fonda, Johnstown, and Gloversville Railroad station stands in Sacandaga Park. Much of the remaining railroad bed throughout the county is being developed into a rail trail for hikers, skaters, and bikers.

The Northville Bridge—once the terminus of the Fonda, Johnstown, and Gloversville Railroad—was a collecting site for the Adirondack logs, which were floated down the Sacandaga River during the great river drives beginning in the 1850s. Enterprising settlers to the north also made shingles, initialed them, and sent them down the river to be taken out and counted at the Northville sawmill.

Today, the entrance to the 133-mile Northville-Lake Placid Hiking Trail through the heart of the Adirondack Mountains is at the Northville Bridge. The village has the old Hotel Northville, a country store, and an antiques shop, in addition to two museums: the old Gifford's Valley Schoolhouse and the Paul Bradt Wildlife and Artifact Museum.

Above the Northville Bridge, Route 30 follows the Sacandaga River and passes a beach and a state boat-launching site and an industrial quarry before reaching the Hamilton County line.

Hamilton County, completely within the Adirondack Park, is the least populated county in the state. The settlements, with their history of tanneries and sawmills, have tourism as an economic base today, with some contribution from the longtime hunting and fishing traditions along this section of the Adirondack Trail.

The route passes the sites of numerous Adirondack hotels, one of the first health farms, the Sacandaga State Campsite, the water-measuring gauge station in use since the early 1900s to record the waters of the Great Sacandaga Lake, and the home of the Bennet brothers, who spent time in bed to avoid World War II.

Wells, on Lake Algonquin, provides electrical power at the dam and maintains a public beach. The county museum is in the old Baptist church, and the community museum is in the old Buyce Homestead. A community hall and library reflect the small-town spirit found in the Adirondack hamlets.

The Camp-of-the-Woods religious camp has been located in Speculator since 1917. The settlement, planned by Philip Rinelander Jr. as early as 1815, has been a tourist destination since the Adirondacks opened. State surveyor Verplanck Colvin made a speech promoting the preservation of the Adirondacks from the post office steps in 1865.

Lewey Lake, site of another state campsite, was home to Adirondack hermit Louis "French Louie" Seymour. For sports, Indian Lake has white water and Chimney Mountain.

Blue Mountain Lake is home to the famous Adirondack Museum. Long Lake has one of the vintage Adirondack hotels and a seaplane base. Tupper Lake, in Franklin County, once the center of the Adirondack logging industry, is the site of the future Adirondack Natural History Museum.

The Adirondack four-year college, Paul Smiths College, carries on the settlement of Paul Smiths, founded by Adirondack guide-hotel keeper Paul Smith in 1858. McColloms is known for its mountain recreation. Malone was settled by Vermont farmers who dared the dense forest to clear the lands in 1802. Old factory buildings built for power along the Salmon River in Malone are being restored and converted to modern use.

A 1950s *New York State Vacationland* guidebook described the Adirondack Trail: "Completion of the Adirondack Trail, a new scenic pathway through the heart of the Forest Preserve, makes it easy for motorists to more fully enjoy the beauty of the Adirondack Mountains. The Trail actually links sections of Route 30, 10, 3, and 86 which have been reconstructed and improved. It starts at Mayfield and extends northward 140 miles through forest wilderness. Along the Trail are the resort villages of Sacandaga Park, Northville, Hope, Wells, Speculator, Lewey Lake, Indian Lake, Blue Mountain Lake, Long Lake and Tupper Lake."

One
Mohawk and Johnstown

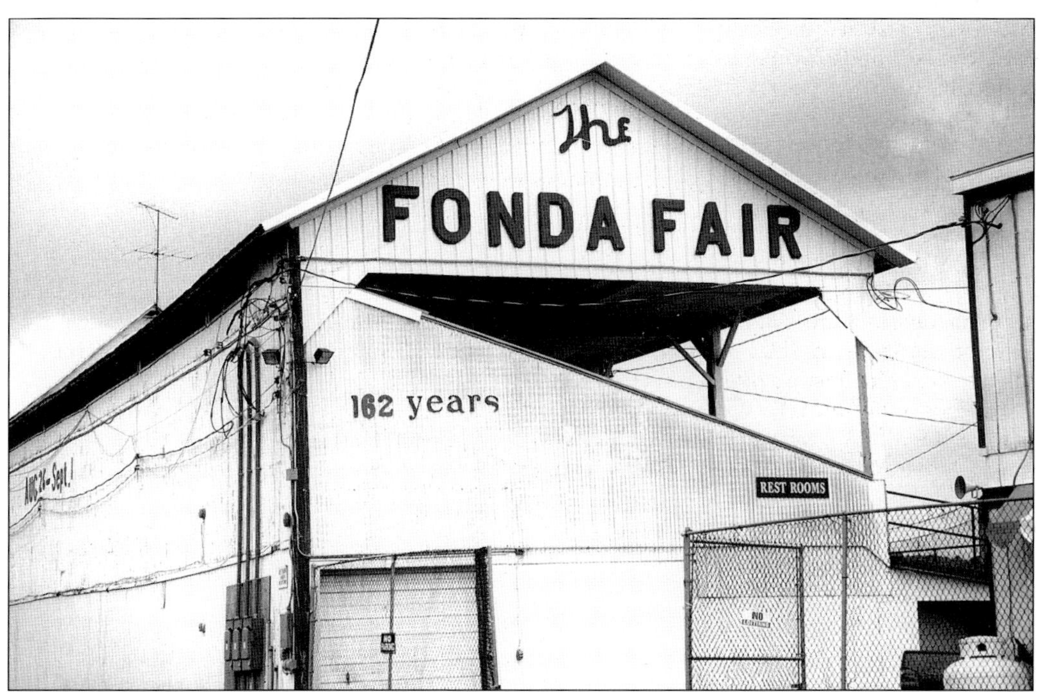

The "Fonda Fair," at the Montgomery County Fairgrounds, celebrated its 162nd year in 2003. The Fulton and Montgomery Counties Fair at Fonda continues to focus on agriculture, presenting ribbons and awards for entries in animal, plant, and craft categories. Exhibits, food, entertainment, the carnival, the midway, and the fireworks are all highlights of the annual event held at the entrance of the Adirondack Trail.

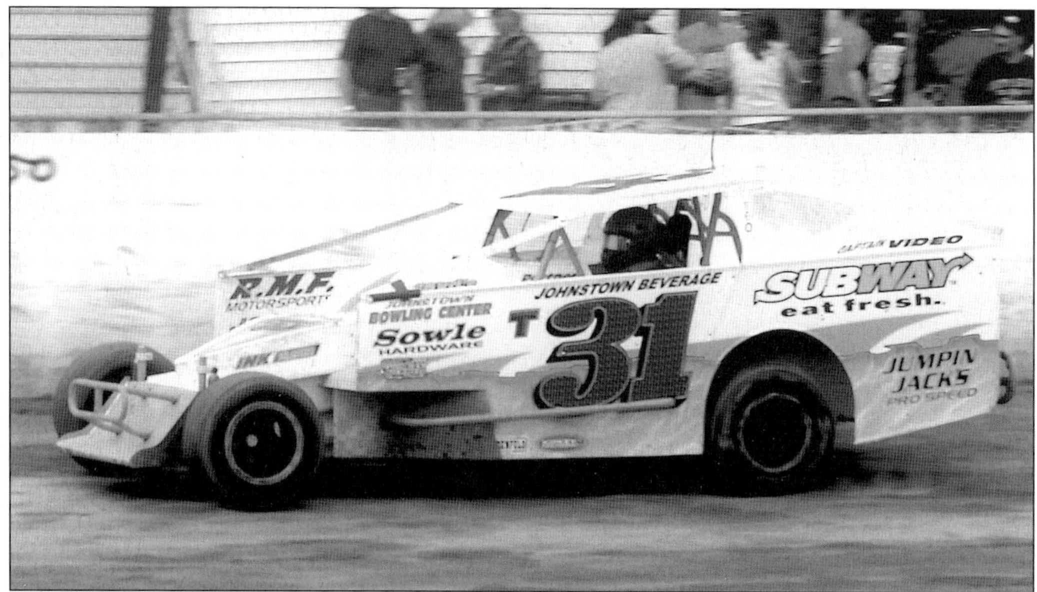

The Fonda Speedway, at the Montgomery County Fairgrounds, began a seasonal auto racing program in 1953. Today, it still draws thousands of fans from all over the country. The half-mile egg-shaped clay oval offers a regular show of modified, sportsman, and street stock racing on Saturdays from April through August. Called the "Track of Champions," it hosts some of the best drivers in the Northeast.

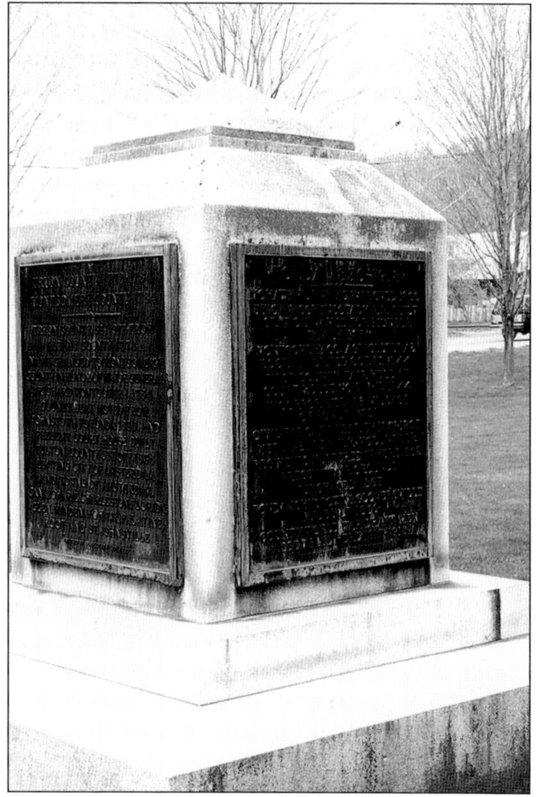

Three monuments have been erected on the grounds of the old courthouse at Fonda. This four-sided obelisk traces the history of Caughnawaga from the 1667 Mohawk village to the Tory-Indian raids of the Revolution. On its other three sides are the dates of the establishment of the counties, significant dates of Fonda history, and a short biography of county namesake Maj. Gen. Richard Montgomery. The other monuments are a memorial to the 115th and 153rd Regiments of the Civil War and a tree-planting monument to honor the delegates to the 1788 Constitution Ratification Convention.

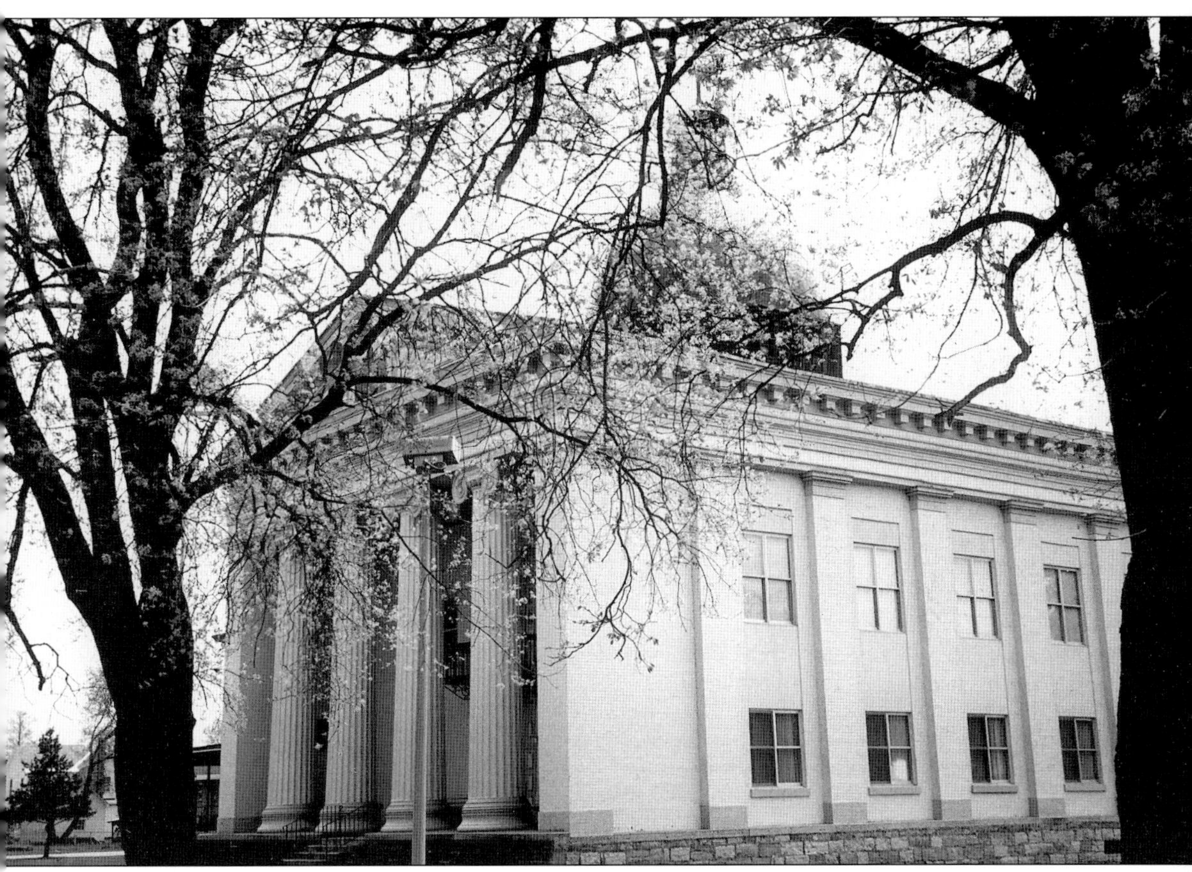

Montgomery County, with its county seat in Johnstown, was growing. The Utica and Schenectady Railroad was routed through Fonda, which, with its central location, was made the new county seat in 1836. Erected in Fonda was this copper-domed courthouse, one of the finest examples of Greek Revival architecture in the state, the current site of the Montgomery County Department of History and Archives. In 1838, Montgomery County was divided, and part of it became Fulton County, of which Johnstown became the county seat.

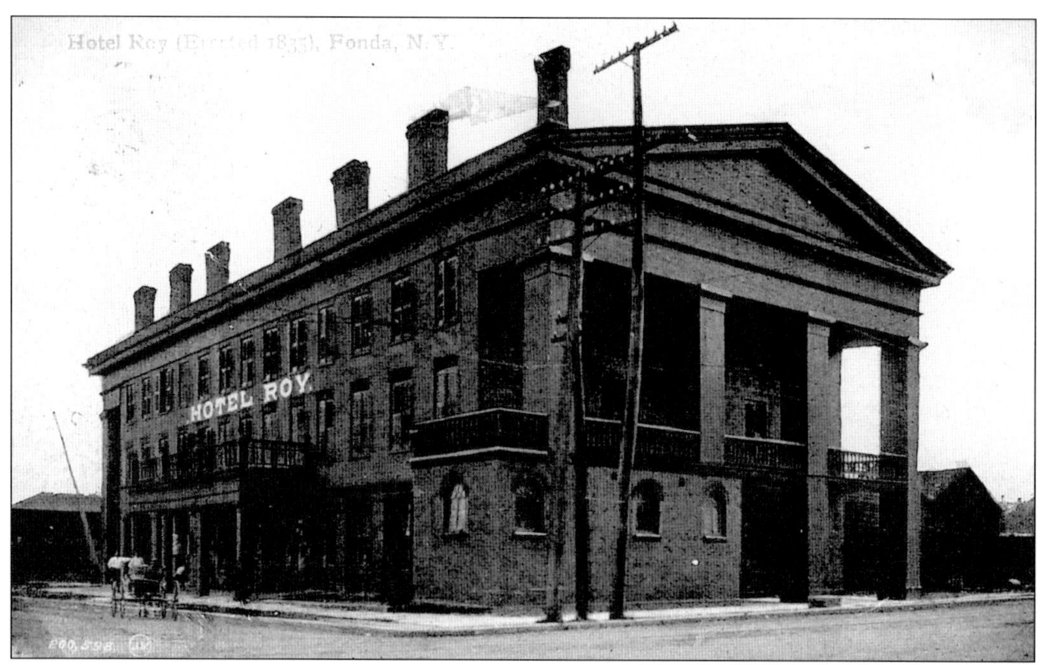

Once established as a railroad town, Fonda became well provided with hotels. By 1878, there were three hotels on Main Street. The three-story Fonda Hotel, with an imposing colonnade at each end, was the largest. It appeared in print in 1840. Later, it may have been renamed Hotel Roy, shown here, erected in 1838 and destroyed by fire in January 1909. The Johnson House had 35 guest rooms and an attached livery stable. The third hotel took its name from a local creek that the Native Americans called *Cayadutta*, or "muddy waters." Three other hotels were located on side streets.

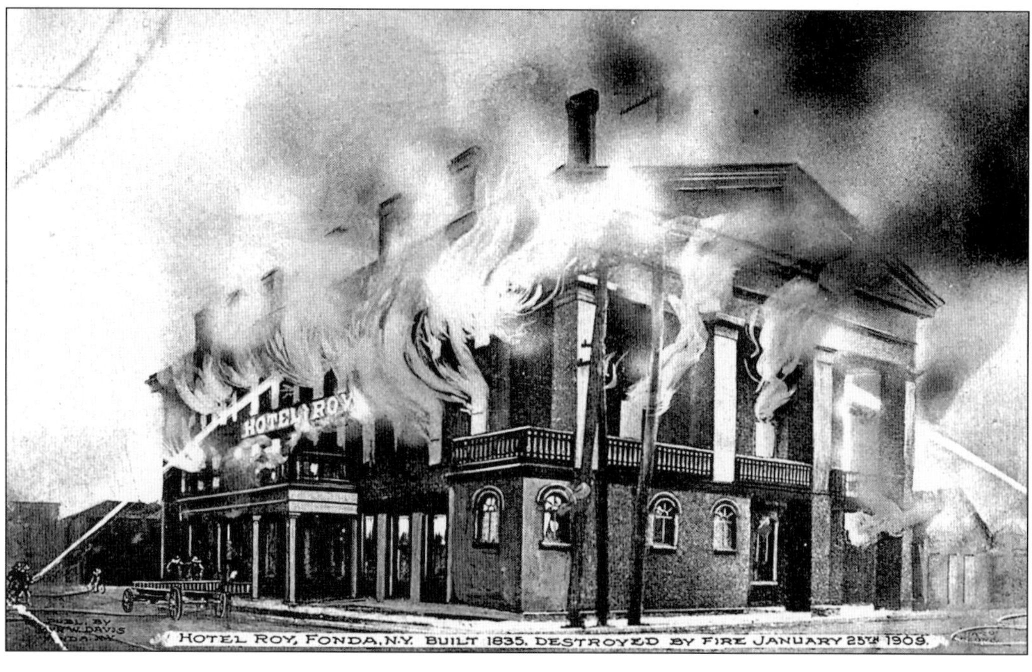

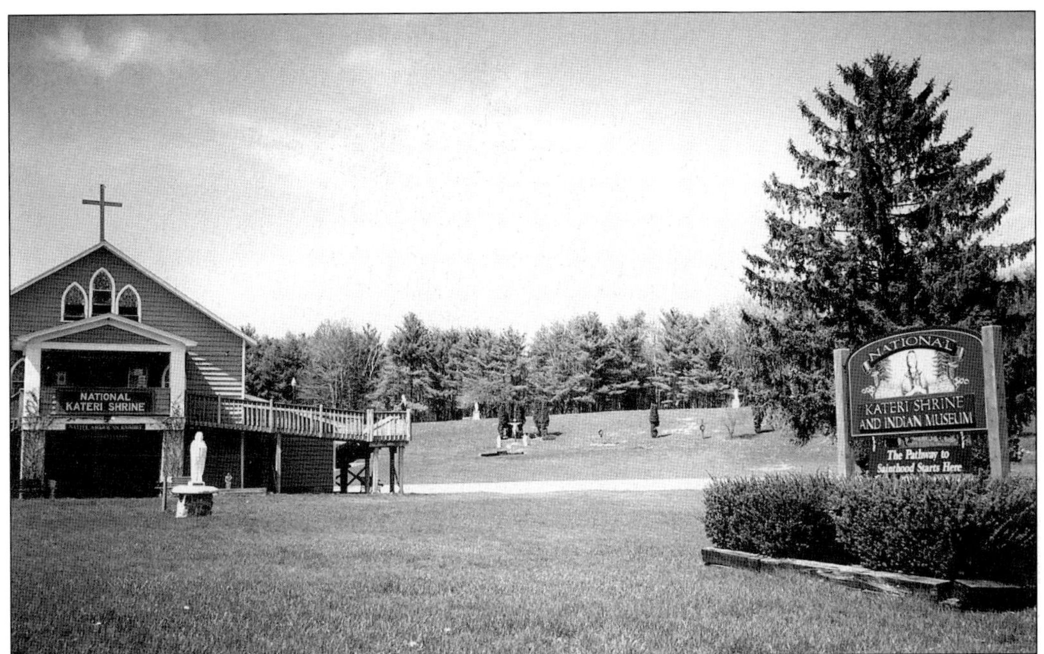

In 1980, Kateri Tekakwitha became the first Native American to be beatified by the Roman Catholic Church. The Mohawk Indian girl was baptized at Fonda in 1676 by early Jesuit missionaries. She died in 1680 at the age of 24 after leading an earthly life of love, gentleness, and kindness. Today, the Mohawk village where she spent half her life has been excavated, and her home and the site of her baptism have become the Fonda National Shrine of Blessed Kateri Tekakwitha and Museum.

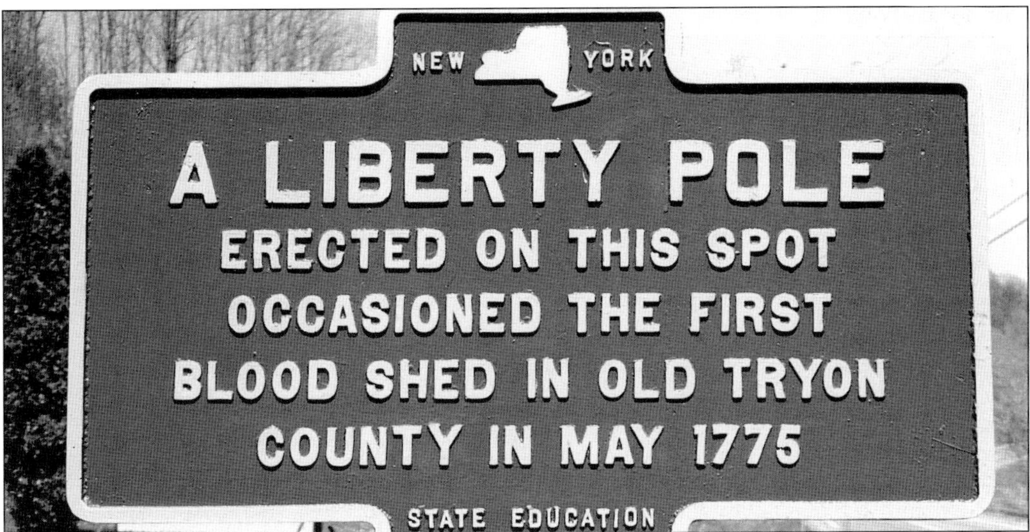

In a time of unrest, some 300 Whigs gathered at the Tekakwitha Shrine and erected a liberty pole to express their support of the Colonial policy toward England. Speaking for the loyalists and supported by a force of men with pitchforks and knives, Sir William Johnson's nephew Guy Johnson told the patriots that the power of the crown would overcome them. Jacob Sammons called Johnson a liar and a traitor. Sammons was pushed to the ground, beaten, and sent down the road. The group dispersed, and the first skirmish of the Revolution was over.

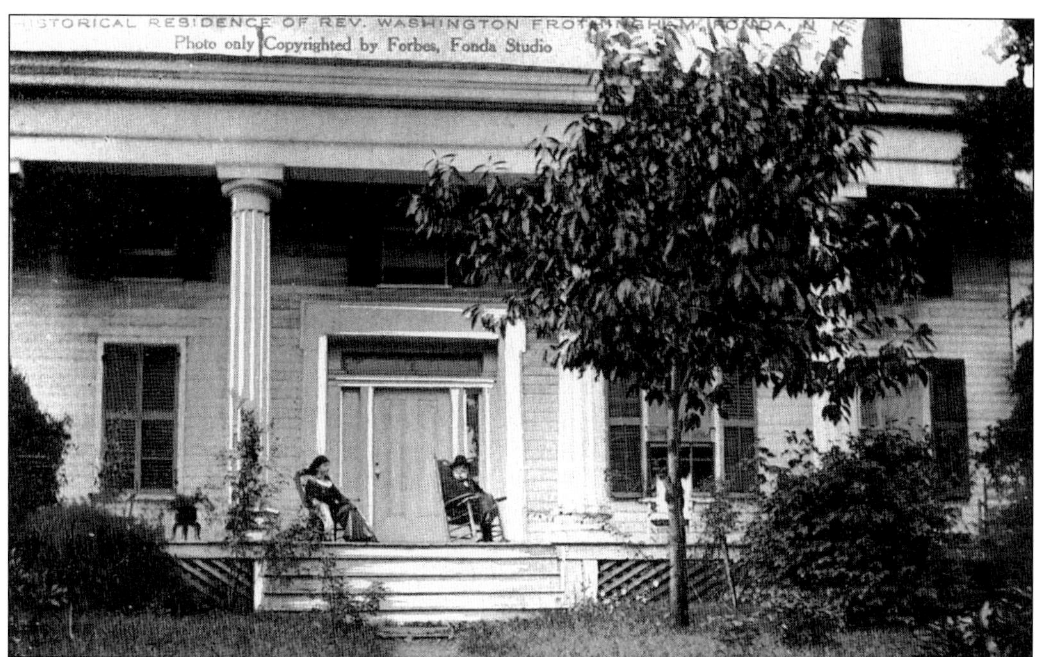

In the 1800s, Rev. Washington Frothingham was an active minister, as well as a journalist, philanthropist, and author of several books. He wrote the massive *History of Montgomery County* in 1892. He made a bequest for the establishment of the Frothingham Free Library, which is still operating on Fonda's Main Street today. His home is shown here.

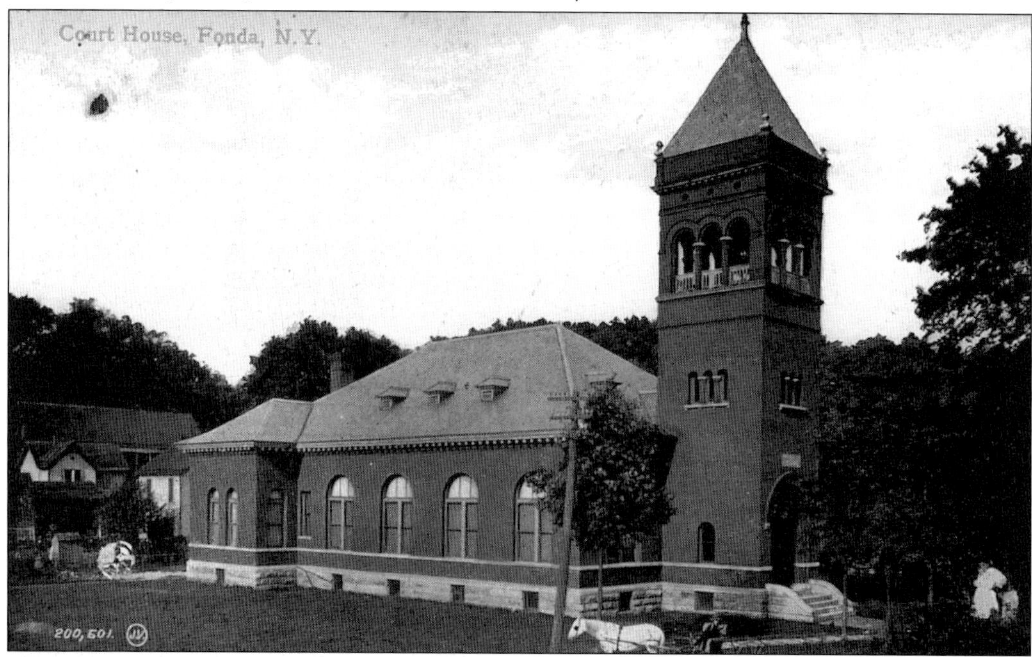

The second county courthouse, shown here, was built in 1892 at the north end of Fonda, away from the railroad, because proceedings in the old 1836 courthouse, beside the railroad tracks, were interrupted by the noise of the passing trains. A new county office building was added next-door in 1965.

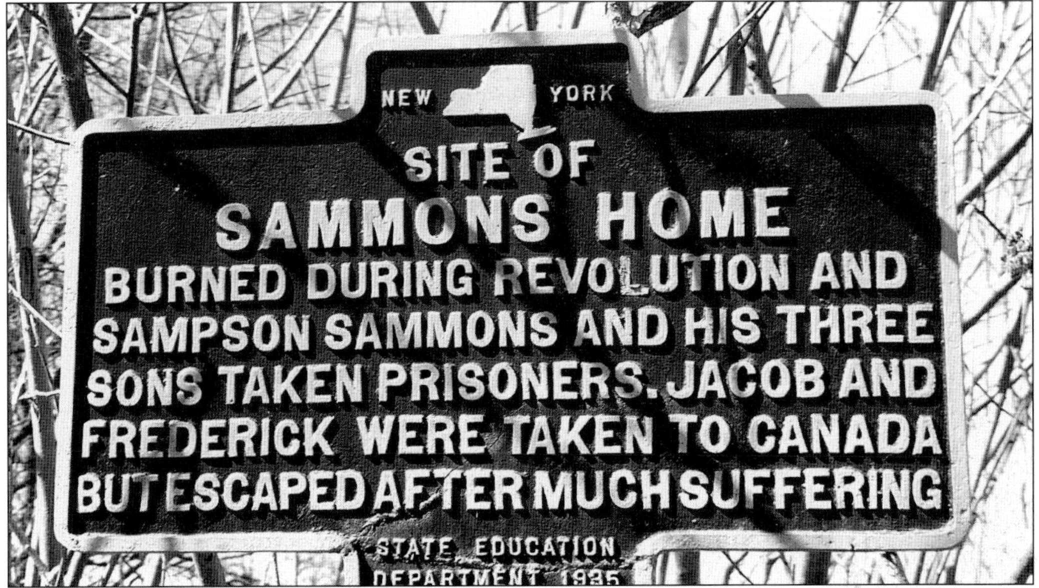

The Revolutionary War was fought and won in the Mohawk Valley. A total of 92 of Revolutionary battles were fought in the valley, where the patriots kept the British from splitting the Colonies. Sampson Sammons and his three sons were typical of the valley farmers who joined the militia and fought to defend their lands. The Sammons homesite is located between Fonda and Johnstown on the Adirondack Trail near the Sammonsville Road intersection.

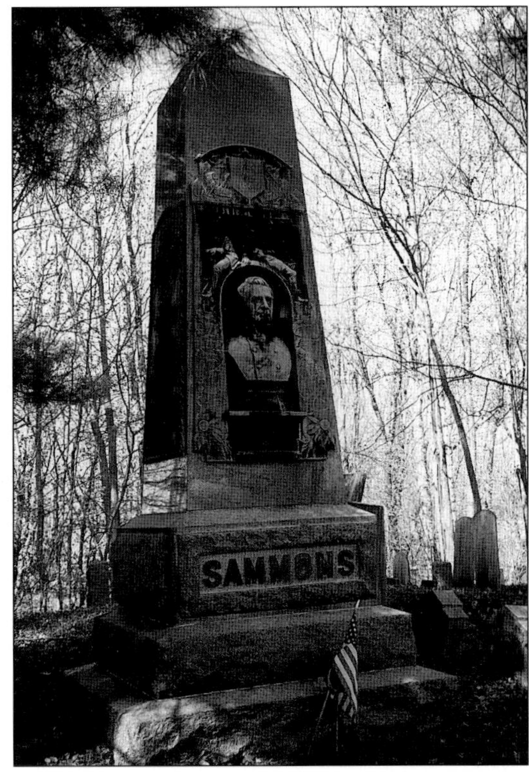

Members of the Sammons family of Mohawk served their country in the Revolutionary and Civil Wars. Sampson Sammons and his three sons, Frederick, Thomas, and Jacob, joined with the militia to protect their homes and farms in the Mohawk Valley, successfully holding off the British. Simeon Sammons served as a colonel in the Civil War, leading the 115th New York Regiment in several battles in the South. The Sammons Graveyard can be found on the road to Sammonsville, just off the Adirondack Trail between Fonda and Johnstown.

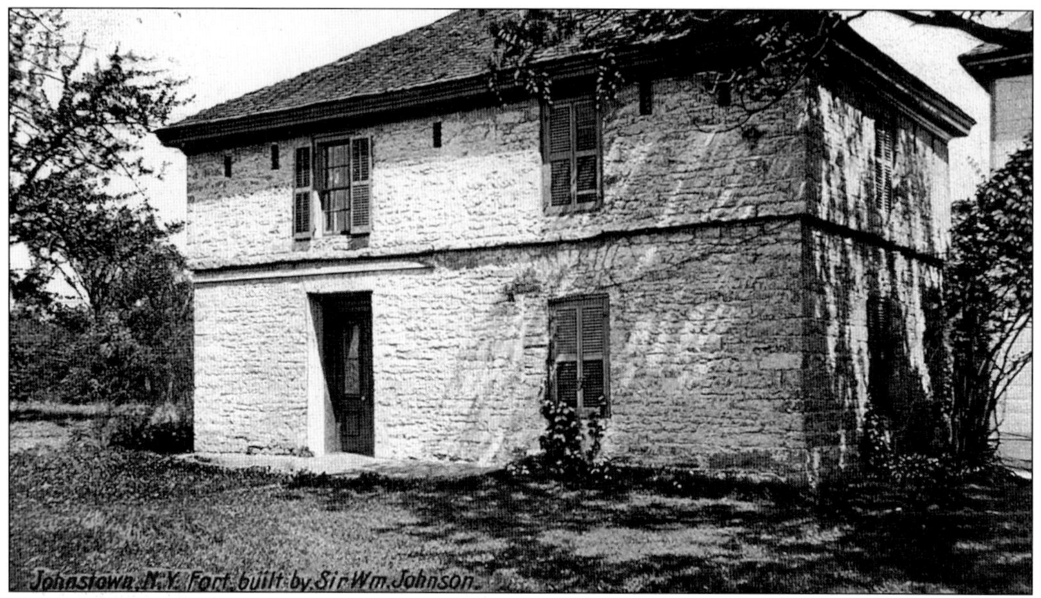
Johnstown, N.Y. Fort built by Sir Wm. Johnson.

This blockhouse, built by Sir William Johnson at his 1763 baronial mansion at Johnstown, is still standing today, along with a second one that was rebuilt. Johnson Hall, a state historic site open to the public, has been the subject of intensive study and restoration since the state purchased it in 1906. An excavation project in 1958 uncovered the remains of a blacksmith shop, a Native American store, and other buildings once part of the estate. New studies will lead to a special exhibit on slavery, which was part of life at Johnson Hall.

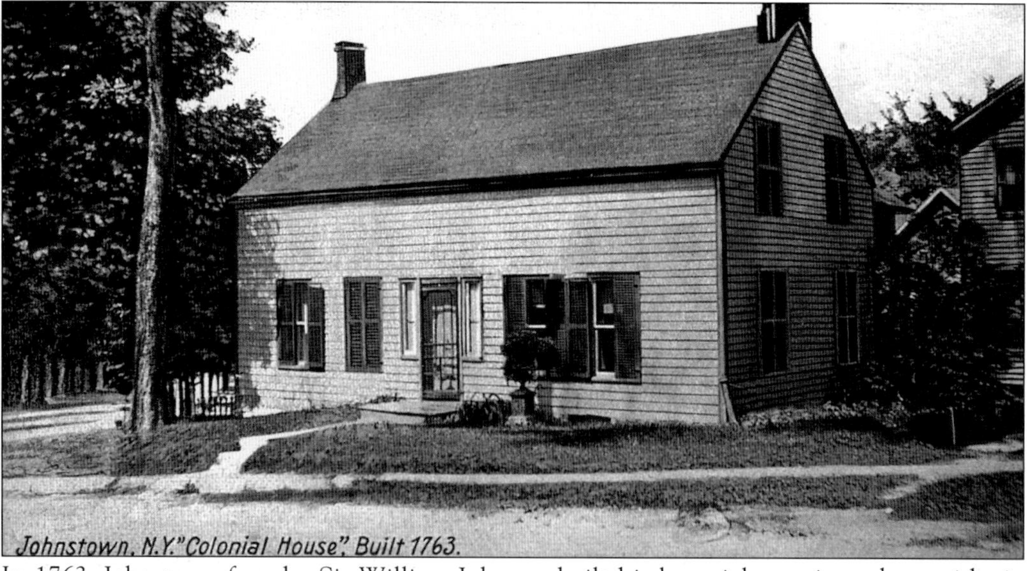
Johnstown, N.Y. "Colonial House", Built 1763.

In 1763, Johnstown founder Sir William Johnson built his baronial mansion, along with six other homes for people whom he brought in to create a community. One of these homes, the oldest in Johnstown still standing, is the Drumm House. It was built for the schoolmaster, Edward Wall, who came from Ireland to teach the Johnson children and others in the first nonsectarian free school in the state. It was later owned by Judge Daniel Cady, Elizabeth Cady Stanton's father. The Drumm family acquired it after Cady's death, and the Kilmer family took title in 1914. In 1980, the Johnstown Historical Society took title and restored it.

The 1772 Johnstown Courthouse is the oldest existing courthouse in New York State and one of the oldest in the nation still being used as for its original purpose today. It served Tryon County before the Revolution and, today, serves as the Fulton County Courthouse. Sir John Johnson, Aaron Burr, Judge Daniel Cady, and Walter Butler, among other notables, have appeared at trials in the historic courthouse.

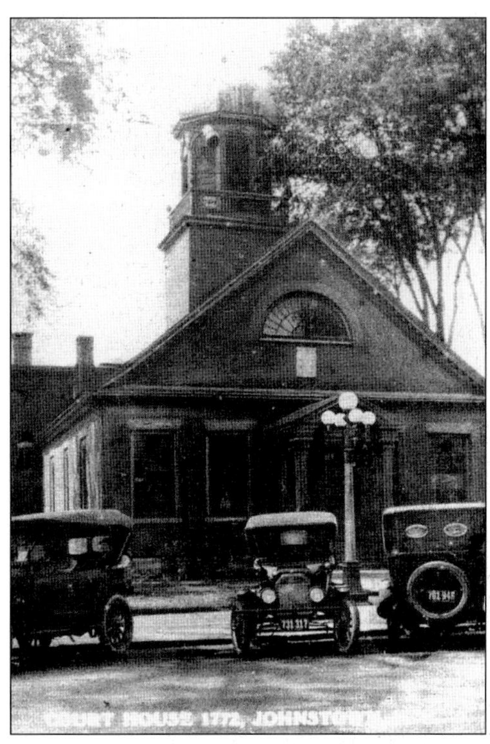

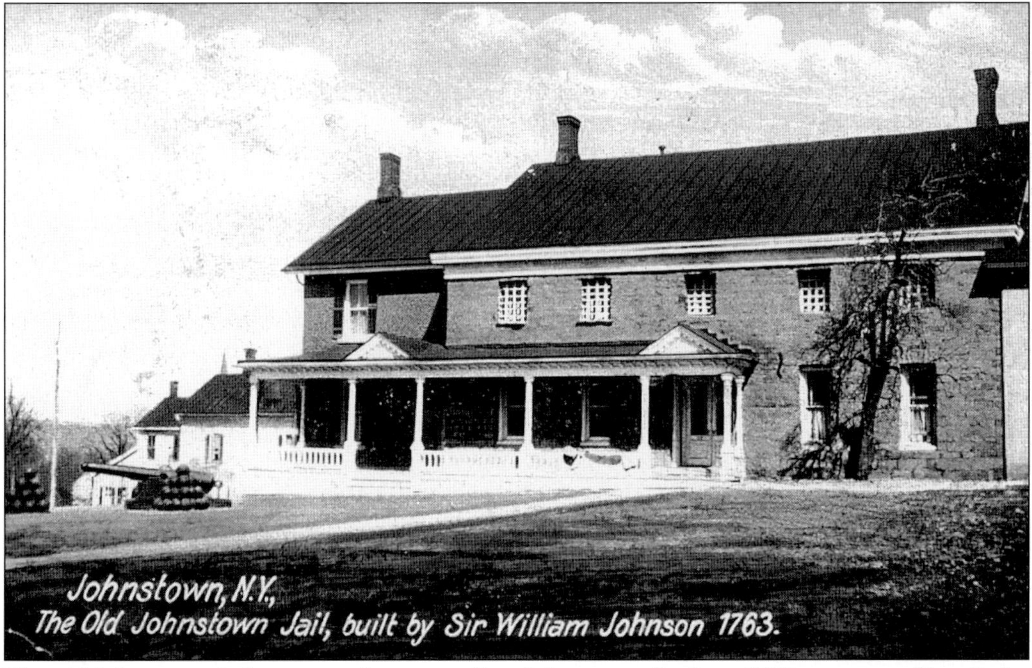

The old Johnstown Jail was once known as Fort Johnstown. Built in 1772, it was used by all the state west of Schenectady County. It became a civil and military prison during the Revolution and was guarded by two blockhouses. Gen. George Washington inspected it in 1783. In 1900, the Johnstown Historical Society placed a cannon and cannonballs on the site in memory of the patriots who fought in the Battle of Johnstown. Today, the building houses government offices.

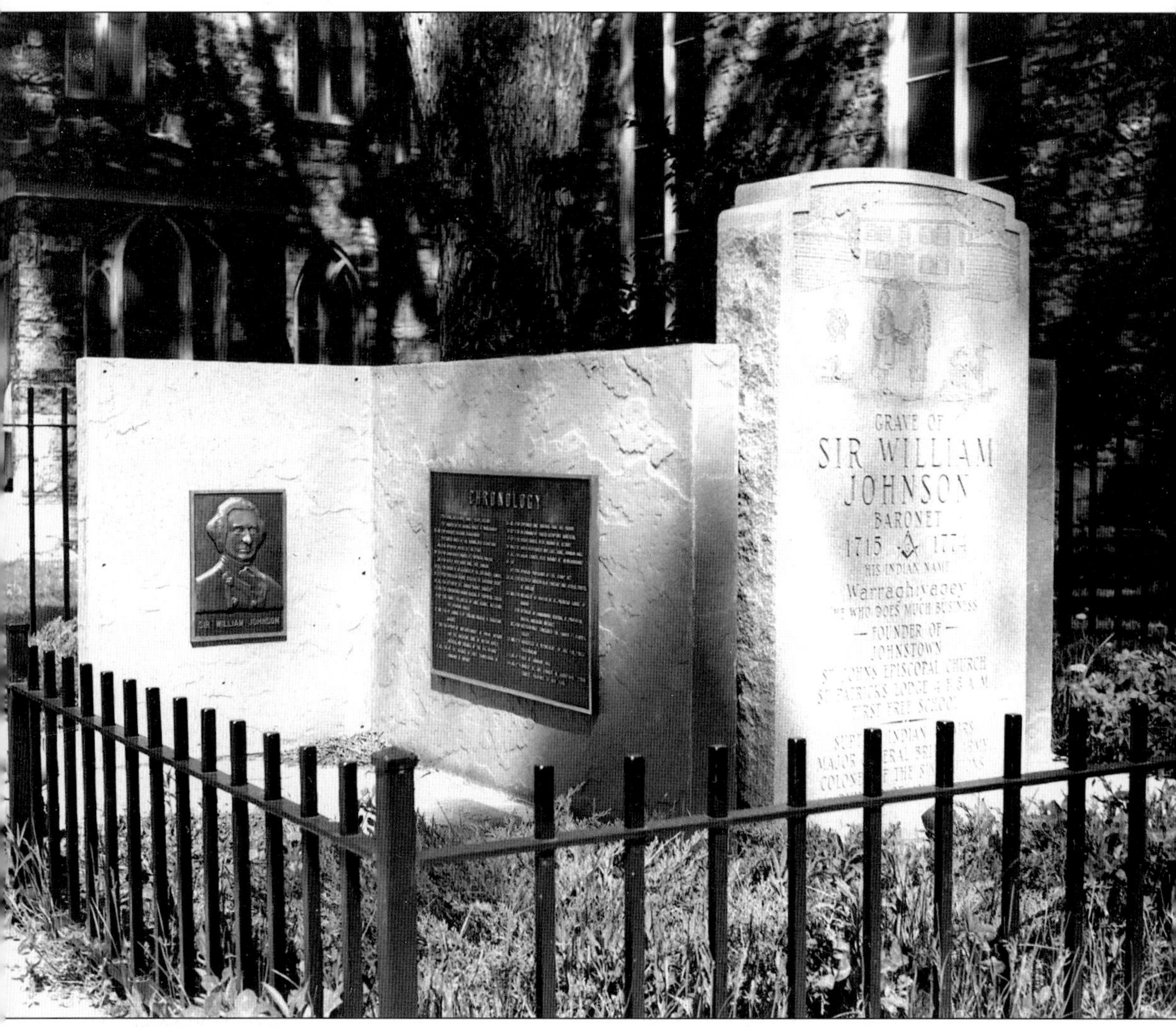

Sir William Johnson's grave can be found in downtown Johnstown. Johnson served as superintendent of Indian affairs for the American colony from 1756 until he passed away in 1774. He was probably the most influential American of his day when it came to Native American affairs, trade, and settlements. He came from Ireland to manage his uncle's estate, and when he passed away, he was the largest landholder in the state. He became a baronet because of his success at the 1755 Battle of Lake George. Johnson built his mansion in the forest at Johnstown in 1763 and laid out the city of Johnstown. Several of his buildings still stand today, including the Colonial Courthouse and the Drumm House. He founded Queens College, was a trustee of Columbia College, and served on the Governor's Council. Able to live as a Native American, he knew the native peoples well and, therefore, could bridge the gap between them and the settlers. His long relationship with Iroquois maiden Molly Brant resulted in eight children and great influence with the New York tribes. Johnson died before the outbreak of the Revolution and, thus, did not have to choose sides. His family stayed loyal to the Crown and eventually lost all that he had spent his lifetime building.

The site of one of the last battles of the American Revolution, on October 25, 1781, is located on the road behind Johnson Hall in Johnstown. Gen. Charles Cornwallis and the British had already surrendered at Yorktown, but news traveled slowly in those days. American Col. Marinus Willert was on his way to defeat a battalion of Royal Greens and Major Butler Rangers near Johnstown. The Johnstown Battlefield Monument, erected by the Daughters of the American Revolution, in the distance, contains a bronze tablet with commentary on the battle, which is also told in *The Saga of Nicholas Stoner,* by Donald R. Williams.

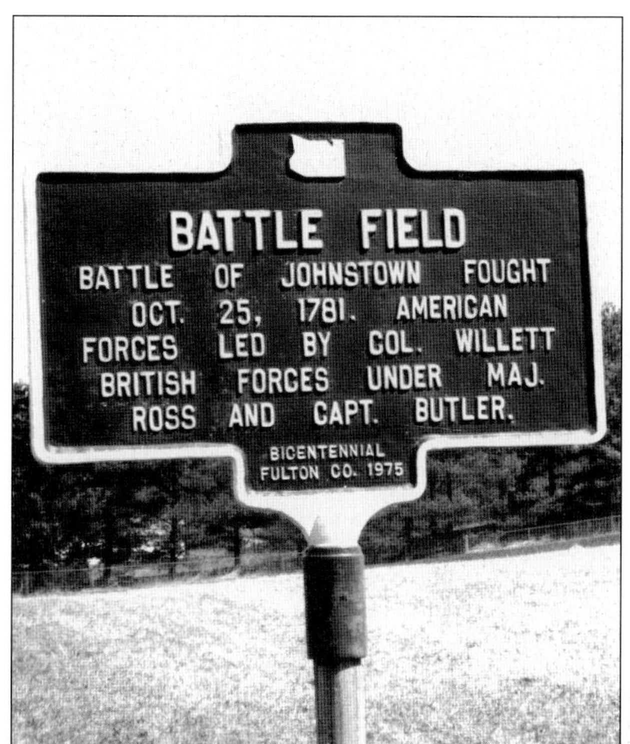

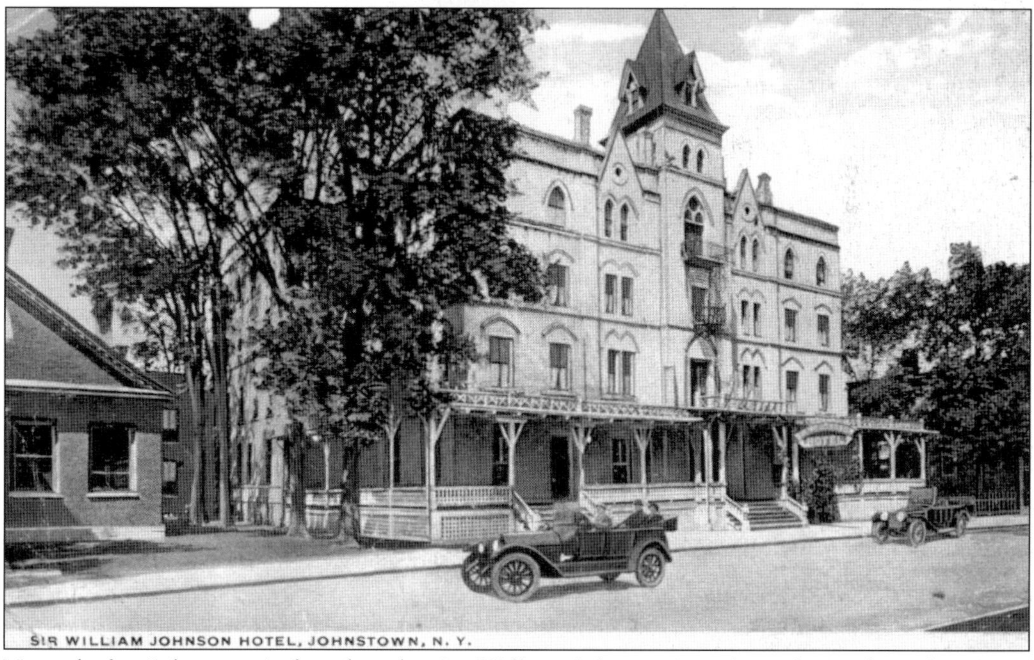

Named after Johnstown's founder, the Sir William Johnson Hotel was located on the site of today's county office building adjacent to the Colonial courthouse. It was one of nine hotels serving businesspeople and travelers in Johnstown in the early 1900s. A busy town, Johnstown was the largest and only prominent place west of Albany when it was the county seat for Tryon County and, later, for Montgomery County.

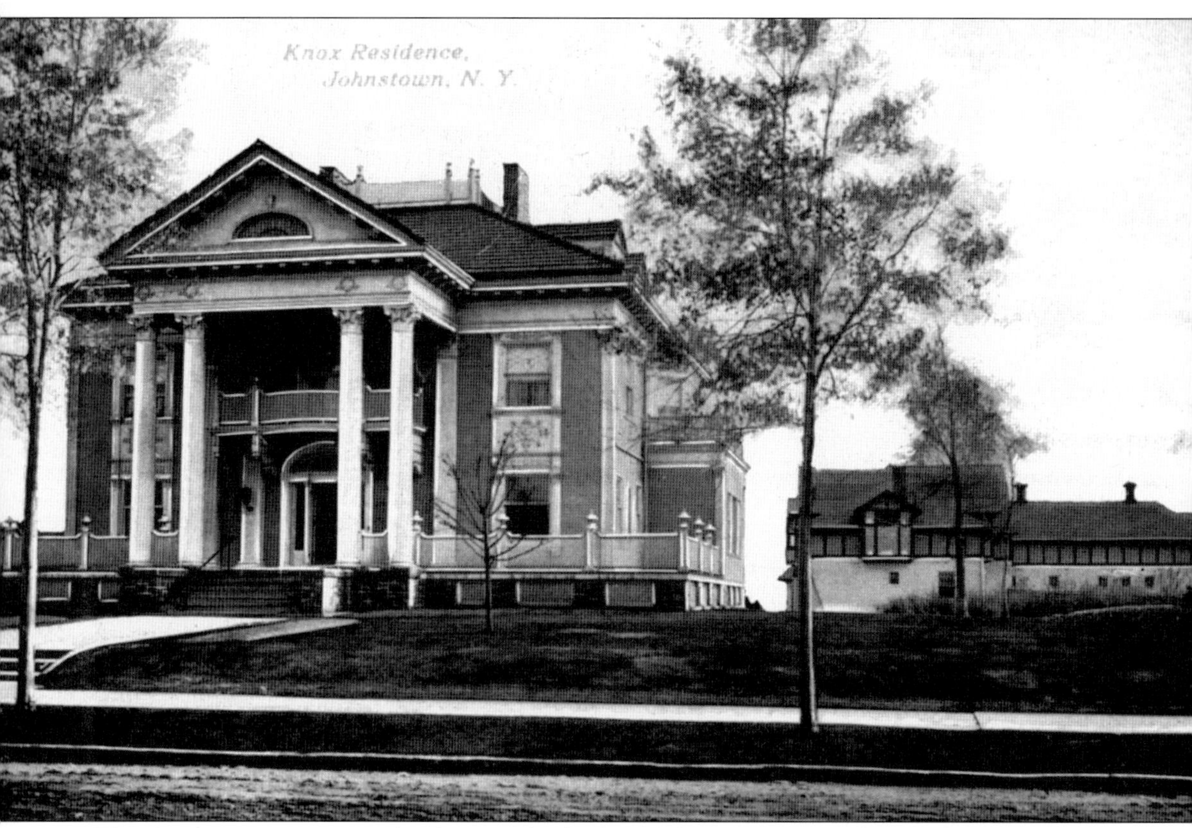

The Knox Mansion was the home of Charles and Rose Knox, who made their fortune manufacturing and marketing Knox gelatin. Built in 1898, the Johnstown home on Second Avenue is now a private bed-and-breakfast establishment that houses a museum of Knox memorabilia. The Knox family made several donations to the community, including the YMCA pool and the Knox Athletic Field. Charles Knox pioneered the use of a blimp to advertise his product in the sky as early as 1905. When he died in 1908, Rose Knox took over the business and ran it successfully for more than 30 years. One of America's most successful women, she was the subject of a December 6, 1937, *Life* magazine article. She authored a number of recipe books, using gelatin in the recipes, and sent out more than two million copies. The Johnstown Knox gelatin plant closed after it was sold and merged with larger companies.

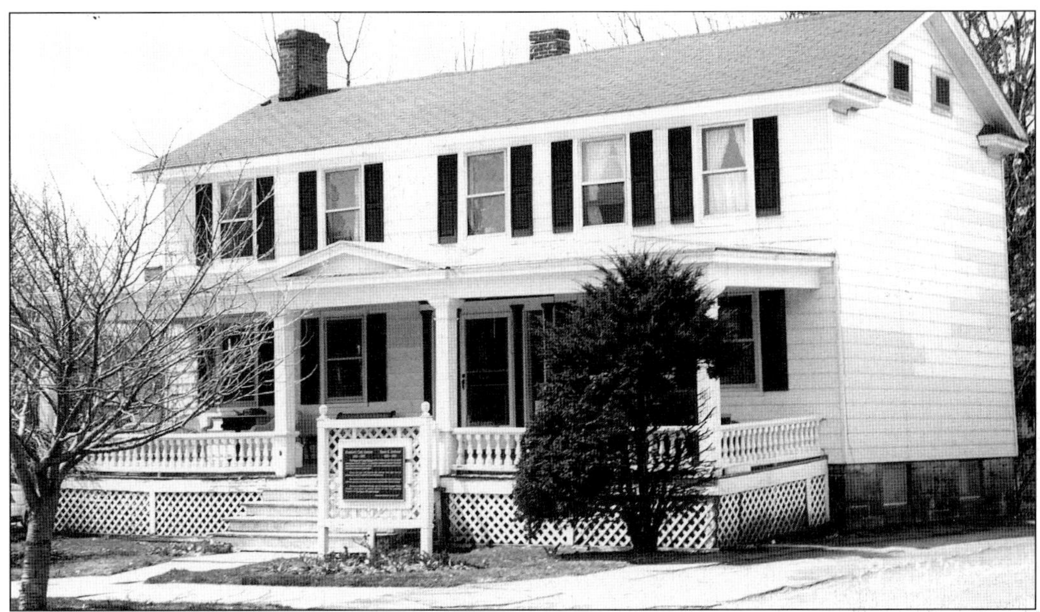

Woman's suffragette Elizabeth Cady Stanton was born in Johnstown in 1815, the daughter of Judge Daniel Cady and Margaret Livingston. As a young child, she listened to the women's problems of unjust laws in her father's law office. To get rid of the negative laws against women, she took her scissors and cut all of the bad laws out of her father's law books. When her brother died, she decided to do what he would have done: she drove horses, learned Greek, studied law, and tried to get into Union College. She originated the American women suffrage movement and, along with Susan B. Anthony, worked on its writings at Mrs. Henry's Boarding House, shown here, on South William Street in Johnstown. The plaque marks her birth site: the corner of Main and Market Streets.

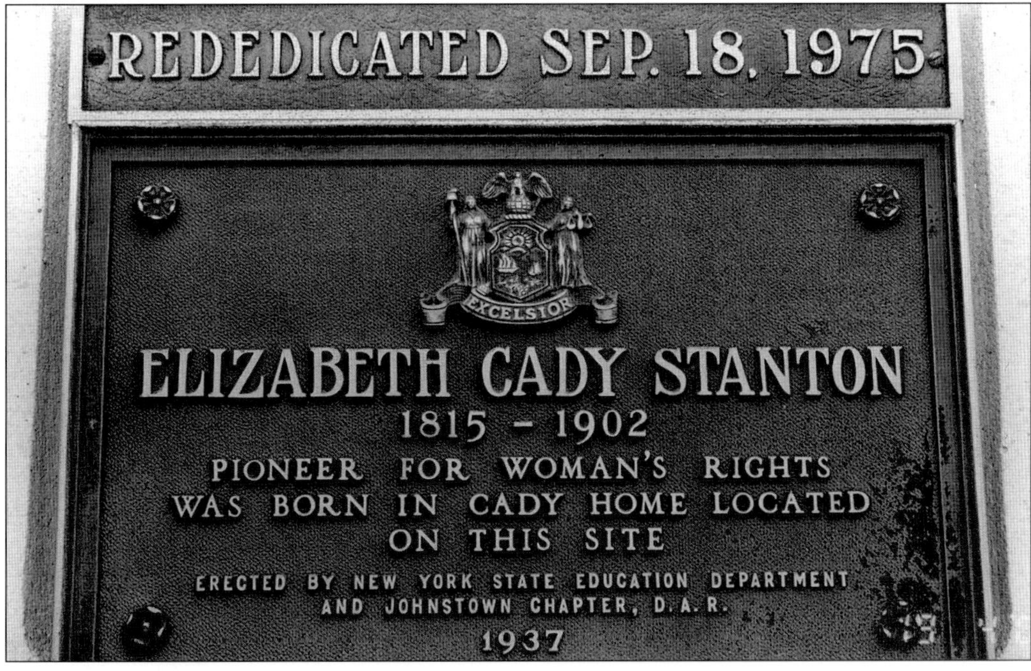

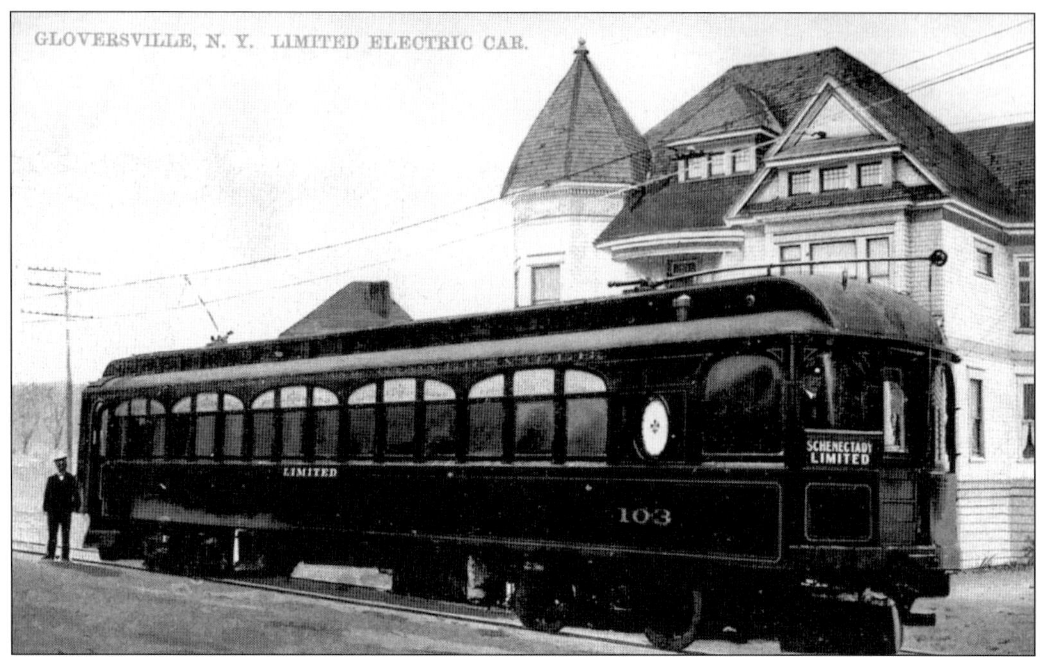

Beginning in 1905, the Fonda, Johnstown, and Gloversville Electric Railway Company provided limited service to Schenectady, making the 33-mile run in less than an hour and a half. The train averaged 45 miles per hour and stopped only in the cities. For safety and high speeds of up to 85 miles per hour, the floors of the cars were made entirely of steel. Four General Electric motors propelled the luxury mahogany coaches, with their green plush seats and smoking compartments.

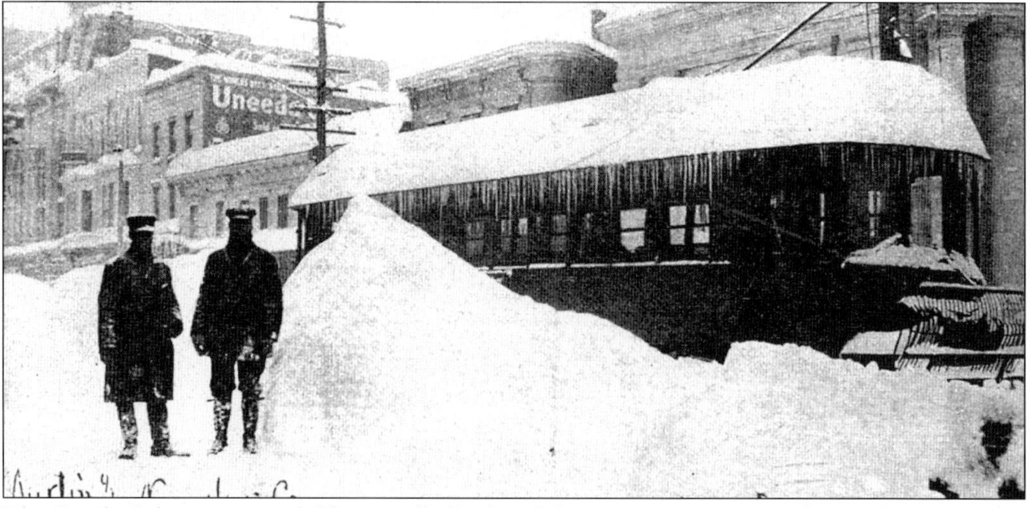

The Fonda, Johnstown, and Gloversville Railroad Company was organized in 1867 to connect with the New York Central Railroad at Fonda. By 1870, the railroad on the southern end of the Adirondack Trail was in business from Fonda to Gloversville. Within five years, another company was formed to build a spur to Northville. The Fonda, Johnstown, and Gloversville took over the Gloversville-Northville Railroad in 1881. Broadalbin was added to the line in 1895. The car from the Electric Division, shown here, appears to be pushing through a severe snowstorm. Some of the railroad line remained in operation until 1984.

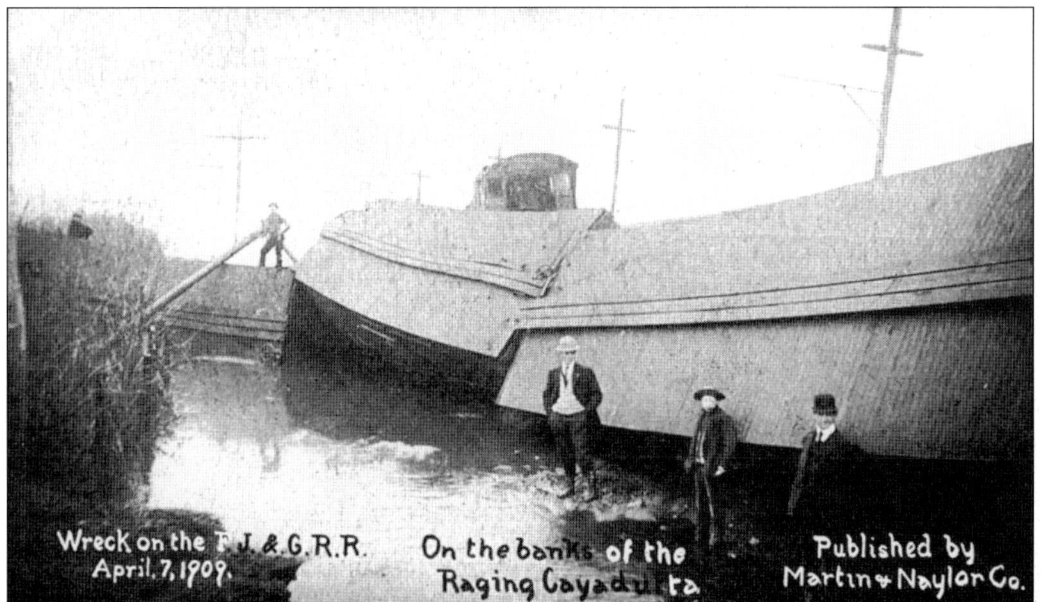

The Fonda, Johnstown, and Gloversville Railroad trains that traveled along the Adirondack Trail from Fonda to Northville met with a few wrecks over the years. In April 1907, conductor Shields and motorman Bowdish of Car No. 79 waited for a baggage car at Fonda. They got the all-clear to head for Johnstown. Unfortunately, Car No. 76 was on its way to Fonda, and No. 79 met No. 76 head-on at Cayadutta Park. Car No. 76 motorman Abe Nellis was killed in the crash.

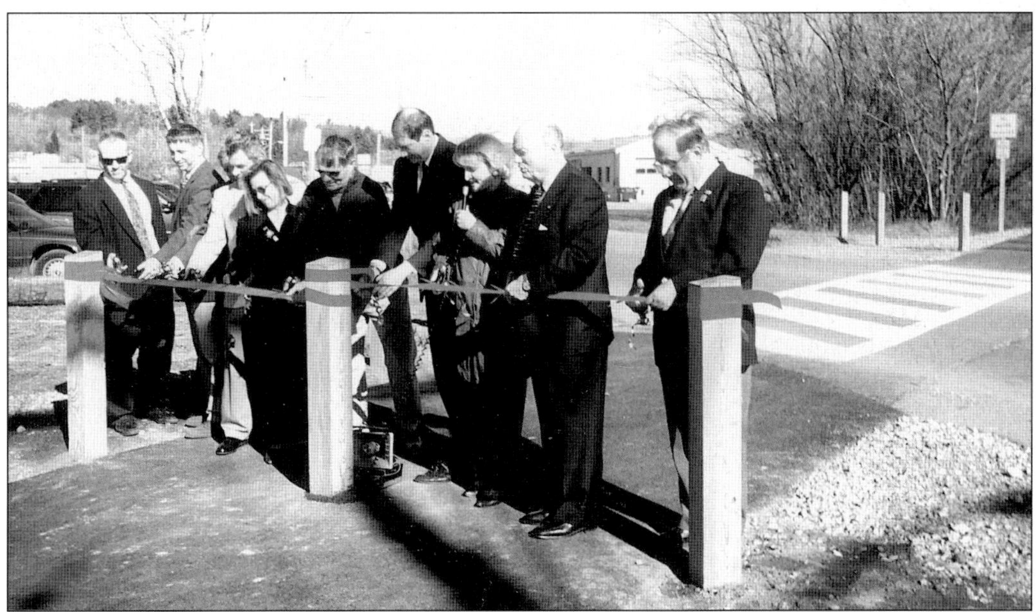
The former Fonda, Johnstown, and Gloversville Railroad tracks have been removed, and a macadam rail trail is being developed through the twin cities of Gloversville and Johnstown, with branch lines to Broadalbin and Fonda. In the fall of 1998, several dignitaries and rail trail promoters gathered to cut the ribbon between the cities and officially open the trail. Pavilions have been constructed along the way for the comfort of the walkers and bikers who use the trail.

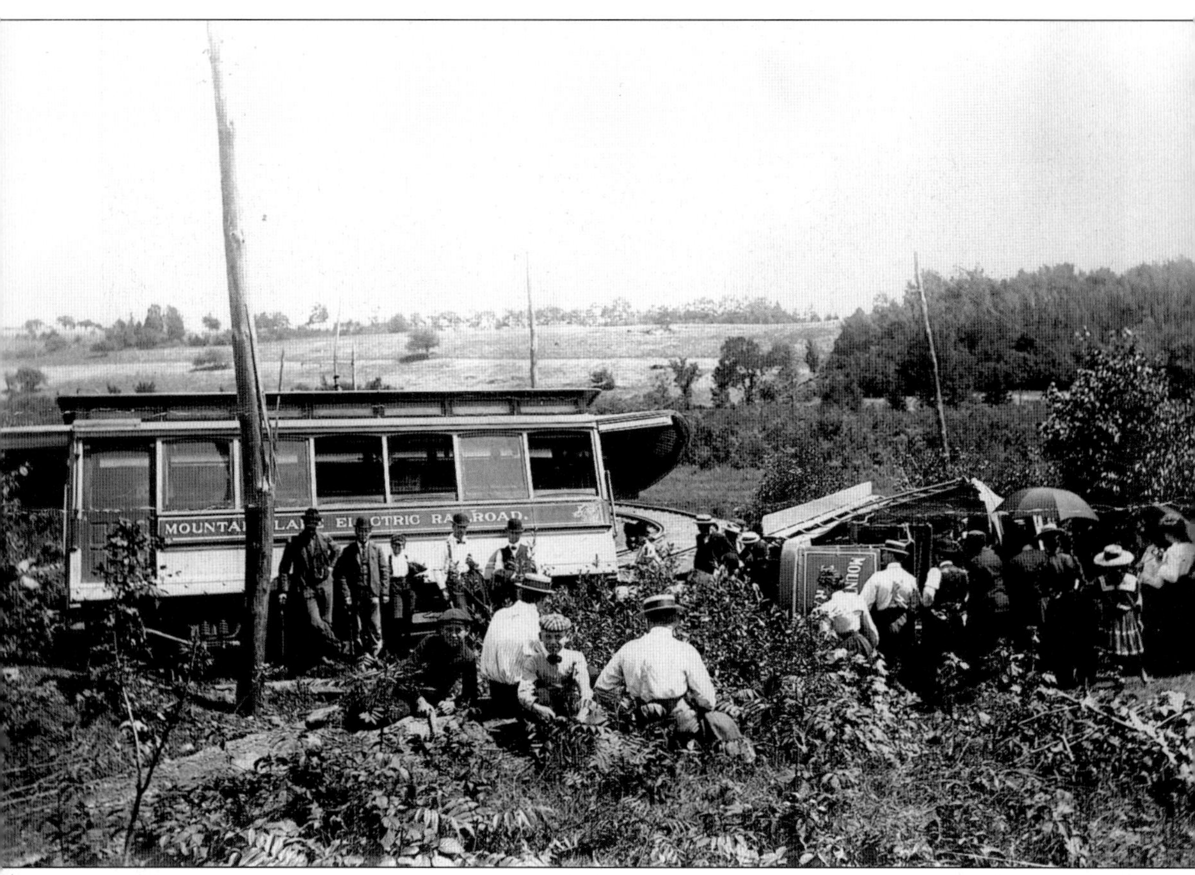

July 4, 1902, was a dark day in the history of the Mountain Lake Resort—a center for dancing, concerts, swimming, sports, and gatherings of all kinds. The resort, served by the Mountain Lake Electric Railroad Company trolley line from Gloversville to Mountain Lake, was established in 1901. After the 1902 Fourth of July celebration, the trolley cars were returning to the city. Unfortunately, a heavier car, No. 5, overtook an open car, No. 1, and crashed into the rear of it. It was dark, and many passengers were trapped in the wreckage, with 13 killed and many injured. Afterward, the Fonda, Johnstown, and Gloversville Railroad bought the line and operated for 15 years.

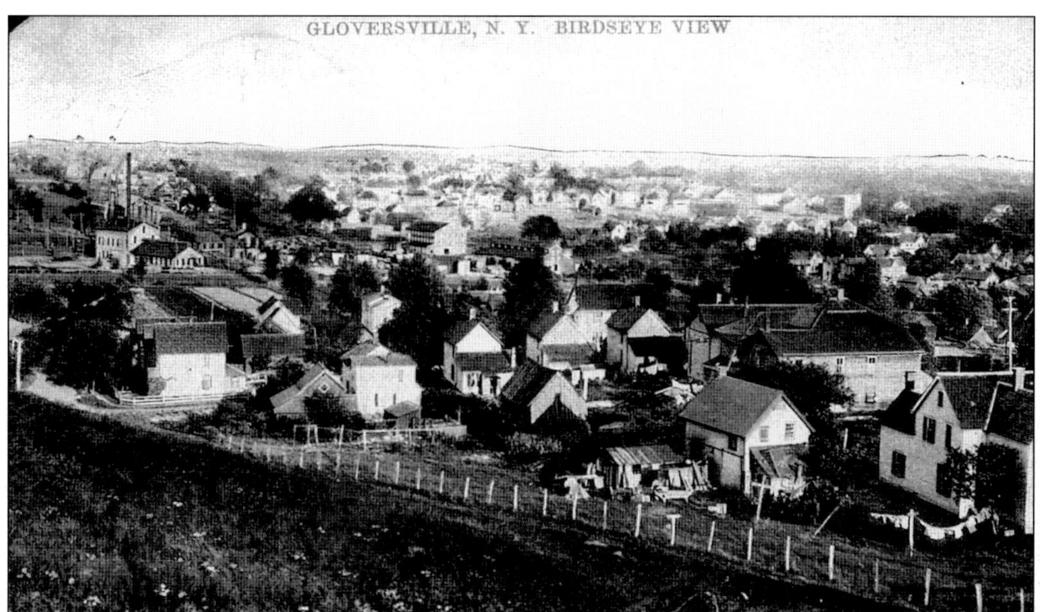

Gloversville, the largest city on the Adirondack Trail, was called "the Gateway City to the Adirondacks." It gained its name in 1828, reflecting the major industry. At one time, more than 275 glove shops operated in the county. Today, the glove industry has gone overseas and only a few shops remain.

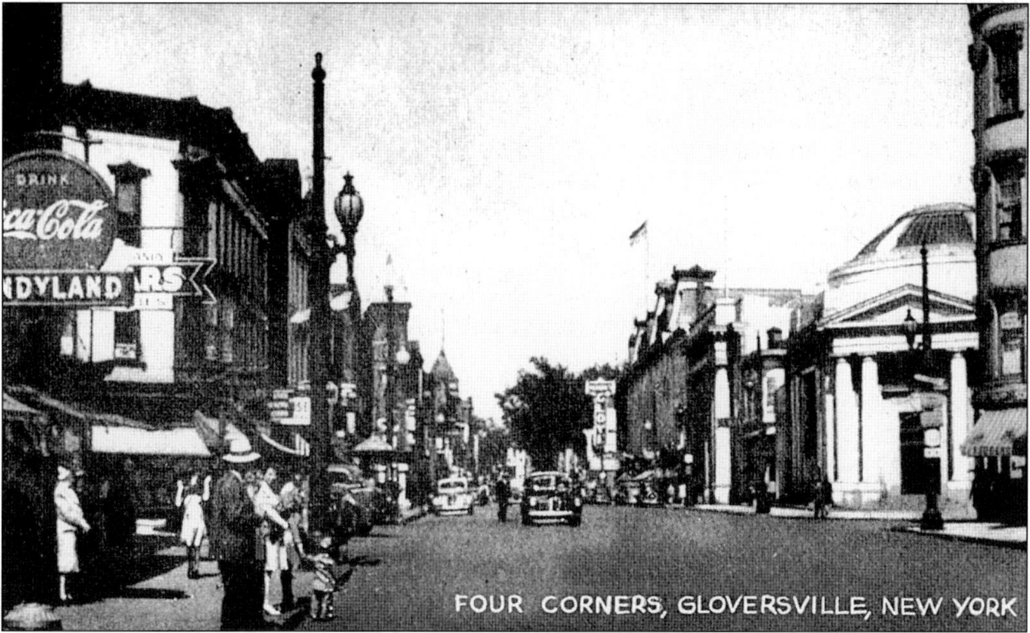

The north–south route from Fonda to Malone originally ran directly through the four corners of downtown Gloversville, a major shopping destination in Fulton County. Named for the glove and leather industries, this city had as its slogan "Gloversville gloves the world." Today, the Fulton County Chamber of Commerce Gallery, the Adirondack Stained Glass Studios, the restored Glove Theater, the Fulton County Museum, and some 100 merchants attract residents and visitors alike.

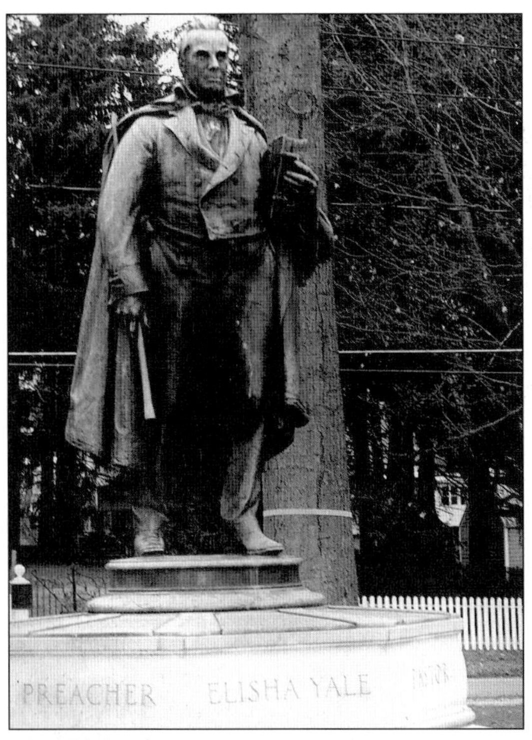

Dr. Elisha Yale stands in the Kingsborough Park in Gloversville, representing those who brought religion to the Adirondack Trail. Serving the Kingsborough Presbyterian Church for more than 40 years, Yale did missionary work up the Adirondack Trail into the remote settlements during the first half of the 1800s. He was the first itinerant minister in the southern Adirondacks. Yale often referred to the Adirondack Trail as a "region of desolation."

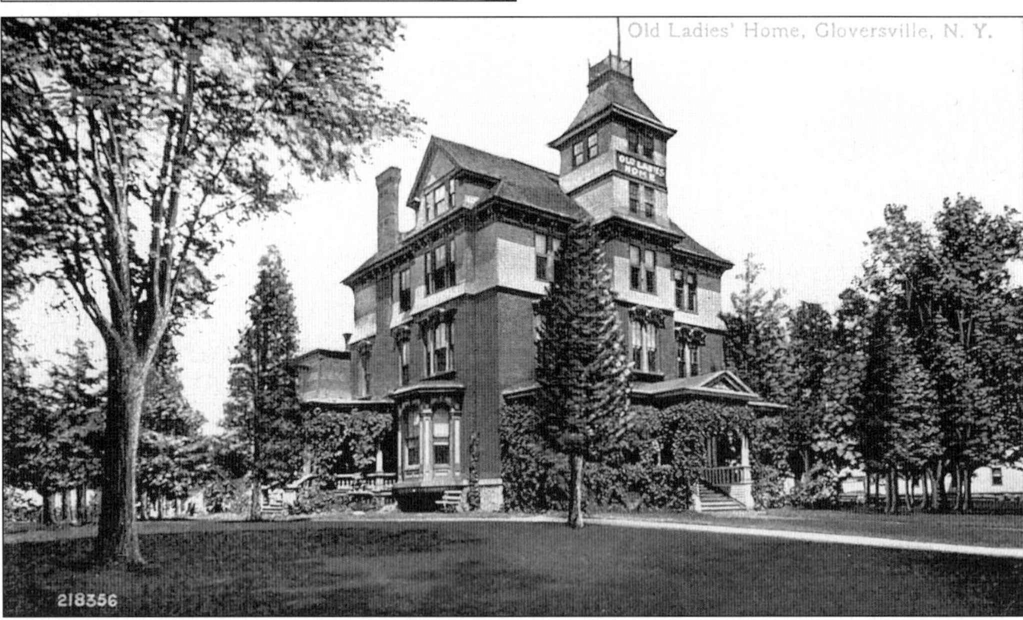

The old sign on the front of the stately mansion on Gloversville's State Street read, "Old Ladies Home." The home was a gift from David and Helen Getman to provide for the "worthy, elderly women of Fulton County." Opened on February 7, 1918, it has operated continuously to this day. Once the home of glove manufacturer Daniel B. Judson, the building served as the Gloversville Business School before being purchased by Getman. Today, as the Getman Memorial Home, it is become coed, also serving men. Civil War veteran Getman also erected a monument to Union soldiers in the Mayfield Cemetery, where he is buried.

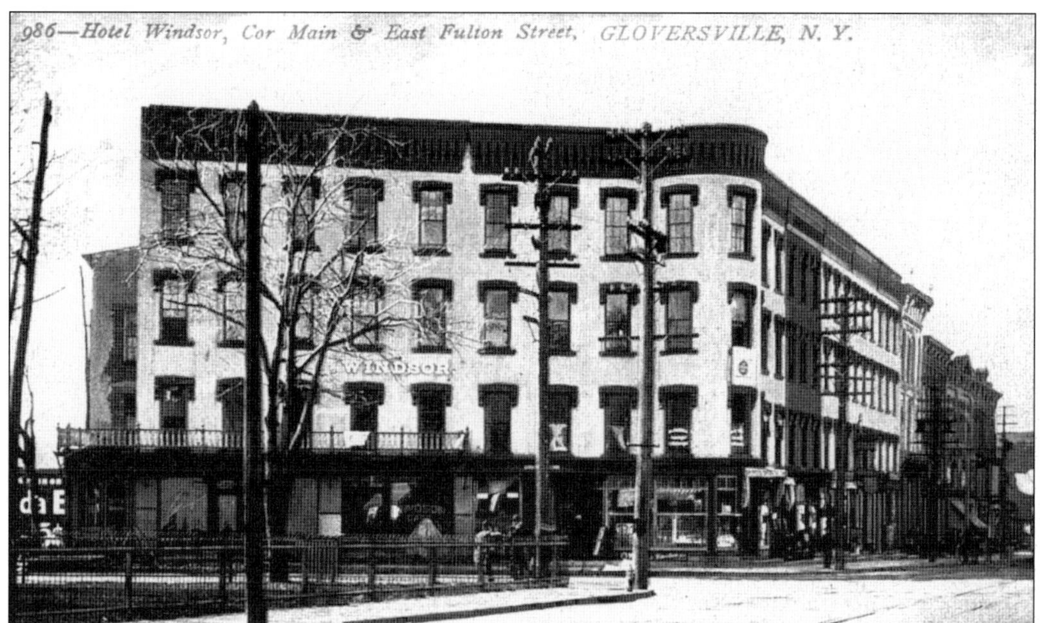

The Hotel Windsor, built in 1856 when the Adirondack Trail was a plank road from Fonda, once stood on the four corners in Gloversville. Originally built by Samuel Stewart Mills, it was called the Mills House. Known as a "palatial gem" in its day, it boasted a magnificent lobby, a ballroom and stage, a circular staircase, and floor-to-ceiling mirrors in the ladies' parlor. A reading room, a barbershop, and public bath facilities were also available. The hotel was lighted by gas from resin gasworks under the kitchen. The four-story $65,000 structure became the tallest building between Albany and Utica at the time it was built. It was demolished in the late 1970s for about the same amount it cost to build it.

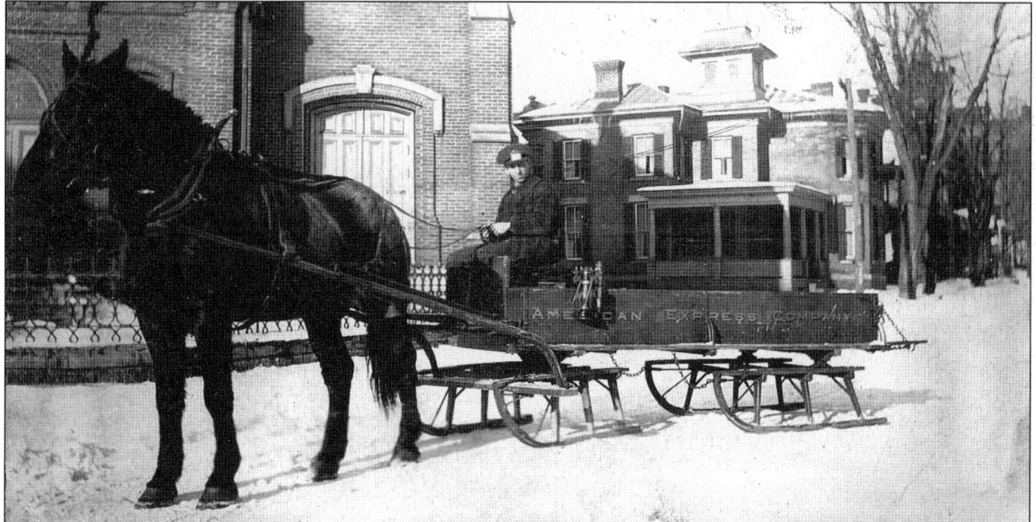

Before the days of automobiles, the American Express Company was making deliveries on the Adirondack Trail. This horse and delivery sleigh, with William Rieth as driver, made good use of the snow-covered roadways. Note the lantern hanging on the wagon; it was probably put to good use when darkness fell before deliveries were over, much the same problem faced by parcel deliverers today.

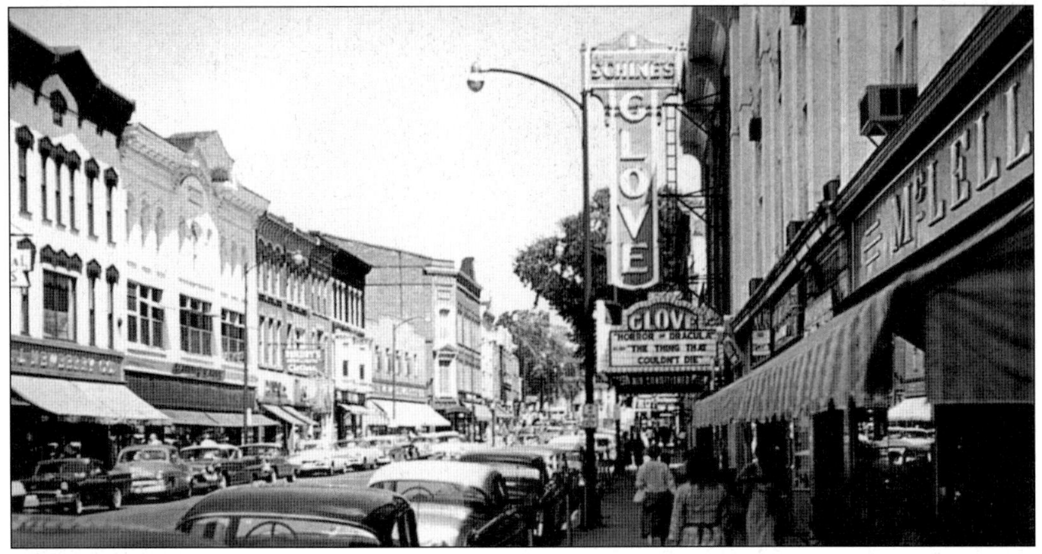

The Glove Theater in Gloversville was once the flagship theater for the Schine movie empire. Major premiere showings were once made here, including *Drums along the Mohawk*, in 1936. The theater was built in 1914 for live performances of opera, vaudeville shows, and orchestra concerts. The Schine brothers bought it in 1920 and opened a movie house, the first of 160 they opened across the country. The Glove Theater closed its doors in the mid-1970s and lay idle for the next 20 years.

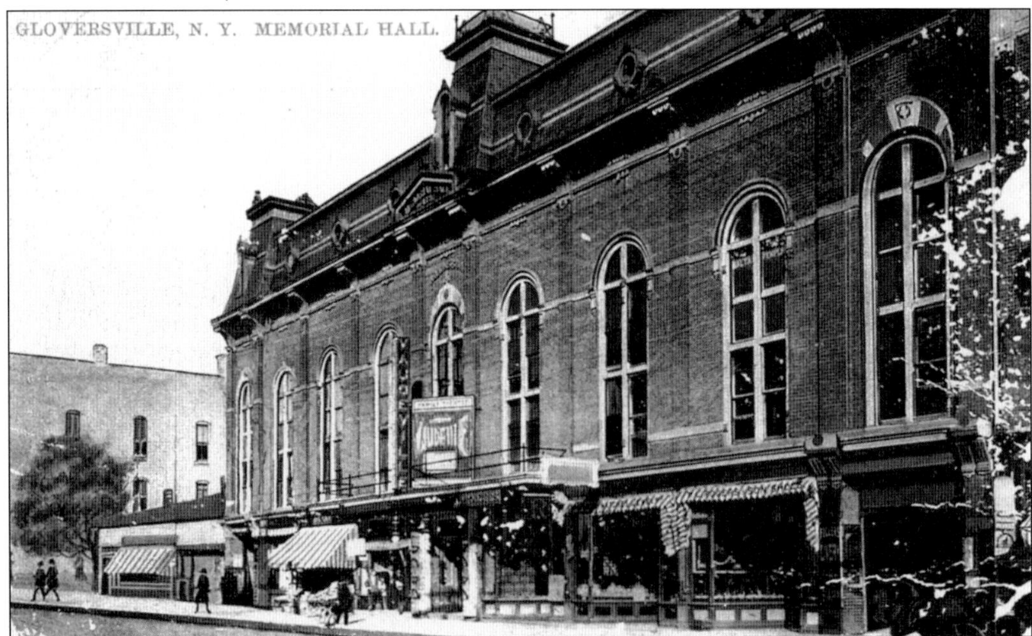

In 1995, a group of community visionaries succeeded in launching a restoration of the historic Glove Theater after two decades of deterioration. Since that time, major progress has been made on what was once a vaudeville theater. It has now reopened as a performing arts center. Plays, concerts, dinner theaters, and musical productions have brought the Glove back to life. A theater museum has been added. Improvements continue, and the Glove has become, once again, the flagship of the old movie houses.

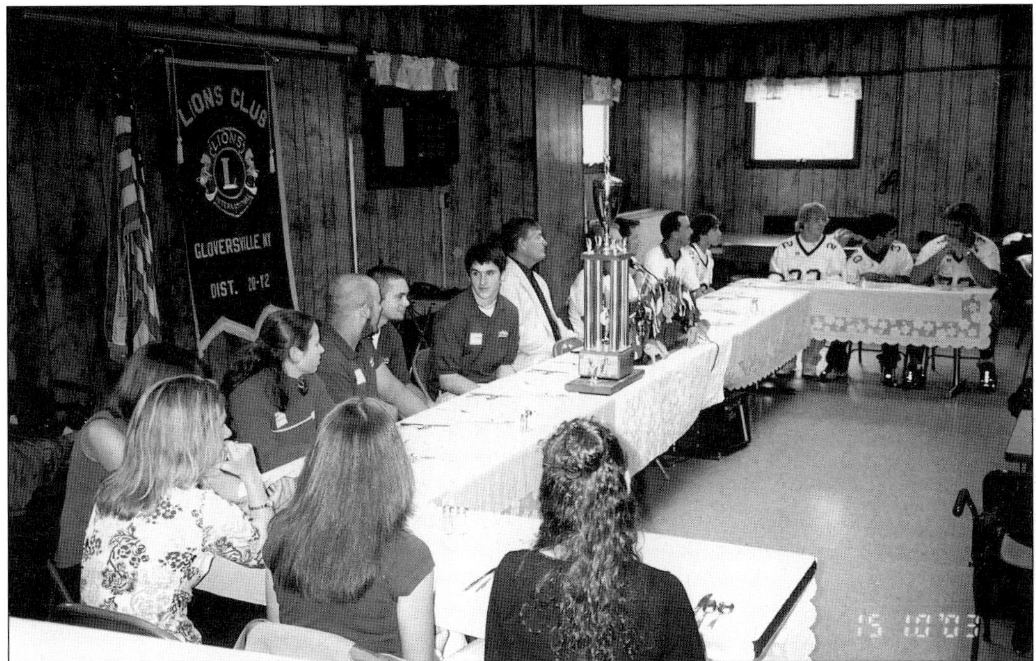

One of the longest running rivalries in New York's school sports is the annual Gloversville-Johnstown football game. The Gloversville Lions Club holds a sportsmanship luncheon with team captains, cheerleaders, and coaches before the game and maintains a perpetual trophy that goes to the winning school each year. It is a tradition that crosses several generations and holds great interest in the twin cities.

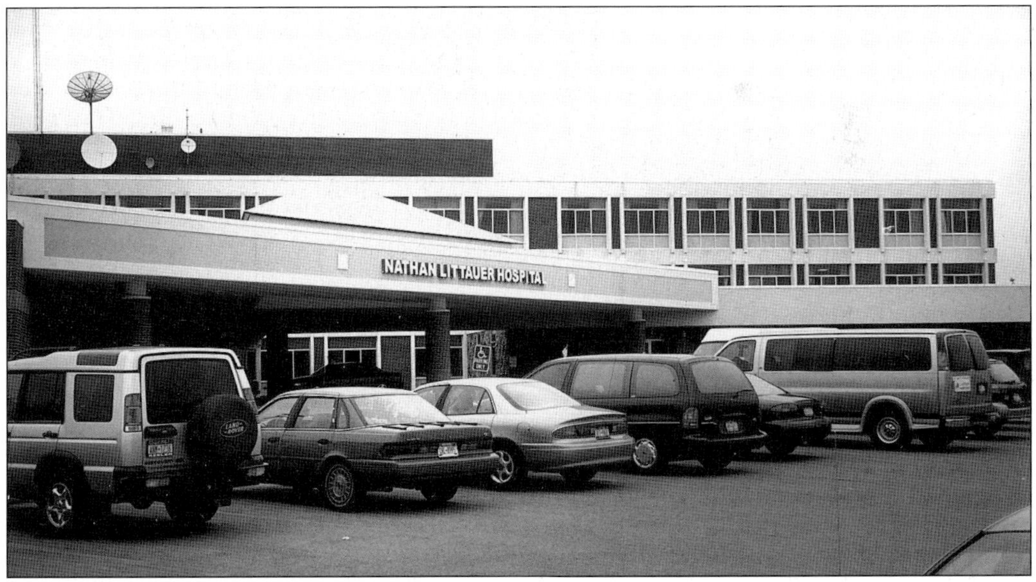

Lucius Littauer, born in Gloversville in 1859, offered, at the age of 32, to build the community a hospital in honor of his father, Nathan Littauer. In 1929, he established the Lucius Littauer Foundation, which provides support to the hospital to this day. The Littauer brothers owned one of the largest glove companies in the country. The original hospital became obsolete in the 1950s, and a new building, shown here, was opened in 1968.

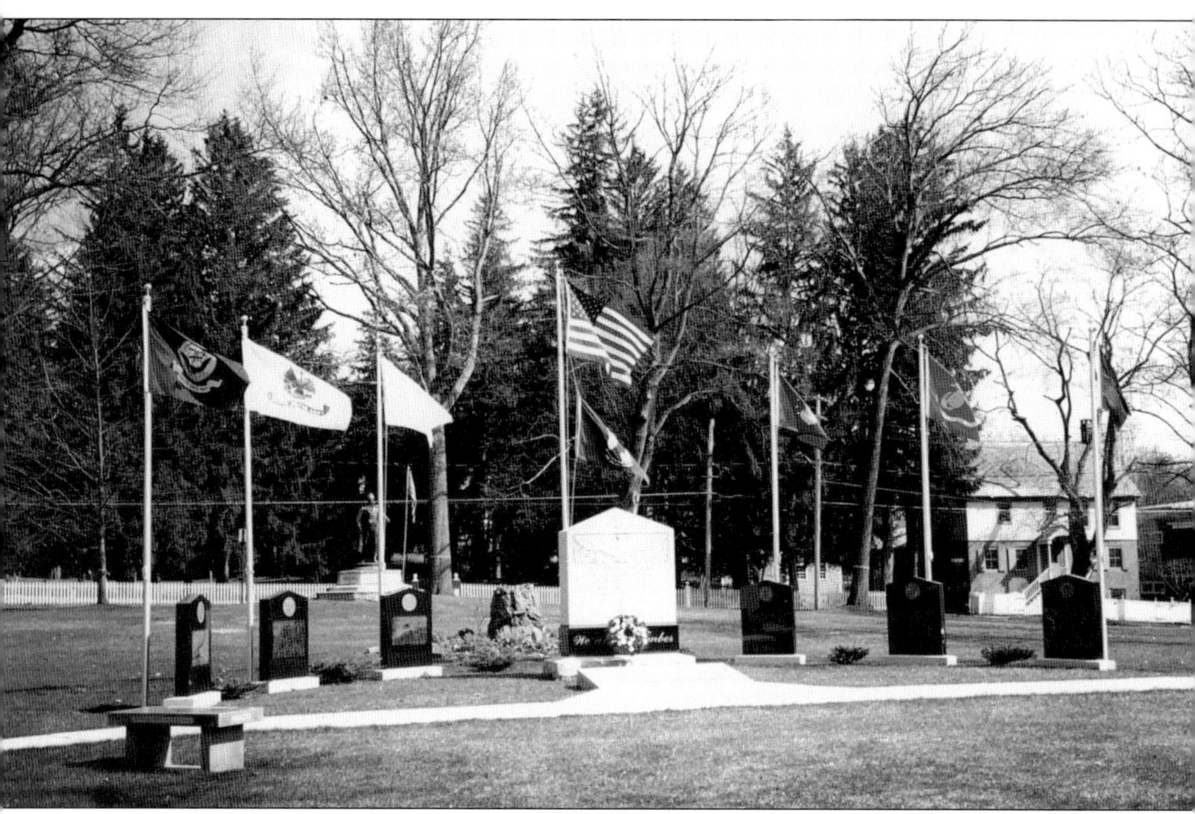

The World War II Memorial for Fulton County stands in Gloversville's Kingsborough Park. It includes seven monuments and the names of those who gave their lives. Each branch of service is represented with a monument that includes an etched picture and a flag flying overhead. Erected at the beginning of the 21st century, the memorial was a community effort spearheaded by World War II veterans. The park is surrounded by a historic church, Underground Railroad sites, a Colonial cemetery, early homes, and the county museum. It also has monuments to early settlers and other notables, along with the original grave site of Revolutionary War and War of 1812 veteran Nicholas Stoner. Settled at the time of Sir William Johnson, Kingsborough was a thriving community before it was swallowed up by Gloversville.

Two
MAYFIELD AND NORTHAMPTON

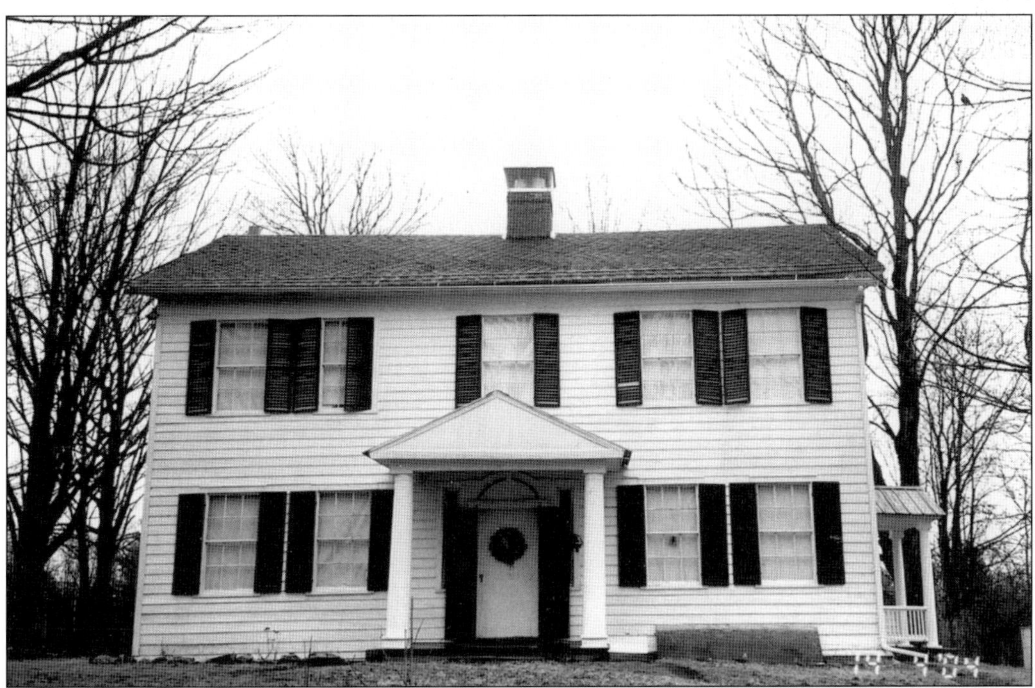

The Rice Homestead, on the Adirondack Trail near Mayfield, was the original home of Revolutionary War veteran Oliver Rice. It remained in the Rice family until it was purchased by the Mayfield Historical Society in 1992. One of the few Colonial houses remaining in America, it now houses a museum collection of the Mayfield area and is open to the public.

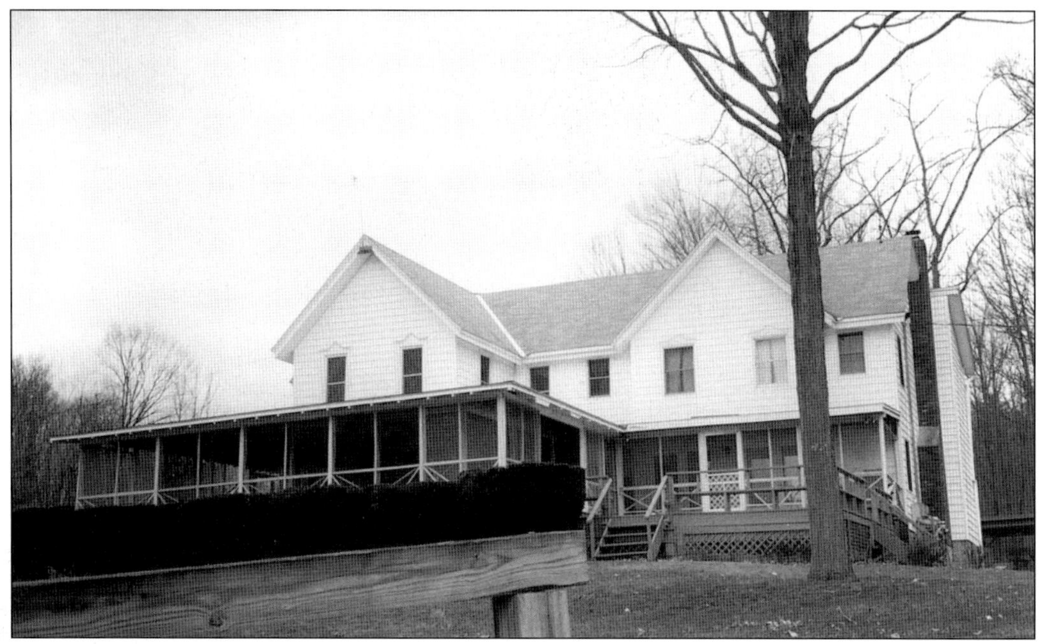

The Great Sacandaga Lake was created by the dam at Conklingville in 1930. In the depths of the Great Depression, 18 men from Mayfield decided to form a boat club. Thus, the Mayfield Yacht Club was born. The members marked a safe channel in the lake with 35 buoys from Mayfield to Northville and carried out other projects to make the reservoir safe for boating. The clubhouse, pictured here, was dedicated on Memorial Day 1937.

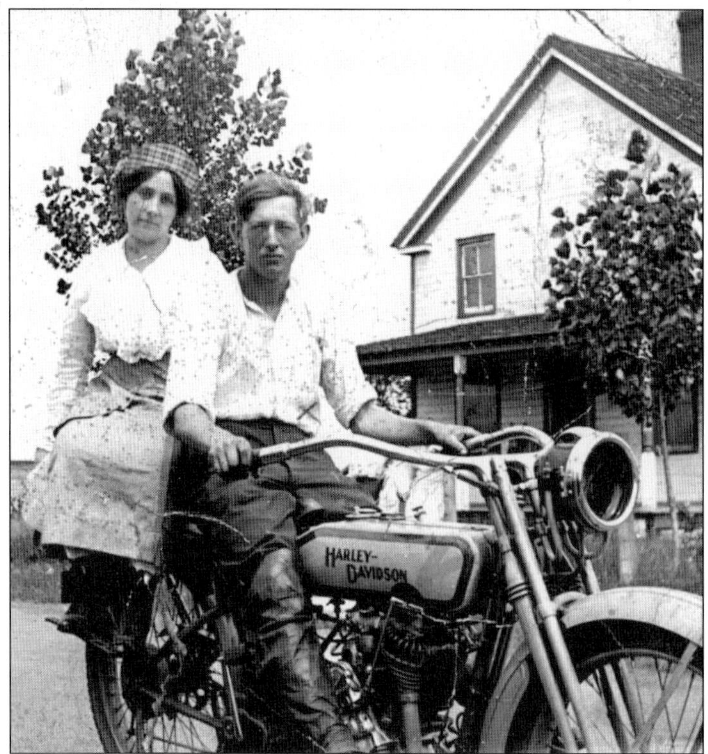

Touring with motorcycles on the Adirondack Trail has long been a popular pastime. Motorcycles were used by the forest rangers in 1923, by those who wanted to take their best girl for a ride, and for skijoring on the winter snows of the northern Adirondacks. Earl Mattice of Mayfield had one of the first Harley-Davidsons in the Adirondack country. Shown are the Warners of Mayfield, who found the Adirondack Trail a good route for motorcycling.

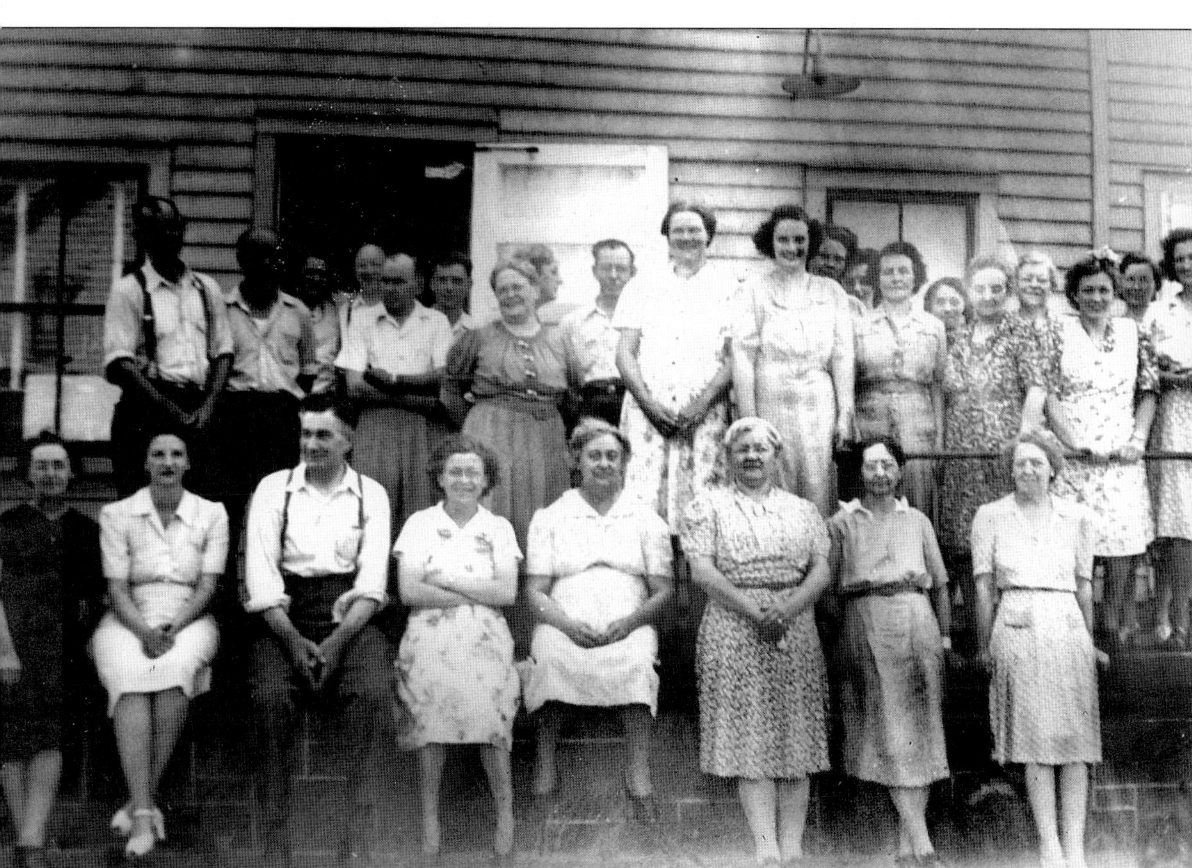

A major industry at the southern end of the Adirondack Trail was glove making. Most of the cities and hamlets had one or more glove shops, and some people sewed gloves at home. Shown in 1930 are employees of the Dixon Glove Company of Mayfield. From left to right are the following: (first row) Anna Proper, Francis Hollenbeck, E. J. Delany, June Hitchcock, Maggie Whitman, Chloe Genter, Edna Mason, and Nettie James; (second row) Jerry Ferguson, Lyman Richardson, Arthur Miller, Lillian Bennett, Lucindie Van Ostrand, Mildred Brower, Matie Hart, Effie Richardson, Aletha Hollenbeck, and Olive Elphie; (third row) Julia Traver, Harland Fonda, Earl Exchler, Ida Eslner, Rupert Warner, Betty Van Ostrand, Evelyn Flood, Carrie Pettingale, Linda Haynes, and Viola Handy.

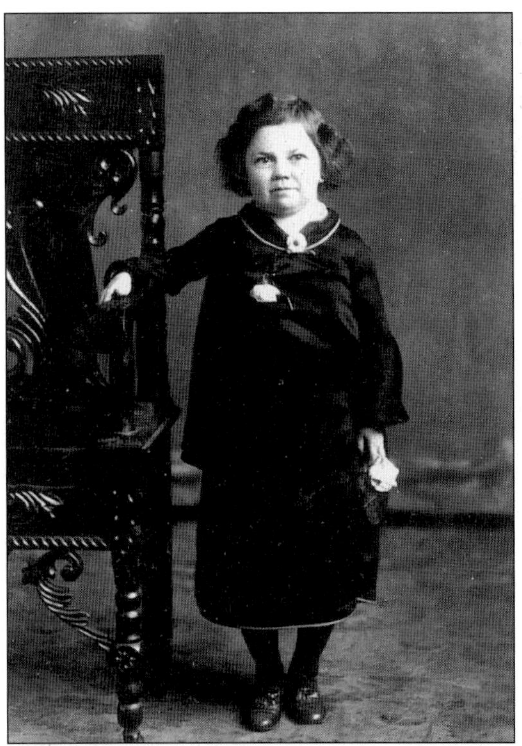

The Adirondack Trail was once home to a princess: Princess Marguerite, 27 inches tall and weighing 25 pounds, who performed with several circuses and played in the movie *The Wizard of Oz*. She was born Cynthia Nickloy in Mayfield in 1900. She attended school in Mayfield, later lived on Route 30 near Northville, and joined the Methodist church in Gloversville.

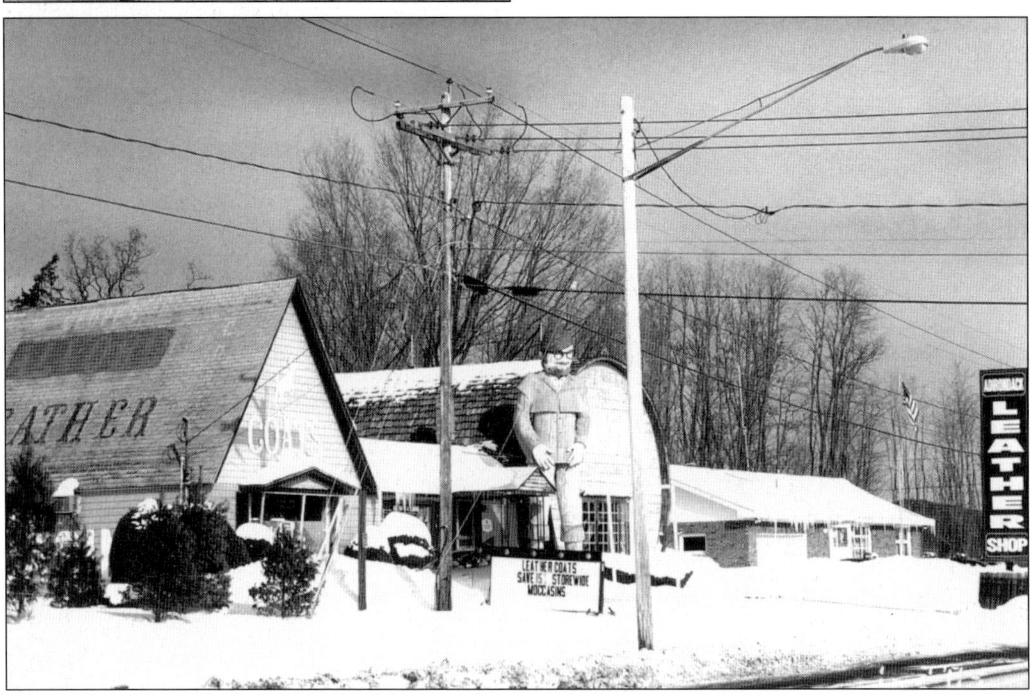

Route 30 was the trail to "Leatherland U.S.A." when all of the tanneries and glove shops were in full operation. Today, a few shops and outlets carry on the leather tradition. The giant leather-clad statue and the tannery barrel-shaped building near Mayfield mark the Adirondack Leather Shop, formerly the Alvord Glove Company, owned by the Alvord family for four generations.

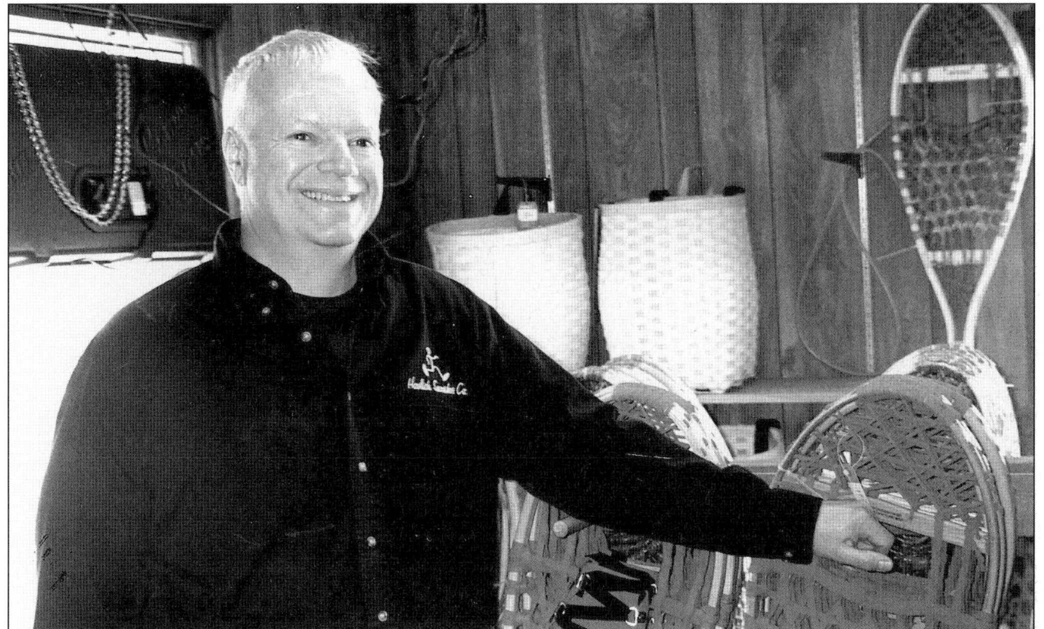

Snowshoes originated in the Adirondacks when the early natives and trappers tied tree branches to their feet to walk on the deep snow. Today, hiking in the woods along the Adirondack Trail in winter is a popular sport. Dick Havlick has been in the snowshoe business since the 1960s. His shop in Mayfield offers everything up-to-date in snowshoeing, including the Havlick modified Bearpaw and a line of metal shoes.

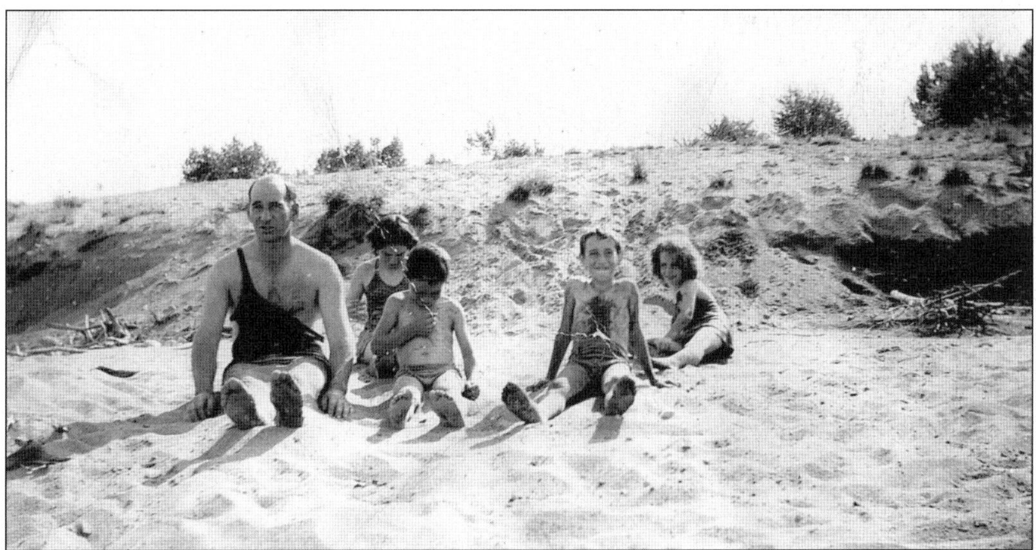

The Adirondack Trail is noted for its many beaches, visited by thousands during the summer. Mayfield has a new town beach, and other hamlets along the Adirondack Trail offer much the same. State campsites usually include a beach with a lifeguard on duty in season. This family enjoys one of the beaches at Great Sacandaga Lake.

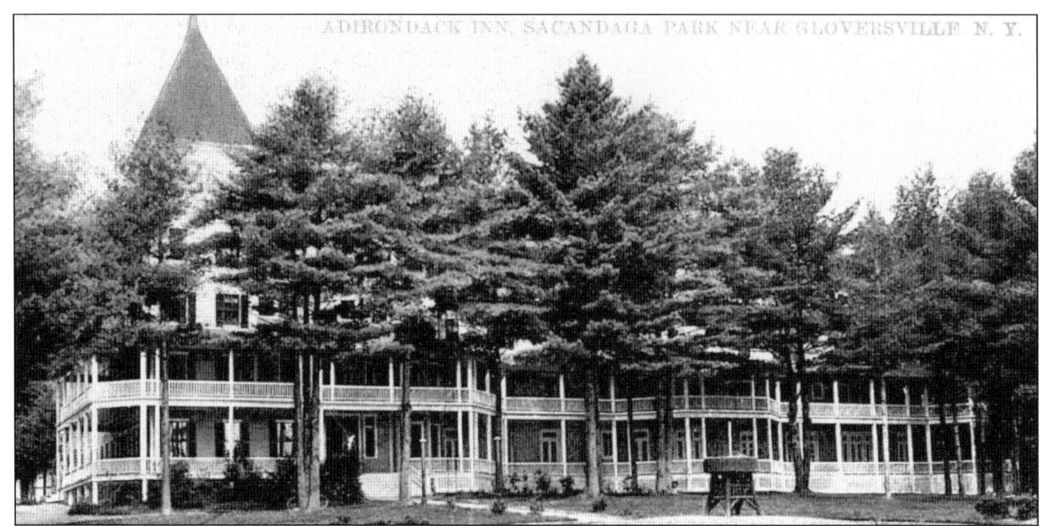

In June 1937, the Adirondack Inn at Sacandaga Park opened for the summer season with 23 new rooms added to the 47-year-old hotel. With these additional third-floor rooms, the hotel had 160 rooms, all with telephone service and hot and cold running water. Owned by the Fonda, Johnstown, and Gloversville Railroad, the inn later grew to 250 rooms, added a four-lane indoor bowling alley and a water-operated elevator, and catered to conventions. It burned down in September 1975.

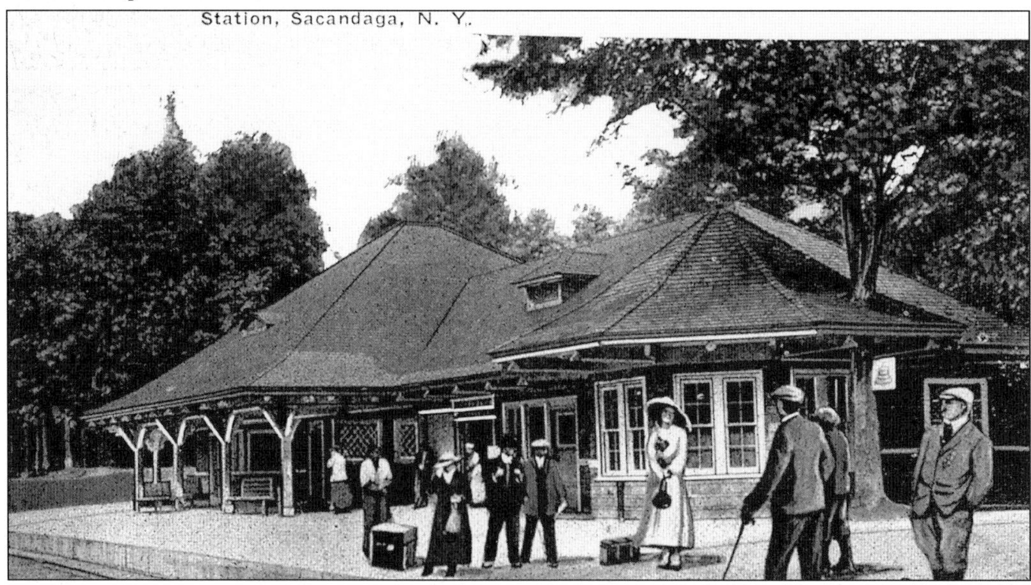

Sacandaga Park, once the Coney Island of the Adirondacks, was established by the Fonda, Johnstown, and Gloversville Railroad Company on the banks of the Sacandaga River near Northville in 1876. It was landscaped with an Adirondack theme of rustic log bridges, walkways, and benches. The amusement park had a midway, a dance hall, water slides, and a sport island. Thousands of visitors arrived by railroad to enjoy the merry-go-rounds, bowling alley, donkey rides, roller-skating rink, and other attractions. The park closed in 1930, when the Sacandaga River flooded much of the land. The railroad station shown here is the second one built in the park. Now renovated, it houses retail space, rental units, community meeting rooms, and offices.

A Methodist camp meeting ground was founded on the shores of the Sacandaga River on the Adirondack Trail near Northville *c.* 1880. Camp meetings attracted thousands, who first stayed in tents on tent platforms, which later evolved into small cottages. More than 100 of these gingerbread-style cottages burned in a major fire in 1898. Many were rebuilt and are still in use in today's Sacandaga Park.

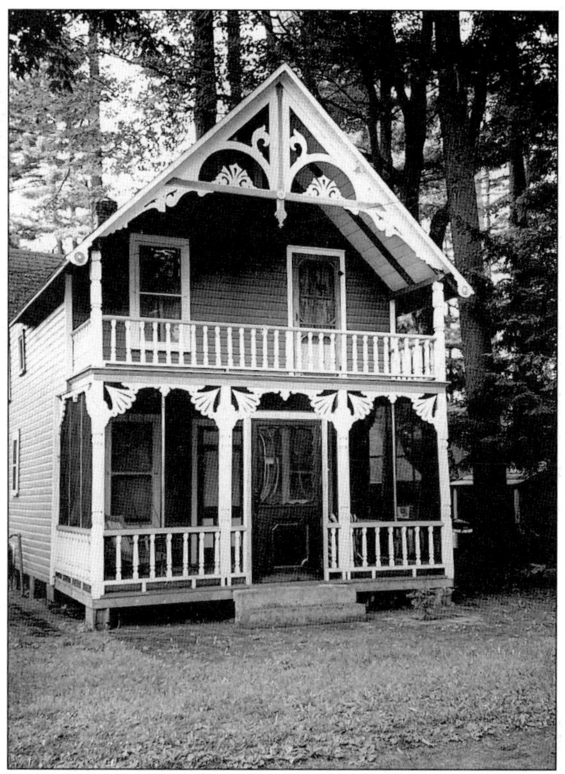

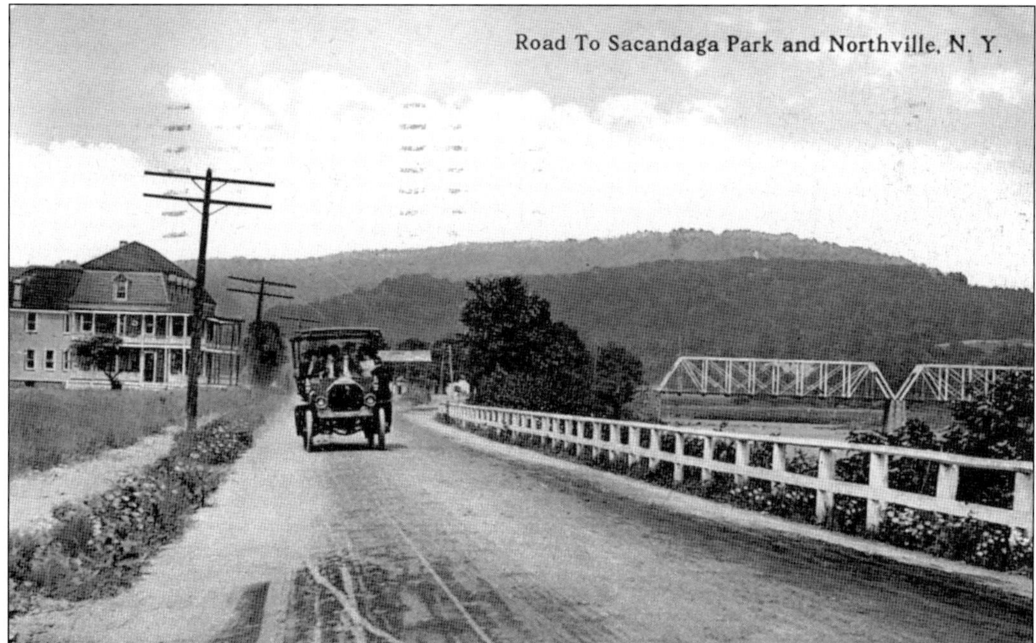

The Adirondack Trail once went through Sacandaga Park on then Route 152 to Northville. A gravel footpath was used by summer residents to walk to Northville to shop. The path was also used by Northville residents to walk to the park for amusements, movies at the Rustic Theater, a swim at the beach, the arcade at the old railroad station, or roller-skating in the old dance pavilion.

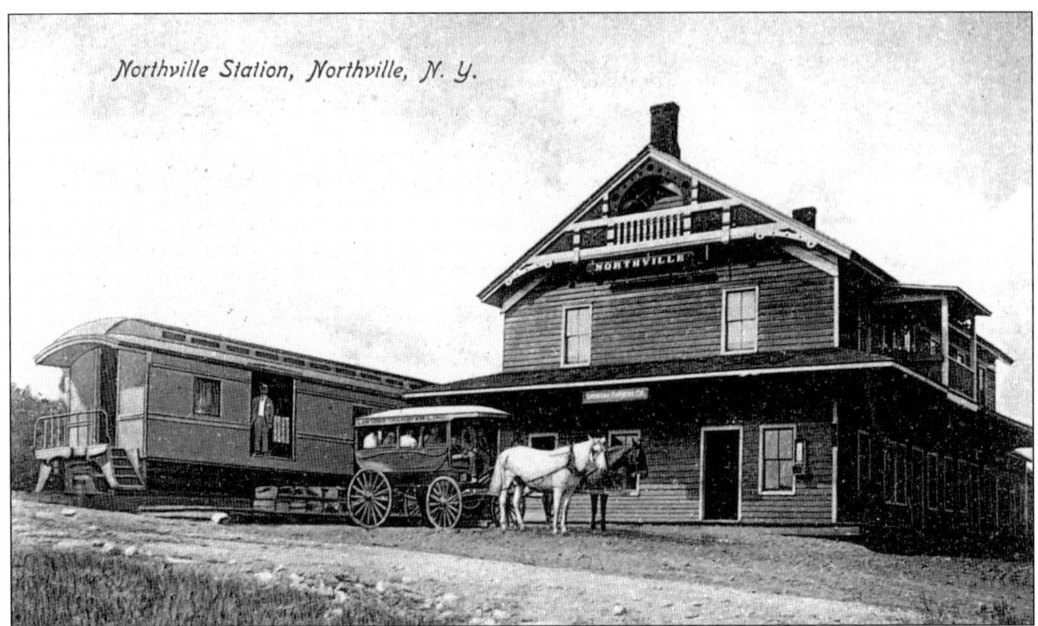

Beginning in 1875, trains carried passengers to the railroad's northern terminus at Northville, which closed in 1930. Connecting to the New York Central at Fonda, the line brought thousands to the Adirondack Trail, where they continued their journey north by stagecoach. This 10-seated horse-drawn hack, owned by the Charles Lawton Coal Company, transported passengers and mail to Northville for a fee. Today, a state historic marker marks the site of the station near the Northville Bridge.

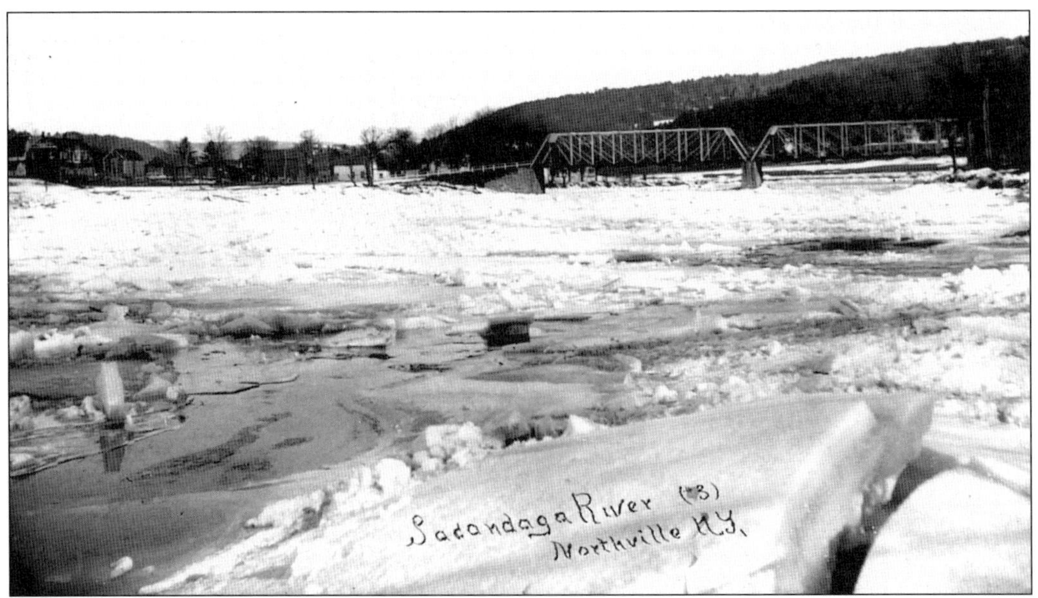

Ice has caused problems on the Adirondack Trail over the years, flooding the roadways and taking out bridges. In 1929, it took out buildings near the Northville Bridge, including Giffords Store. Until some work was done along the river, flooding of the flats between Northville and Wells was a recurring problem, closing the road until the water and ice chunks could be cleared.

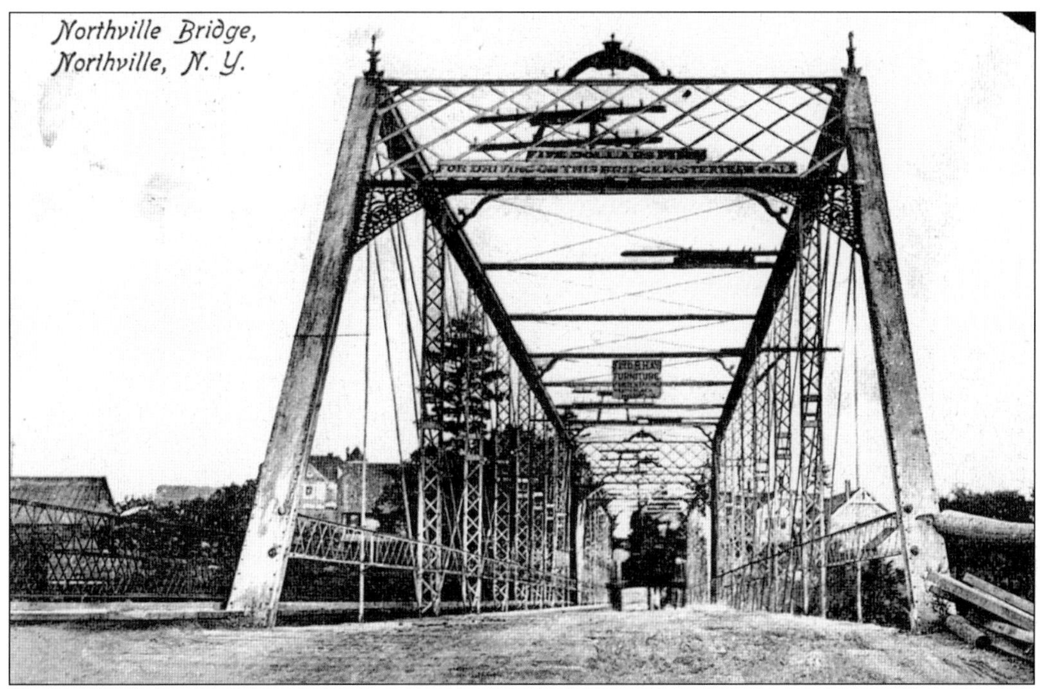

Bridges were important links on the Adirondack Trail. Rivers had to be crossed to keep the hamlets from being isolated from the outside world. The Sacandaga River at Northville had an 1860 wooden bridge until a spring flood took it away in 1882. The replacement, the two-span bridge shown here, served another 49 years. The sign on the bridge states, "Five dollars fine for traveling on this bridge faster than a walk." The small advertising sign on the top of the bridge is for Fred Hay Furniture.

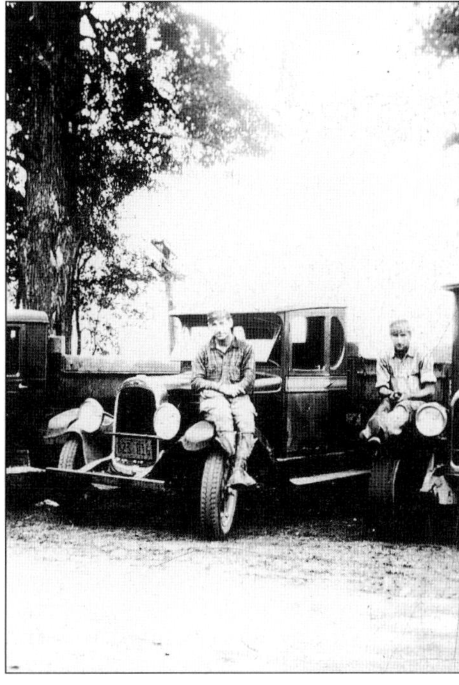

When the Great Sacandaga Lake was created in 1930 by the damming of the Sacandaga River, a new bridge had to be built over the rising waters at Northville. Ross Williams of Dolgeville quit school in his senior year, left his father's dairy farm, bought a truck, and moved to Fulton County to work on the bridge project. He is pictured sitting on his truck, along with other men who worked on the project. The bridge was replaced in recent years.

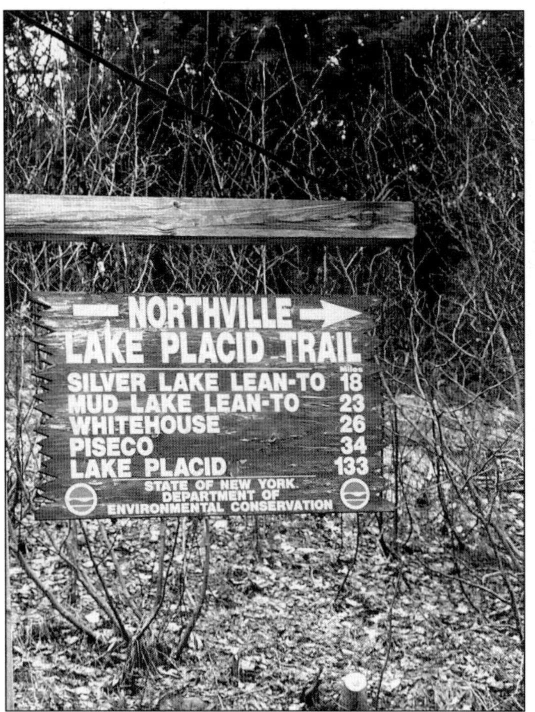

From the Northville Bridge, the 133-mile Northville-Lake Placid Trail follows the roadway until branching off at Benson to enter the forested lands. Established in 1922 by the Adirondack Mountain Club, the trail began at the terminus of the railroad, where the train dropped off the hikers. At the end of the trail, the hikers caught a train at Lake Placid. Plans are now under way to move the portion of the trail that follows the roadway into the woods through Giffords Valley.

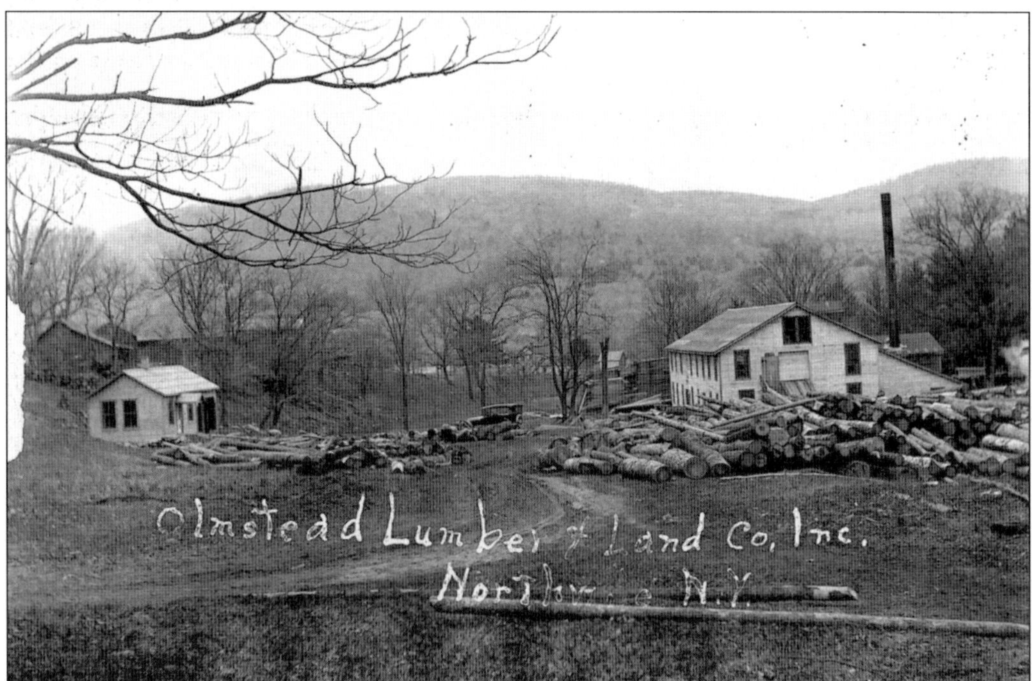

Lumber companies arose along the Adirondack Trail with the advent of the early settlements. Employment during the logging season and work in the sawmills helped Adirondack families make their homes in the great wilderness. Land and lumber companies made use of the timber from the forests and then sold lands to the growing population. The Olmstead Lumber and Land Company was on the Adirondack Trail along the Sacandaga River at Northville.

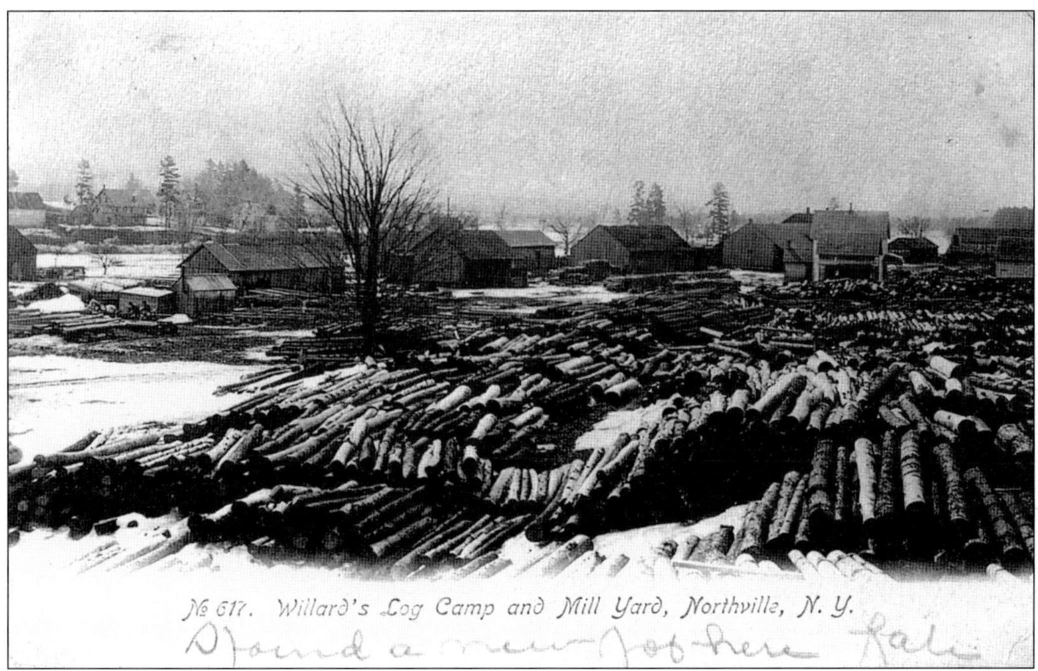

The Adirondack Trail is no stranger to the logging industry. Adirondack logs have traveled its roadways and waterways since Sir William Johnson built the first sawmill in 1760 at Johnstown. Willard Lumber Company was located near the Northville Bridge, where logs were floated down from the north on the Sacandaga River. Today's logs are transported by trucks on the Adirondack Trail.

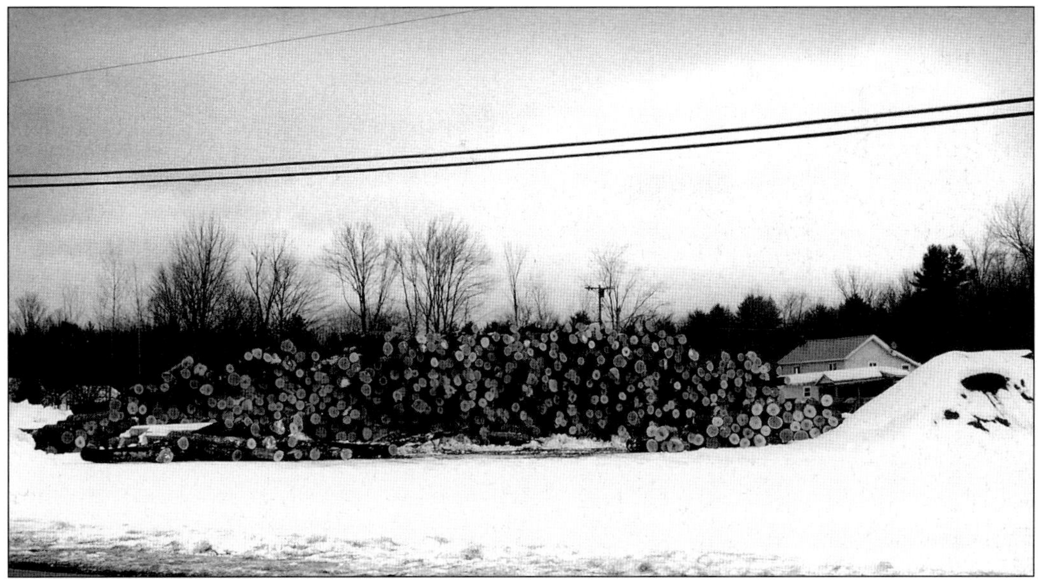

Logging still survives in the forested Adirondacks, and logs are shipped out to other lands. The staging area shown here is on the Adirondack Trail between Mayfield and Northville. Logs are sorted and graded at this central location and then trucked to their destinations. In the days of the river drives, the standard log was set at 13 feet long to help prevent the rustling of logs by cutting off the brands.

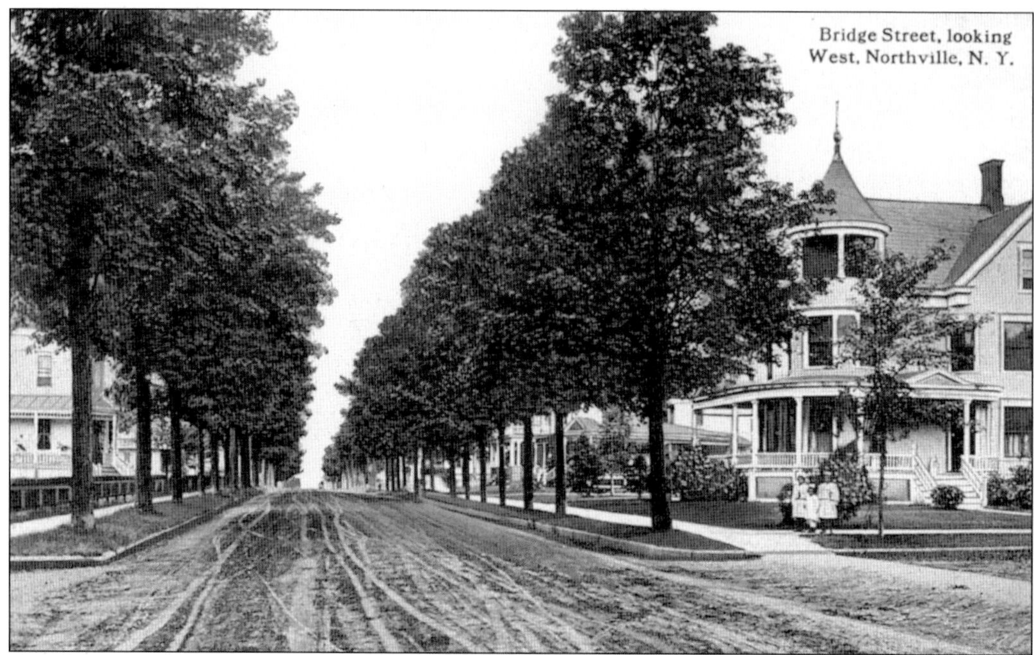

The original Adirondack Trail went up Bridge Street in Northville and along the east side of the Sacandaga River. The road from Gloversville to Northville was surfaced with macadam in 1908, but the road at Northville remained a dirt road until 1912–1913, when the paved road was established to Wells. The large home on the right was built by Richard Weaver for the William P. Harris family. In 1938, it became a funeral home, which continues to this day.

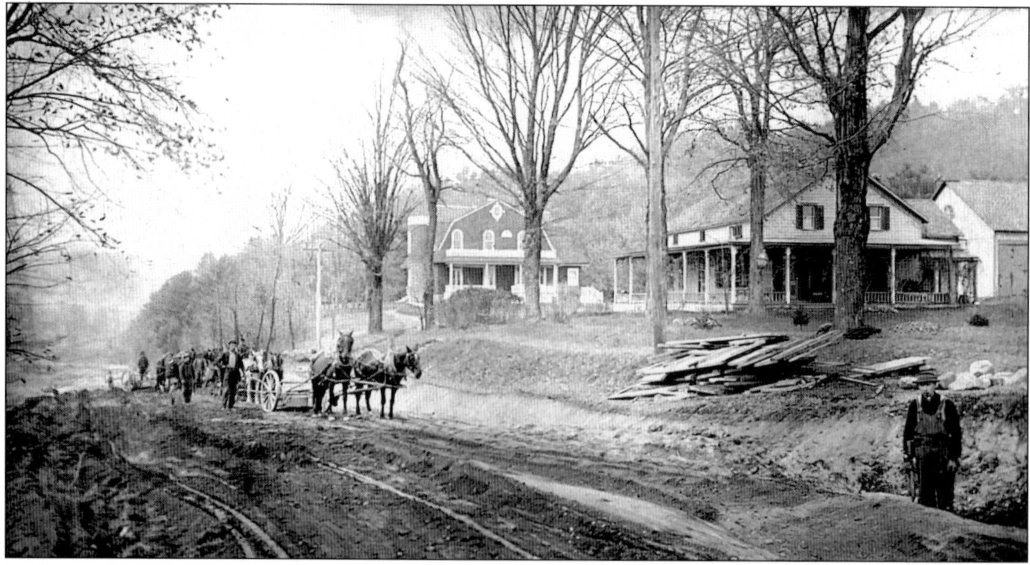

Early road building required extensive labor in the days before heavy equipment was put to use. Here, workers make good use of horses to move the soil and level the roadway on Lamb's Hill north of Northville. The Lamb house, on the right, burned in 1914, and the Randolph house, on the left, is still in use. Oral history tells of Mr. Randolph building the house for his wife. Upon his unexpected death, his widow, who loved the house, was forced to sell it because she could not afford the upkeep.

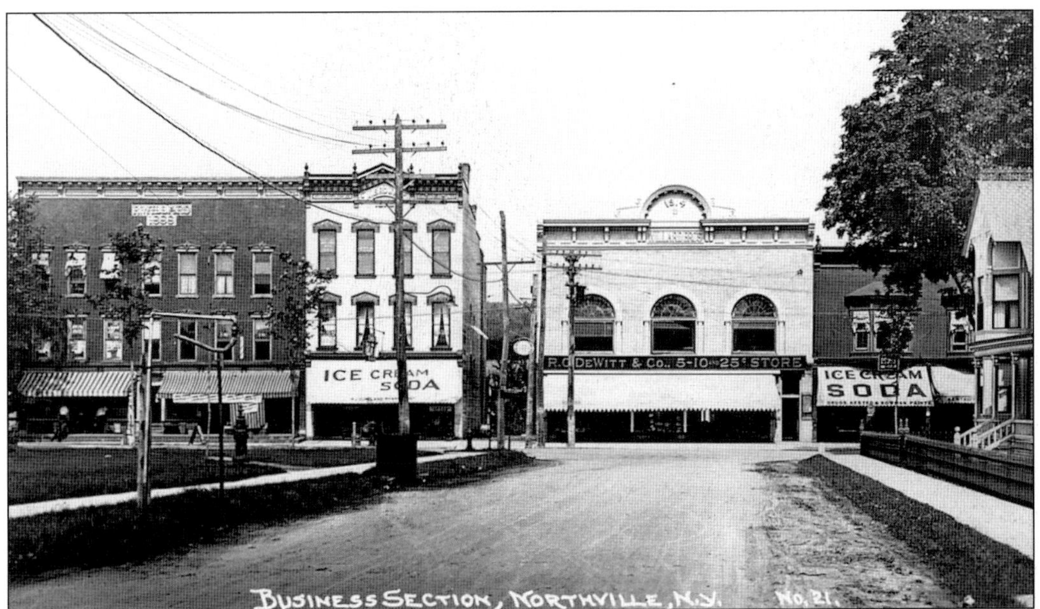

Until the bypass west of the river was constructed in 1960, the Adirondack Trail followed a route through the village of Northville. The 1914 DeWitt Dime Store, on Main Street at the head of Bridge Street, later a J. J. Newberry, is still open as a five-and-ten-cent store. From left to right, the old stores are the Smith Ice Cream Parlor, a confectionery, a fruit and vegetable market, Kested and Bowmans Drug Store, Dr. Meter's upstairs dentist's office, the five-and-ten, Wright's Drug Store, and Kested's Harness Shop.

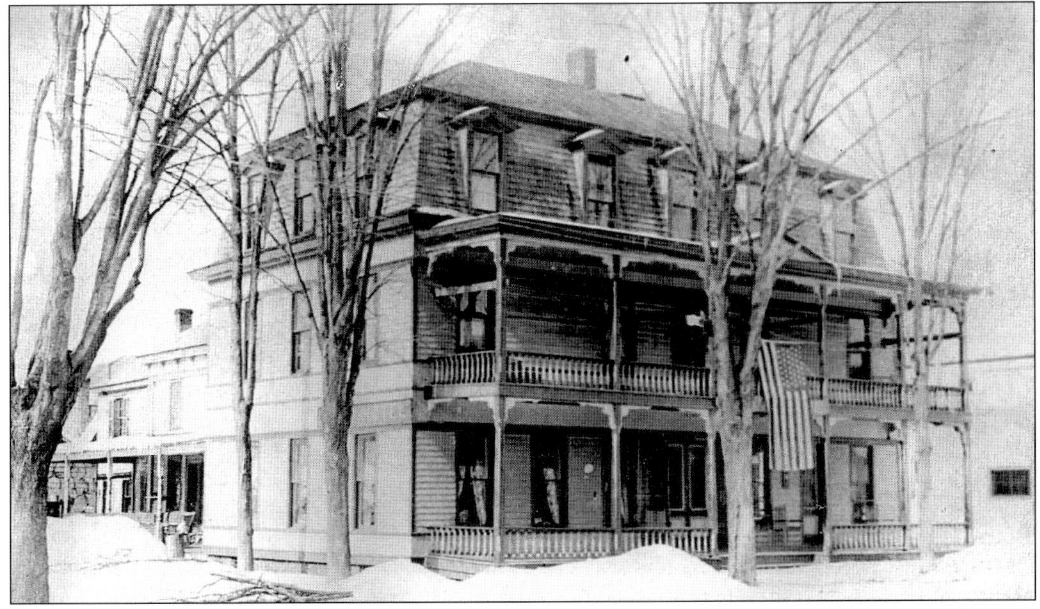

The Adirondack Trail brought lumberjacks to the mountain hamlets during the winter logging jobs, creating a need for hotels. The lumberjacks were followed by the tourists, who came summer and winter for recreation. The Lyon House, one of several hotels in Northville, "the Southern Gate to the Adirondacks," was built in the 1800s as the Arlington Hotel. For a time it was the Dopp House, and it was the Truman A. Lyon House when it burned down in 1910.

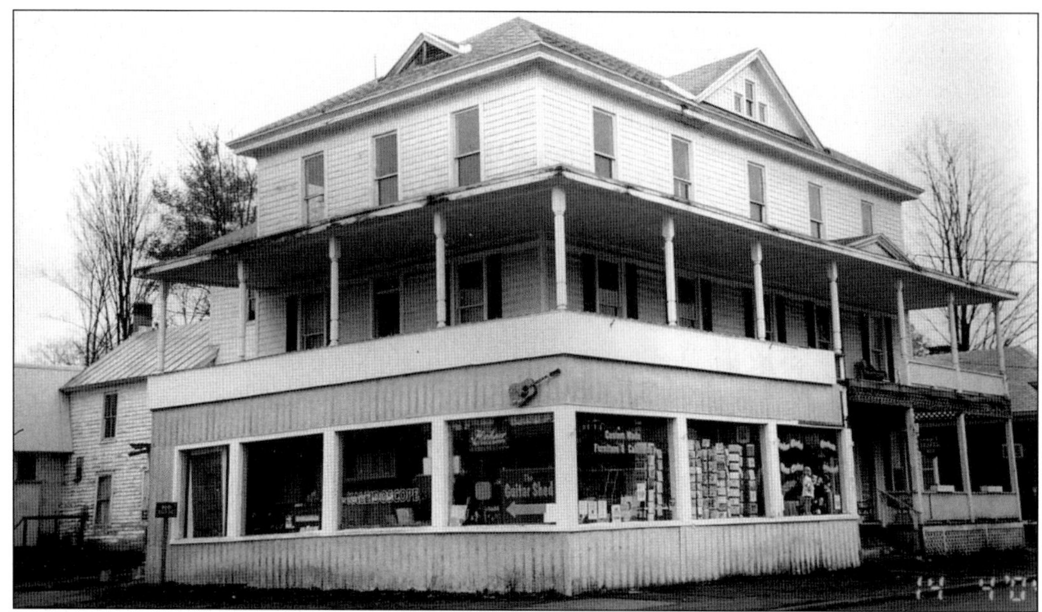

The Hotel Northville was built on Main Street in 1813 by Abraham VanArnum as a home for his daughter and her husband. VanArnum's brother, Jacob, soon opened it as a guesthouse and restaurant. Over the years it welcomed many famous guests, including J. D. Rockefeller. The hotel's colorful history includes "hooch holes" in the floor to hide illegal booze during Prohibition, cock fights in the basement, a secret code on the hotel register, and an Underground Railroad site.

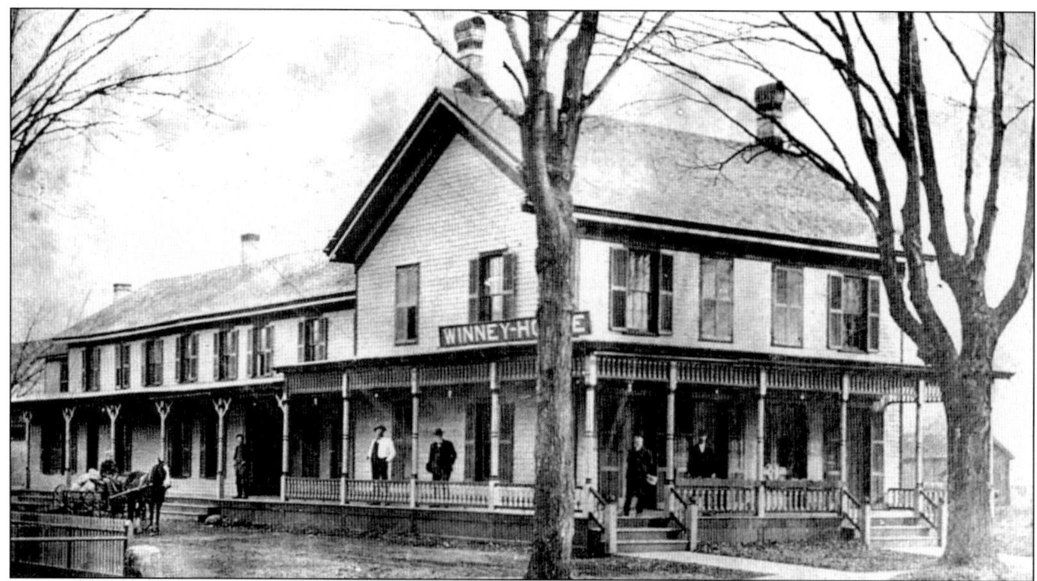

Northville was once a village of hotels, many of which were first built to house the loggers. Thus, Northville became known as "the Gateway to the Adirondack Lumber Industry." Later, tourists traveling the Adirondack Trail stayed at the Northville hotels. The Winney House, pictured *c.* 1900, was one of the village's original 13 hotels. It was built by Gardner Winney on the site of the former National Hotel in 1788 to replace the Sacandaga Hotel, which had burned down. It, too, was lost to a fire in the first decade of the 1900s.

The swifts of Sacandaga provide a yearly spectacle, returning each May 6 to take up summer residence in the chimney of the old Hubbell factory, in Northville. Each night at dusk, until they depart for their winter homes in Peru and the Upper Amazon on August 20, the tiny birds circle the chimney until they are all in one large mass like swirling smoke. Then, suddenly, they all shoot into the chimney in a huge funnel to spend the night on the vertical walls of the brick chimney.

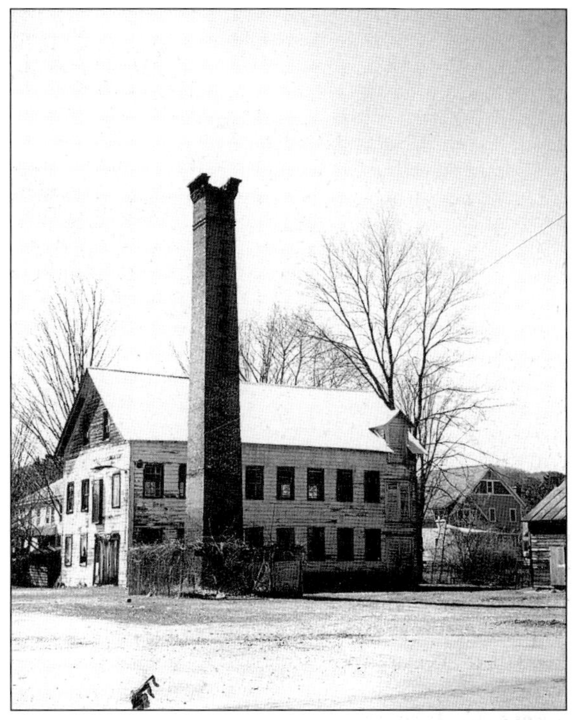

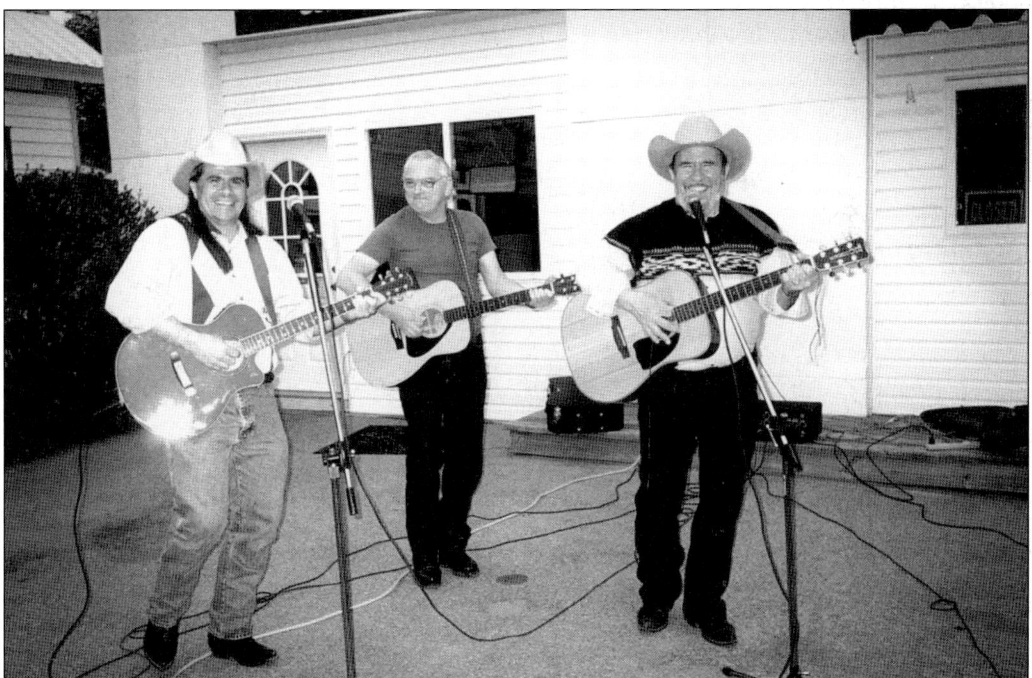

There are many country music fans in the Adirondacks, and the hamlets often had their own country bands. Some groups such as the Pals of the Saddle and Leon Page and the Hope Valley Boys played at Saturday night square dances, on local radio stations, and at the parades. From left to right are Rick Barnes, Nelson Peters, and Dick Barnes playing at the May 6 festival for the return of the swifts of Sacandaga.

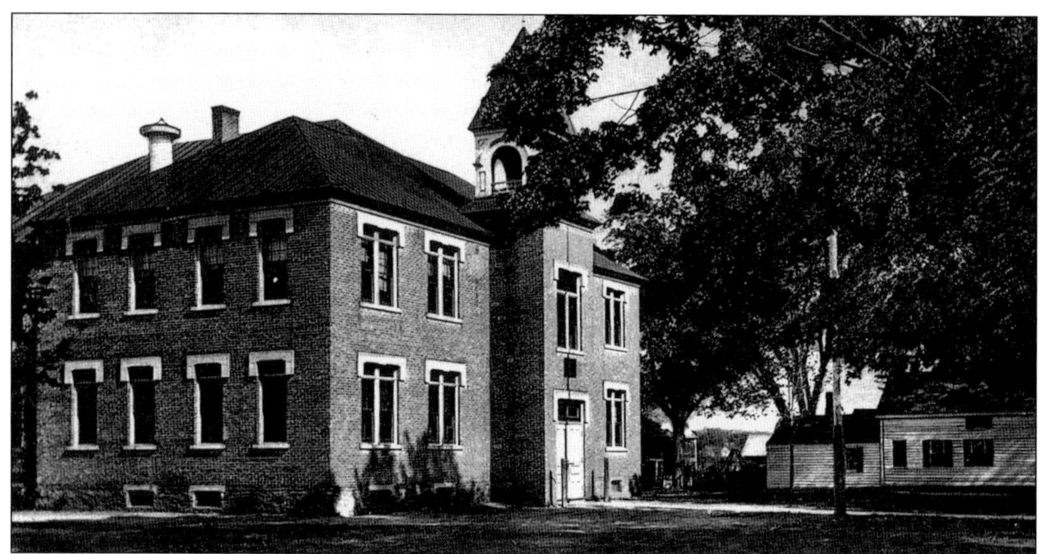

The Northville High School, a Union Free School, was built in 1888. The school's original principal earned $750 and also did the janitorial work. The school got indoor plumbing in 1913 and served the community until 1933, when the new school was built. In 1938, the old building was remodeled for use as the Serfis Glove Company. With a payroll of 150, the company operated until 1969. The building, on the site of today's town offices, was torn down in 1972.

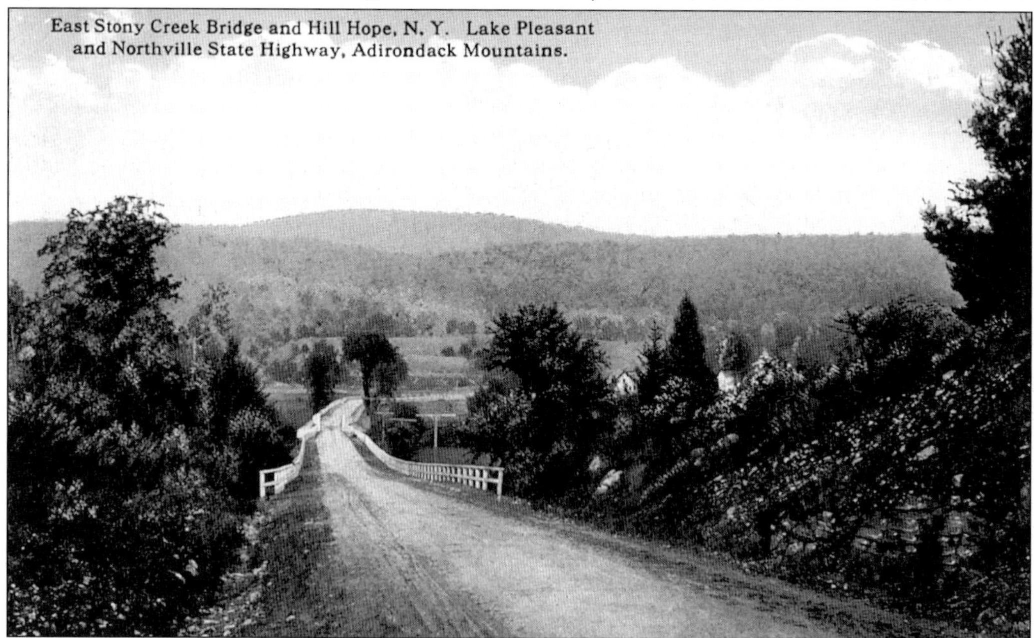

The gravel and graded roadways provided a transition from the footpaths and rutty, muddy trails used by the first people who penetrated the Adirondack wilds to the macadam roads of today. Narrow wooden bridges and wooden roadside fences had to be replaced by steel bridges and cabled guardrails. The history of the hamlets includes many years of raising funds for the roads. The 1930 bridge over Stony Creek hit the news in May 1962, when one end collapsed and dropped into the creek. For the next 16 months, the new Route 30 bypass was used as an alternate route until some $50,000 in repairs could be made.

Three

Benson and Hope

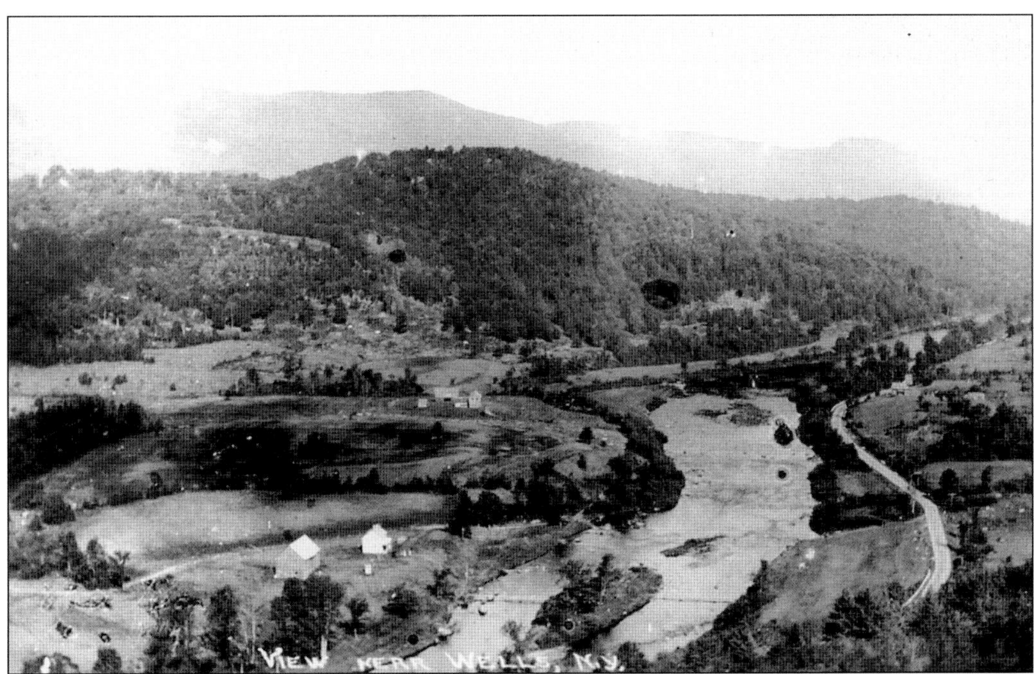

This view shows the Adirondack Trail on the right, heading north between Northville and Hope along the Sacandaga River. The small island in the foreground was once known as Canada Island. When the Adirondack Trail was first used by the Native Americans, the loyalists, and others going to Canada, the island served as a fork in the trail. The right fork led to the Lake George-Lake Champlain corridor, and the left one to Raquette Lake and up the Raquette River or the Grass River to Canada.

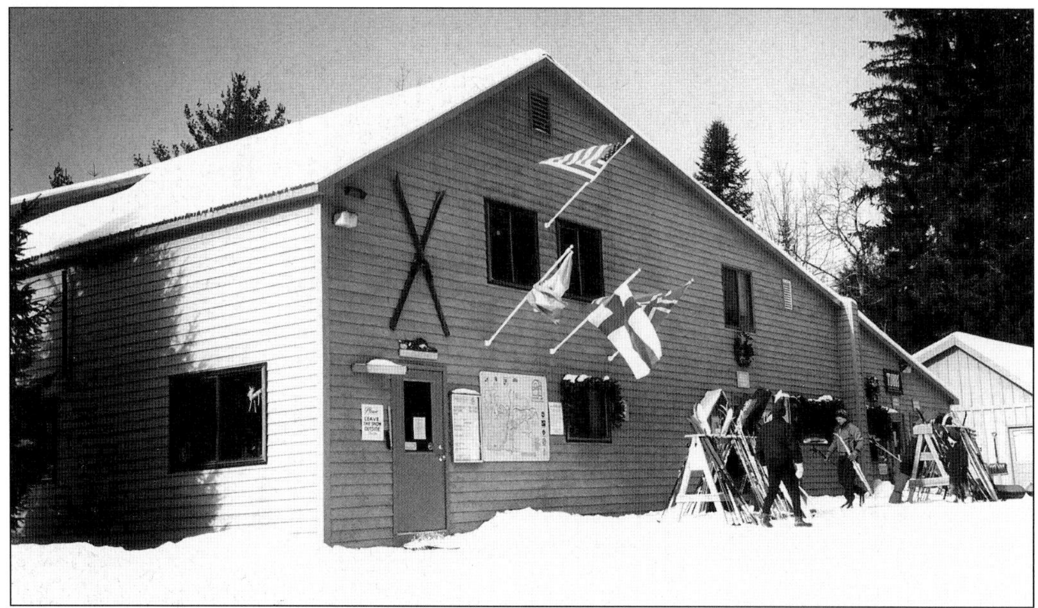

Lapland Lake, in Benson, has become a nationally and internationally known cross-country ski center and resort, run by Olympic skier Olavi Hirvonen, a member of the 1960 U.S. Olympic cross-country ski team and a winner of the Armed Forces Cross-Country Ski Championship. Hirvonen, whose home country is Finland, and his wife, Ann, own the resort. The original owners of the land, the Norm and Ruth Storer family, came to the Adirondacks in 1939 to work and to farm.

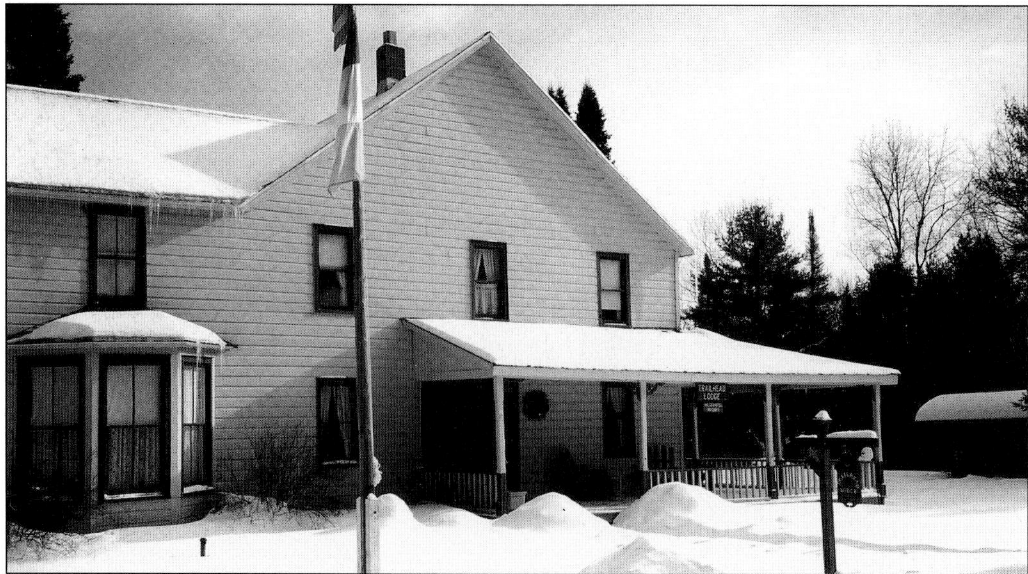

Trailhead Lodge, just off the Adirondack Trail in Benson, began its life in 1850 as a two-room, fireplace-heated, Adirondack cabin. William and Julia Washburn bought it in the 1880s for raising their children, working in the woods, and renting rooms to hunters. The Washburn men served as Adirondack guides, and the lodging and guiding tradition is carried on today by grandson John and his wife, Jane. Additions have been built to create a year-round retreat on the Adirondack-Lake Placid Trail.

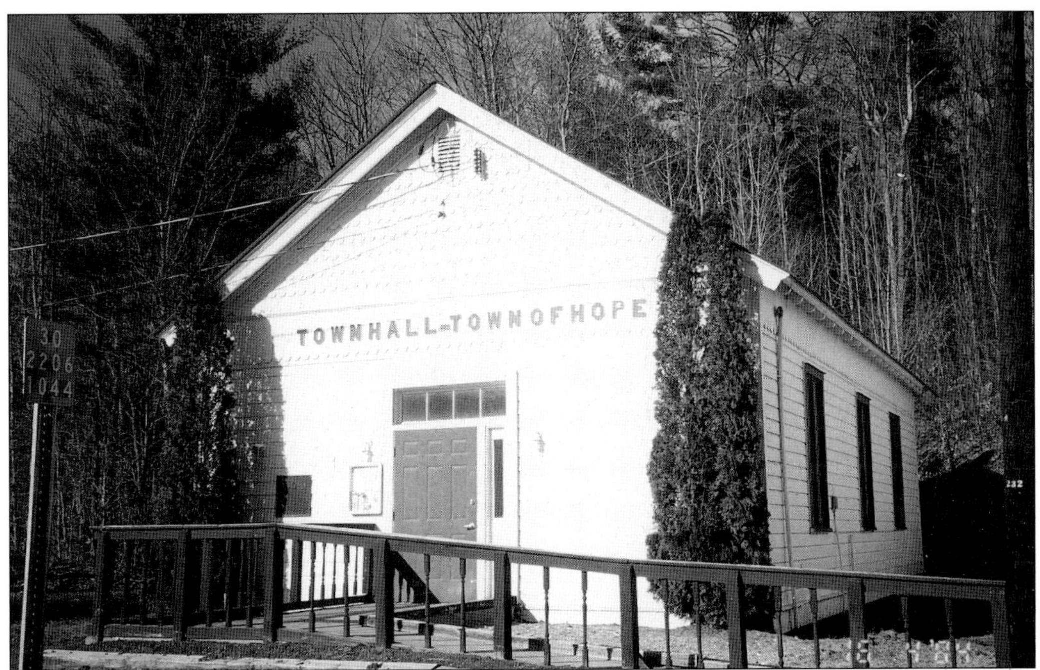

The town of Hope was formed on April 15, 1818. It became a thriving community and in 25 years grew to 650 residents. Seven sawmills were erected in this logging settlement in those early years, and tanneries made use of the hemlock bark for tanning hides. The town hall shown here was the Wesleyan Methodist Church from 1910 to 1925, when it became a public meetinghouse. In 1939, the building was moved to its present site and used for the business of the town.

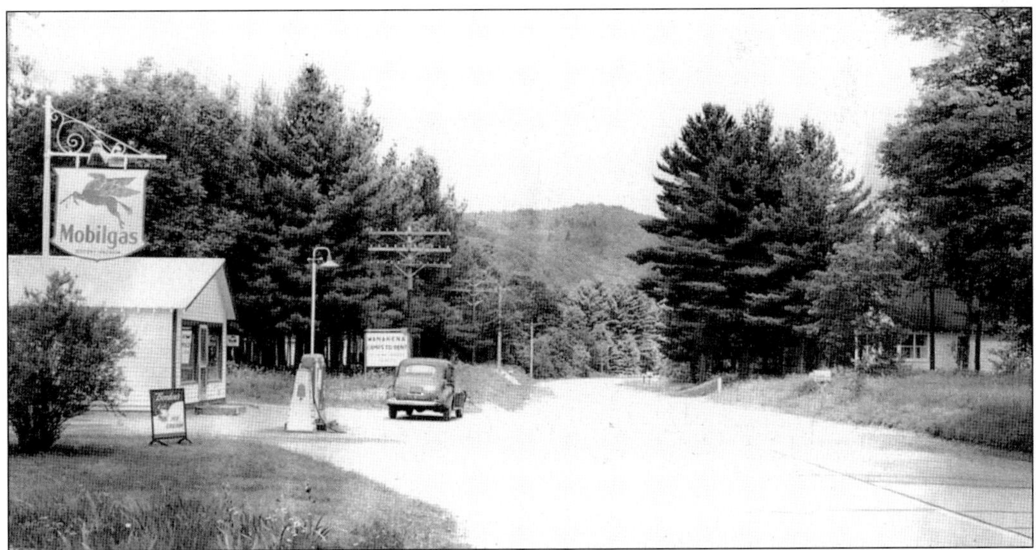

Once the Adirondack Trail became a paved road and automobiles joined the Adirondack scene, new enterprises arose to fill the needs of the traveling public. Howlands Store, in Hope, provided gasoline and groceries; the flying red horse on the Socony stations was a welcomed sight on an Adirondack tour. Next-door, the "Wanakena Camps for Rent" sign advertises one of the many cabin colonies once found along the Adirondack Trail.

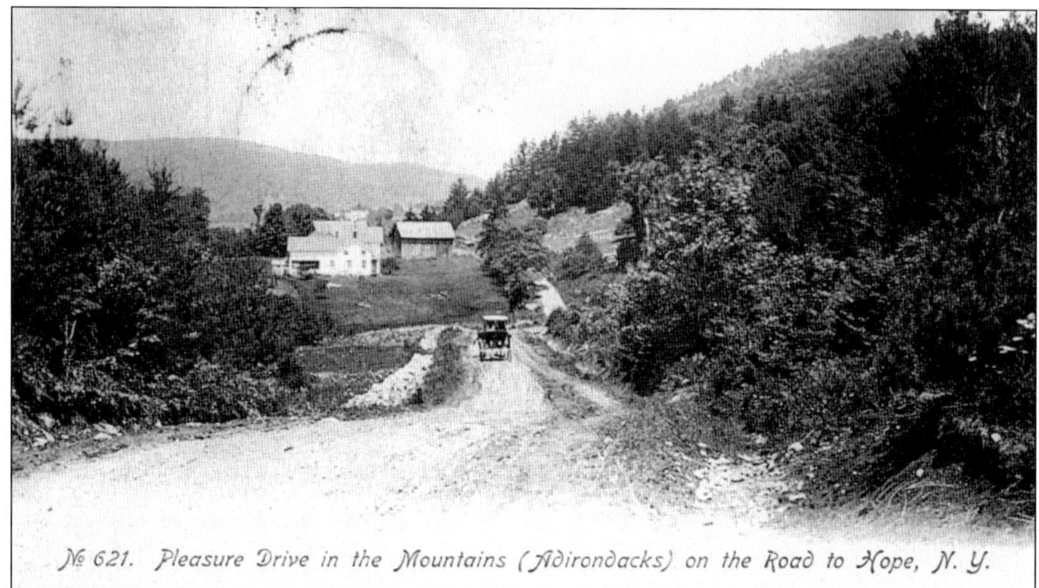

The Adirondack Trail was not always the smooth, well-cared-for macadam road of today; it was once a series of dirt roads connecting the small settlements scattered throughout the mountains. This postcard of a horse and buggy says, "Pleasure Drive in the Mountains (Adirondacks) on the Road to Hope, N.Y." It was mailed in August 1907 to "Juliet" by "Romeo," who was having "the grandest ride!"

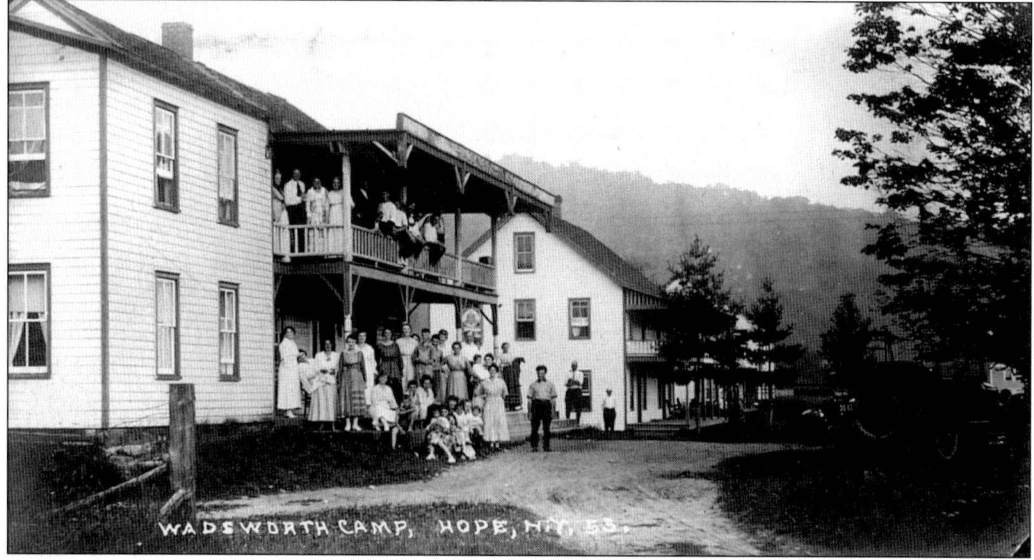

Wadsworth's Hotel, in Hope, was an important stopover on the Adirondack Trail for many years. Built in the 1850s by the Josiah Wadsworth Jr. family, it was a popular summer spot for guests from New York City and Long Island, who often stayed all summer. It originally had a large dining room, a big ballroom, 10 guest rooms, and a two-story front porch overlooking the Adirondack Trail and the Sacandaga River. To handle the crowds, two other buildings were added, the Coop and the Camp. The hotel complex was closed in the 1930s. It later became the residence of Nerie Coulombe, whose picture, taken at the hotel, appeared in *Life* magazine on July 4, 1970.

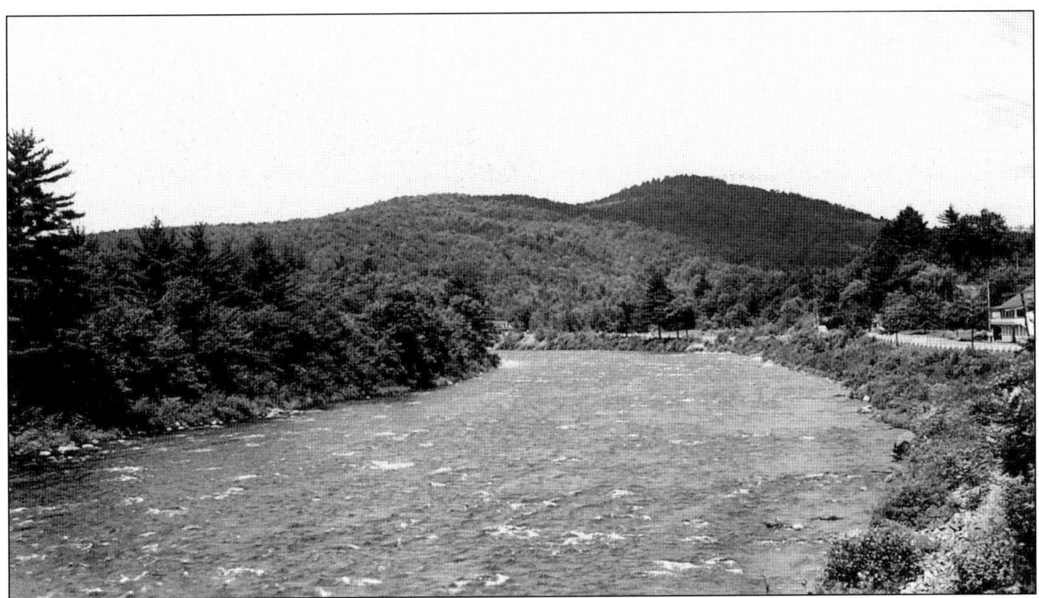

The Adirondack Trail followed the Sacandaga River for many miles through the southern Adirondacks. The Alpine Inn, on the right, was one of the roadside restaurants that provided food for travelers. Still in business today, it sits on the edge of the Adirondack Trail because of road widening over the years.

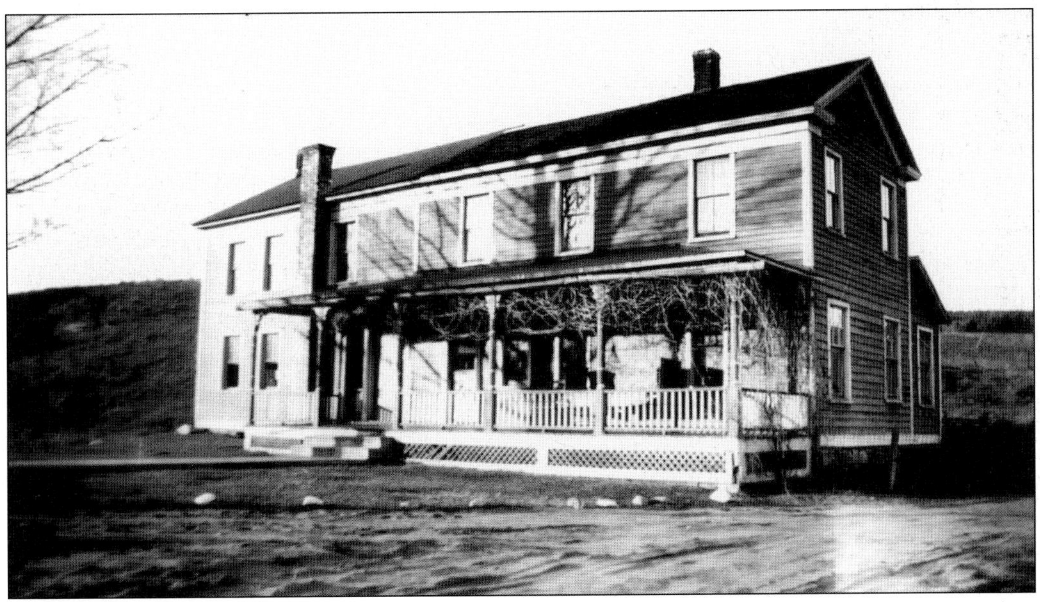

More than two dozen hotels operated in Hope over the years, but none is still in business today. Forest-related workers, travelers, politicians, families, and sportsmen all needed lodging in the days of slower transportation. The hotel pictured was first under the proprietorship of Silas Torrey and later operated by Bud Davison. The Hope Volunteer Fire Company is located on the site today.

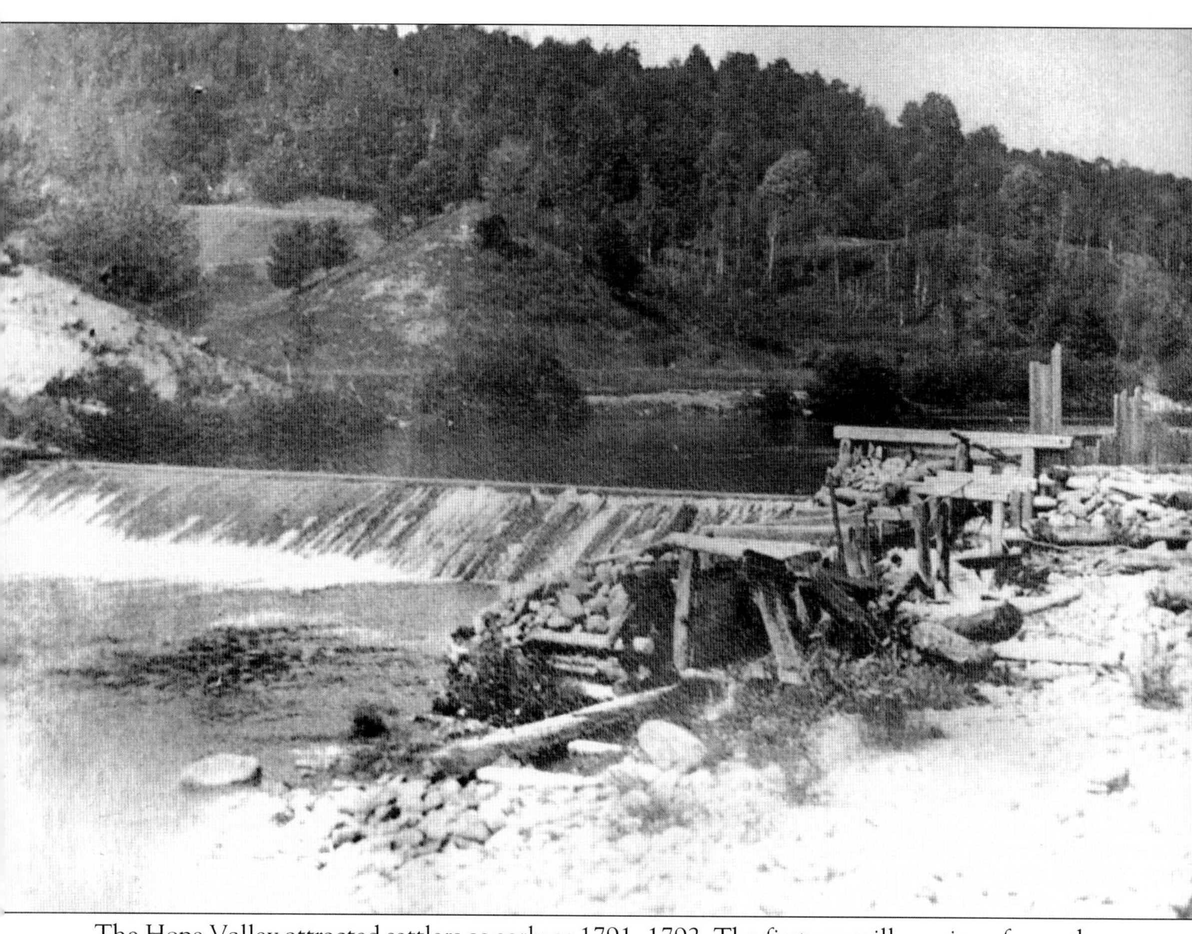

The Hope Valley attracted settlers as early as 1791–1792. The first sawmill—a sign of growth—was operating by 1803, and by 1845, there were six more. In the 1845 census, Hope had 5,373 acres of improved land with 48 farmers, who grew crops and made over 20,000 pounds of butter and over 3,900 pounds of cheese. By 1850, some 1,100 residents lived in Hope. Interestingly, the growing community had two stores and a lawyer but no doctors or clergymen, much like the remote settlements in the Adirondack wilderness. A trip down the Adirondack Trail was required when sickness struck or a wedding was in the works. A total of 15 births—probably with a midwife—and 12 burials were recorded in 1845. Itinerant ministers were often called to the mountains to conduct funerals and other religious rituals. The old dam shown here once provided water and power for the sawmills and tanneries that made up the Hope community. Today, the industries are gone. Seasonal and permanent residents live in this rural setting, and hikers park and follow well-marked trails to the lakes, falls, streams, and mountains.

Four

Wells and Lake Pleasant

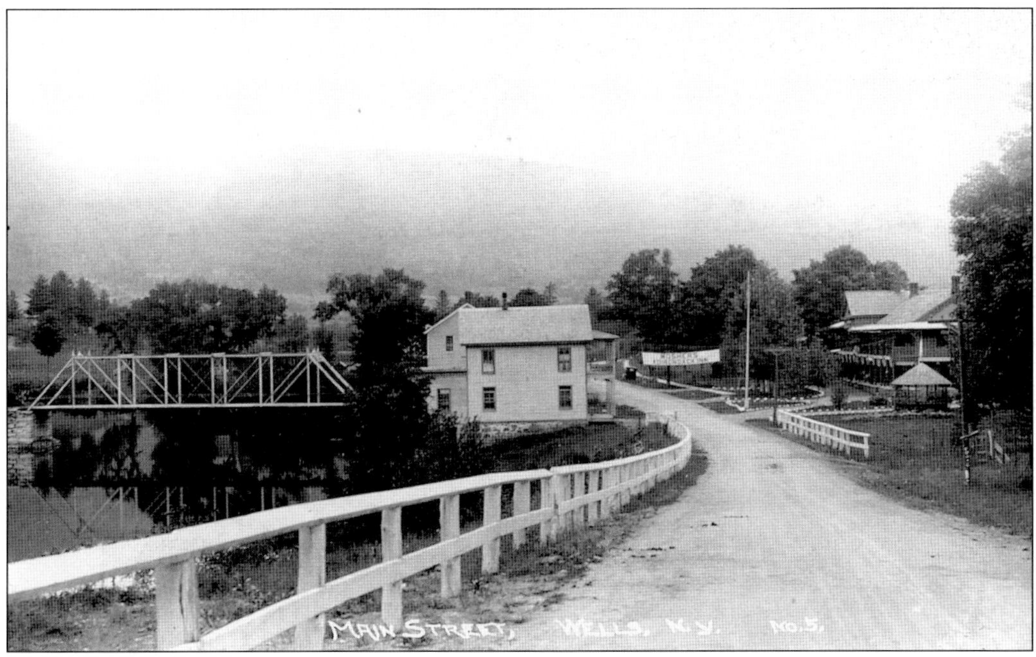

Entering the hamlet of Wells, the Adirondack Trail appeared well traveled and protected by the wooden fence, often seen along roadways of old. When automobiles came into use, the town was often sued by drivers who ran off the road where there were no guardrails. The 1883 bridge took residents and visitors to the west side of Lake Algonquin and up the West Hill road. It was replaced in 1939 with a new bridge. The banner across the road was an early billboard advertising the "Moshers Adirondack Inn." The house and Parkers Store, on the left by the river, have since been replaced by Parkers Corner Memorial Park.

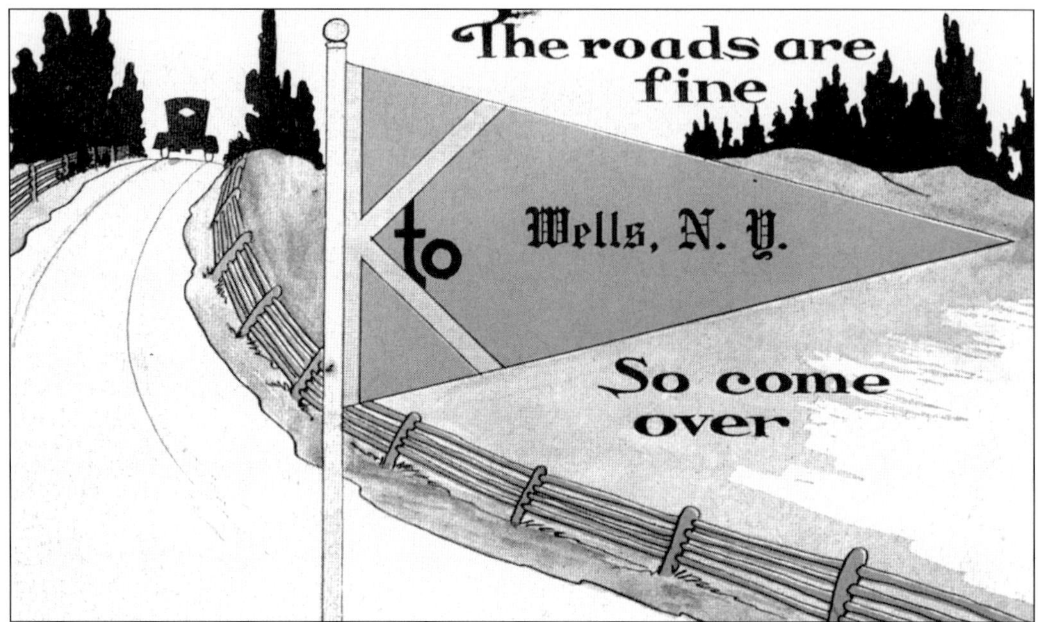

An early postcard supporting the Adirondack Trail was mailed *c.* 1915, stating that "the roads are fine to Wells, N.Y., so come over." The macadam road to Wells from Northville was completed in 1913. It was a great improvement over the rutty dirt road used for 100 or more years. Such improvements led to the growth of accommodations, gas stations, boat liveries, cabins, and campsites along the north–south road through the Adirondacks.

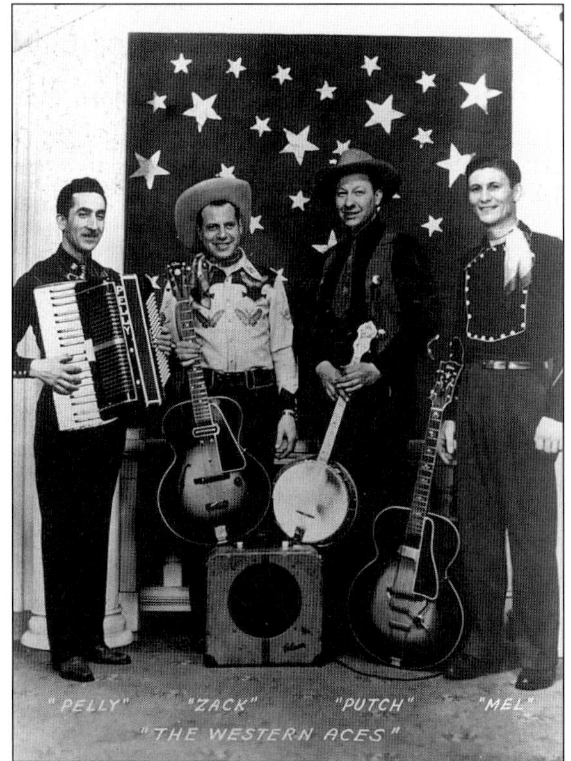

The Veterans of Foreign Wars Post of Northville sponsored a benefit dance in April 1946 at the Forks, a gathering spot near Wells on the Sacandaga River, where two branches came together at the Sacandaga Campsite. Round and square dancing could be enjoyed for the price of a 50¢ ticket. The music was supplied by the Western Aces, who often appeared on local radio stations. The four members of this typical Adirondack band were, from left to right, Pelly, Zack, Putch, and Mel.

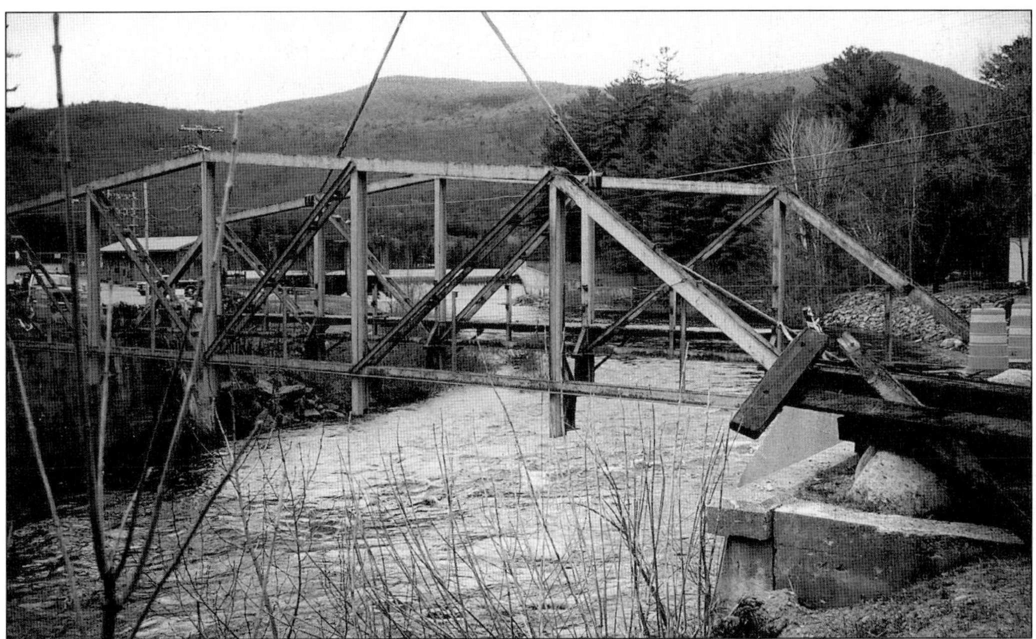

The 1939 bridge over the Sacandaga beside the dam at the southern end of Wells was replaced in 2003. It is shown being lifted off its moorings by a huge crane. It was preserved, refinished, and repositioned farther upriver, replacing the old Griffin Bridge. The first steel bridge at the site was used for over 50 years, and the 1939 bridge served for over 60 years.

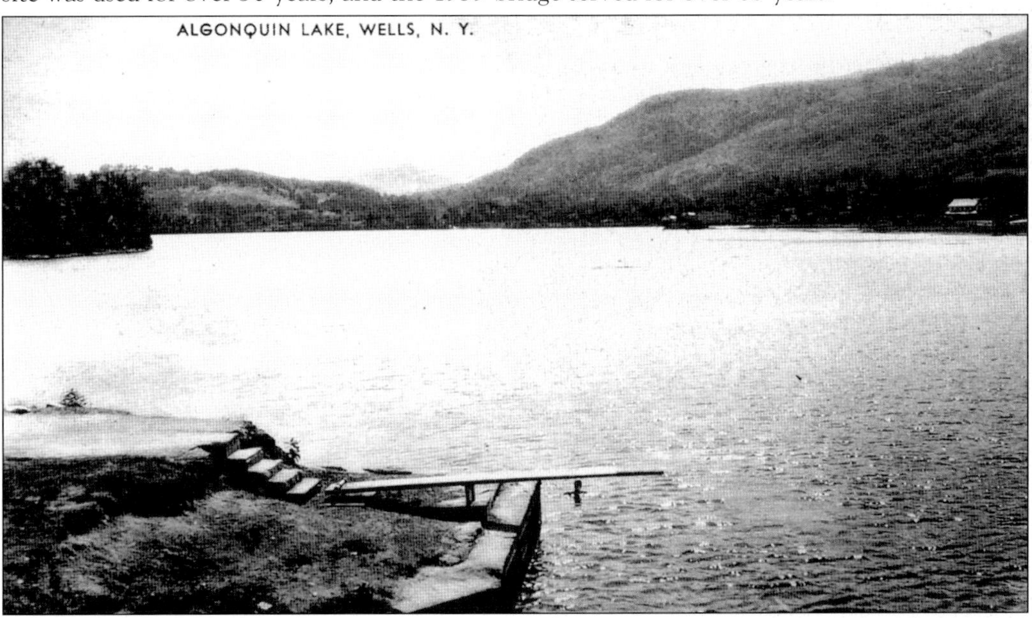

Lake Algonquin is named after a Native American tribe that once used the Adirondacks for their hunting and trapping grounds. Created by a power dam on the Sacandaga River, the lake lies on the bed of an ancient sea in Wells. It is rather shallow except where the original river bed runs through. It is scheduled, pending approval, for draining and dredging in the near future to maintain its original depth of some 10 feet. It has summer homes and camps, and provides fishing, swimming, water-skiing, boating, and ice racing.

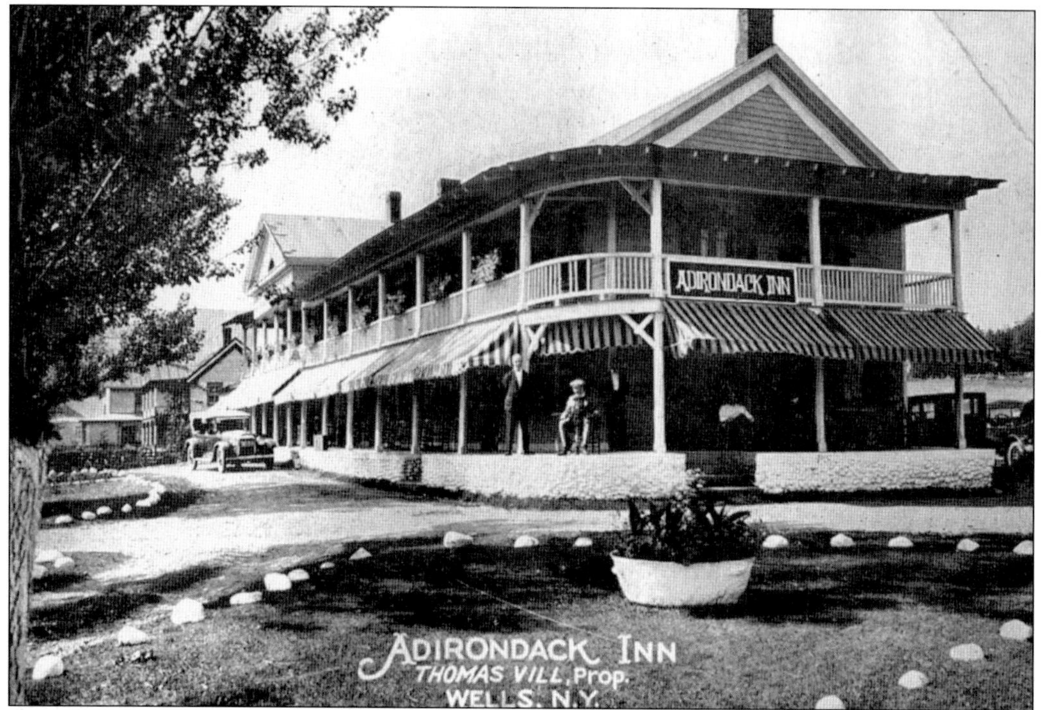

Once the Adirondack Trail opened up the Adirondack Mountain region, new industries emerged. The growing demand for Adirondack guides was followed by the building of guideboats and the construction of hotels for food and lodging. In each of the Adirondack hamlets, several hotels opened to serve the traveling public, hunters, fishermen, and vacationers. Open for 60 years in Wells was one of the many hotels named Adirondack Inn.

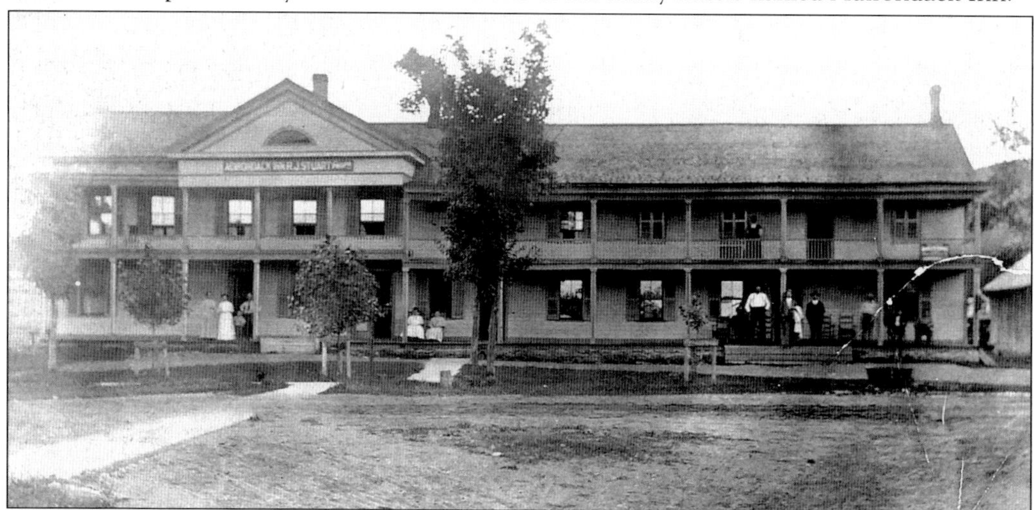

The Adirondack Inn, shown here in an older photograph, served the southern Adirondacks on the Adirondack Trail. It was built by James Mitchell *c.* 1870 on the site of William Wells's 1846 inn and store. In 1900, Lee Anibal took over the operation, and by 1905, the proprietor was Robb Stuart, who exhibited some trained bears there. Some 10 years later, the inn became Moshers Adirondack Inn, and by 1925, it was operated by hotelkeeper Lee Fountain. It burned down in 1929.

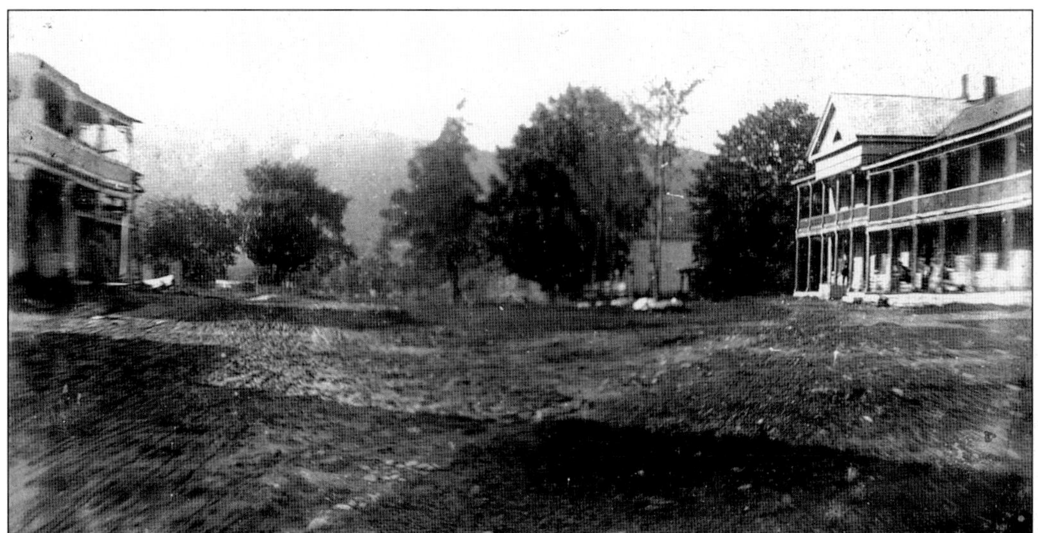

The Adirondack Trail is hardly discernable in this 1900 photograph of the Moshier Hotel and the Adirondack Inn at the entrance to Wells. The roadway appears to be a wide dirt pathway where a stagecoach and others could pull the horses right up to the hotel porch. Most of the people who used these hotels and the dirt roadway arrived by northbound stagecoach from the Northville train station.

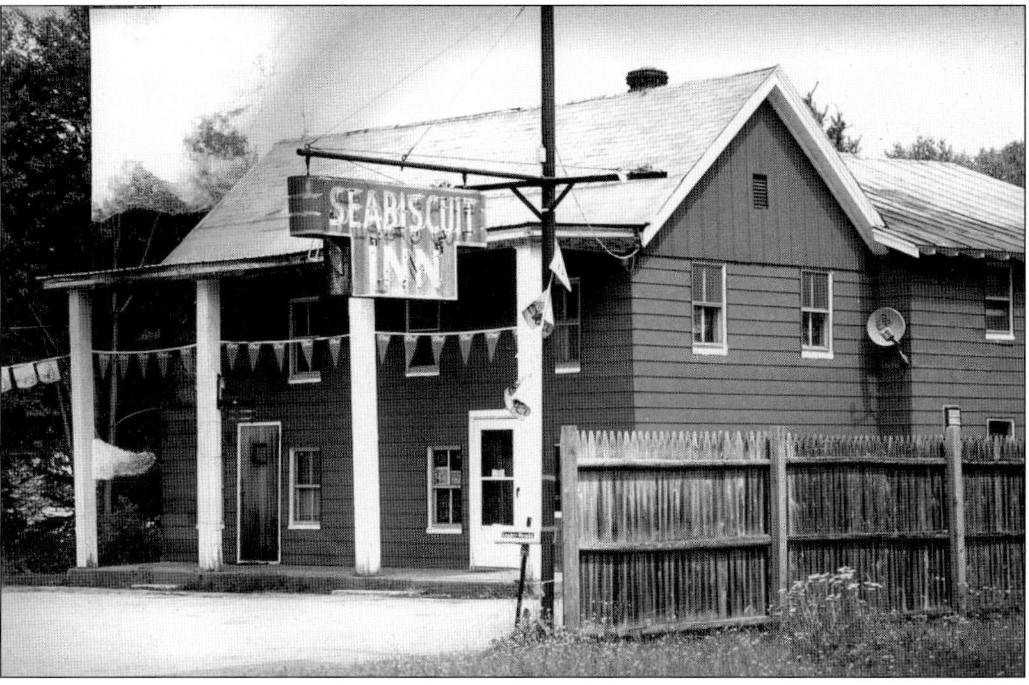

The Seabiscuit Inn has been on the Adirondack Trail at Wells since 1920. Named for one of the nation's greatest racehorses, it has been a gathering spot not only for residents and visitors but also for hunters. During hunting season, it was not uncommon to see deer hanging on the front stoop. The weighing scale for deer is still there for use. The restaurant was built and later named Seabiscuit by Fred Freeman and Harriet Smith, the chauffeur and the nanny, respectively, for the Howards, the owners of the famous horse.

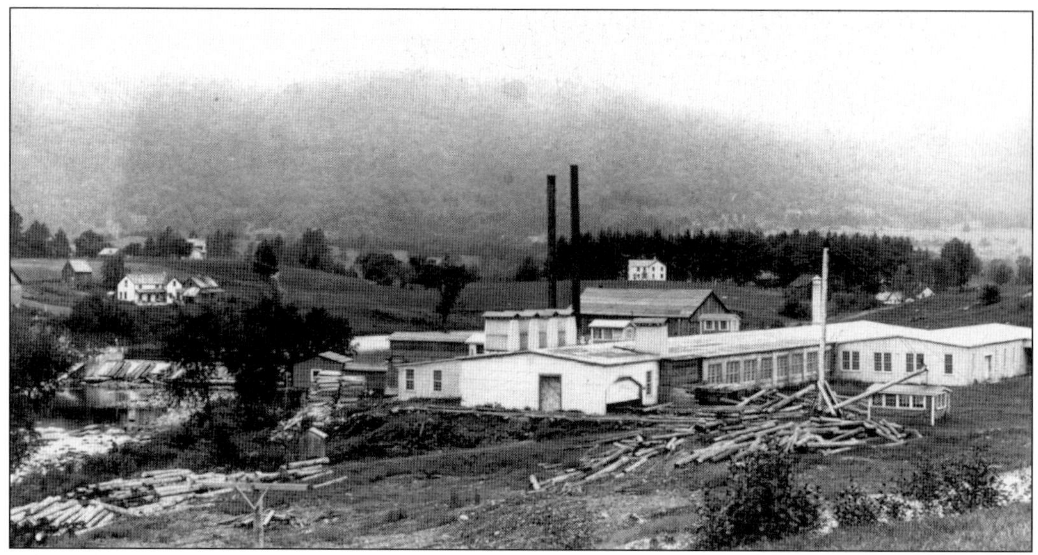

The Adirondack Trail hamlets offered employment to those who wanted to settle in the mountains. The mill at Wells went through several uses. In 1915, Viola Whitman's father, John, worked in the Veneer Mill. He took her and her baby brother to the Mattice family on West Hill on his way to work, where she then went on to the one-room schoolhouse at 9:00 a.m. He worked in the mill all day and picked up the children on the way home. One night they met a bear, whereupon Viola told her father to take the baby and run. She really did not know what she would have done had the bear not run away from them. Such was life on the Adirondack Trail.

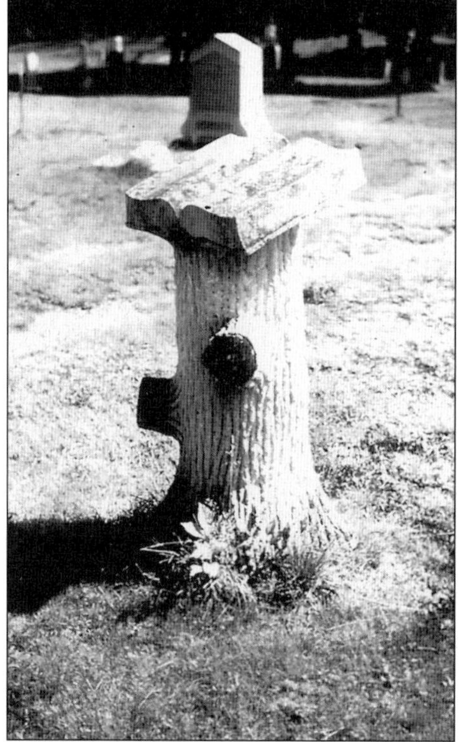

The influence of the Adirondack woodlands on the settlers is reflected in their tombstones. This tree stump monument is in the Methodist Cemetery at Wells. It is the memorial stone for Charles A. Whitman, a Wells blacksmith, and his wife, Emma, the town weaver. The open Bible on the stump records their birth and death dates, 1853–1946 and 1854–1920, respectively.

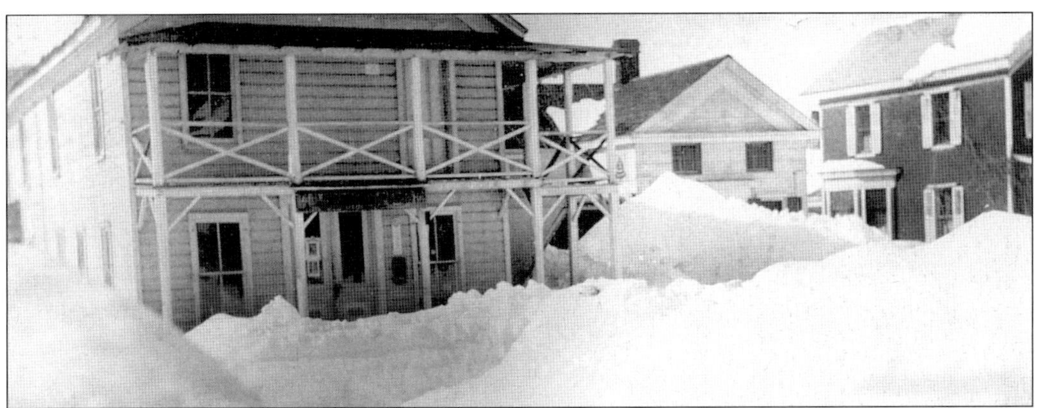

People in the Adirondack Trail settlements craved news from the outside world, and the newspapers of the counties developed with the community needs. The 1845 *Hamilton County Sentinel* was the first newspaper to be published in Hamilton County. By 1882, the *Gloversville Intelligencir*, the *Hamilton County Journal* (later, the *Hamilton County Republican*), the *Hamilton County Press*, the *Hamilton County Democrat*, and the *Adirondack Herald* appeared off and on in the Adirondacks. In 1890, the *Hamilton County Record* appeared. This building was the headquarters of the newspapers up to the 1940s. The *Hamilton County News* began at Inlet in 1947. Now headquartered in Speculator, the newspaper still comes out weekly.

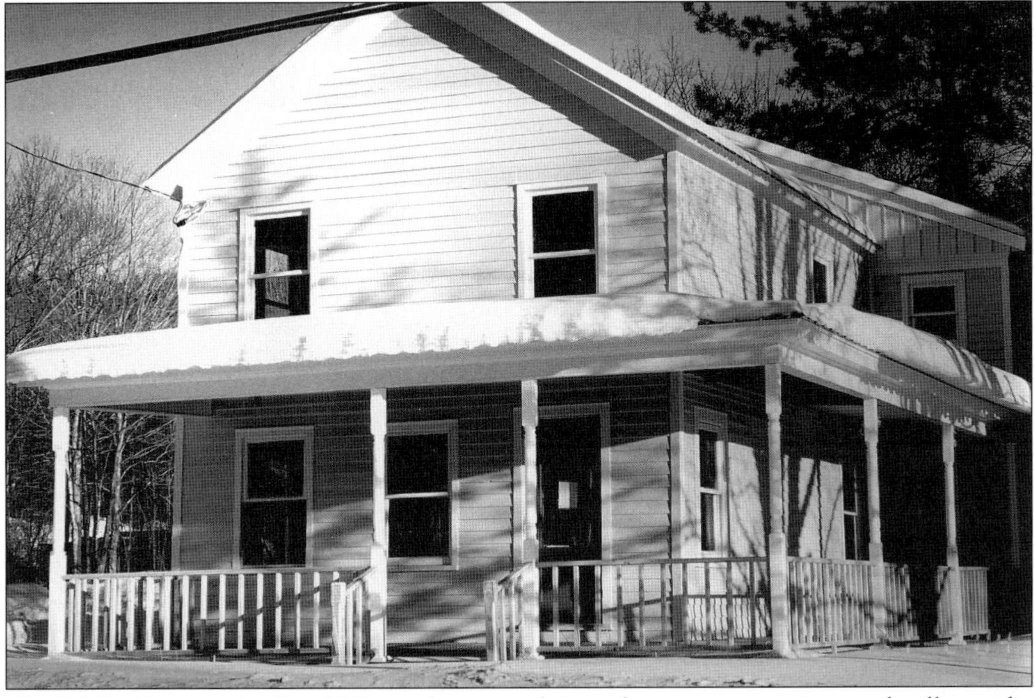

The Wells Museum, in the old Buyce homestead, is undergoing renovations and will soon be open for visitors. Sponsored by the Wells Historical Society, it will house the history of the community including early glove making, lumbering, tourism, furniture making, maple sugaring, and hunting. During the first half of the 20th century, it was the home of general storekeeper Orra Buyce, whose grandfather came to the area to work in the woods, and Mary Hosley Buyce, whose great-grandfather relocated from Edinburgh in 1841 to farm the Sacandaga River flats.

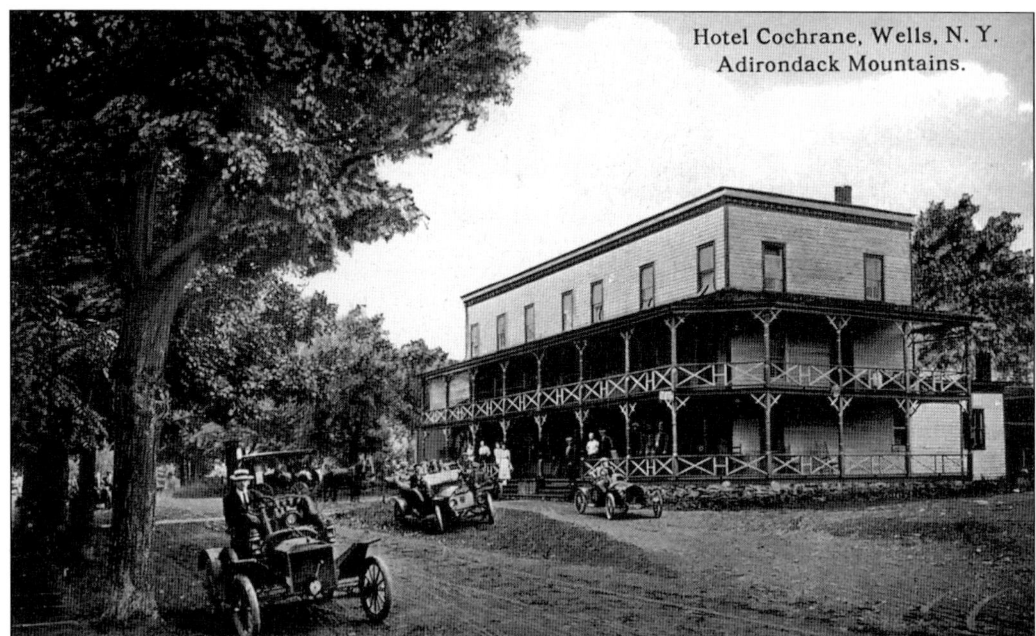

The Hotel Cochrane was as modern as a hotel as could be found at the time it was built, *c.* 1880. With accommodations for 50, it boasted a hot-air furnace. The Wells Town Board held a meeting at the Cochrane Hotel in 1883 to discuss the replacement of the rotting bridge across the river in the southern part of the village. The hotel offered "special dinners" for those traveling on the Adirondack Trail and gave special rates to summer boarders.

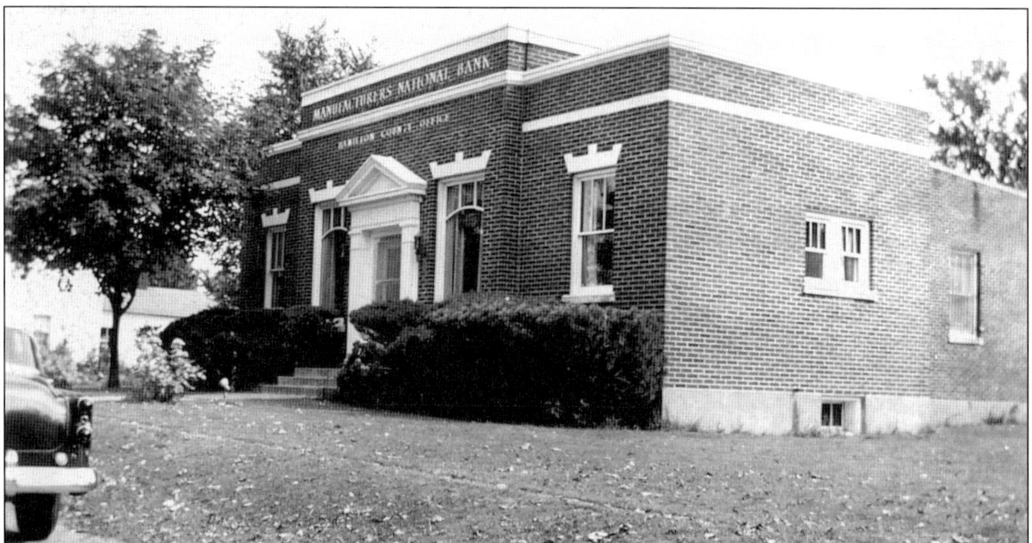

The Adirondack hamlets that grew up once the highway was developed soon found the need for a local bank. The bank in Wells was opened in 1929 as the Hamilton County National Bank on the site of the Cochrane Hotel. It merged in 1955 with the Manufacturers National Bank and became the Hamilton County office of that bank. It relocated to Speculator in 1961 and became a Marine Midland Bank. In 1999, it became an HSBC bank. Today, it is a branch of the City National Bank and Trust Company of Gloversville. The former brick bank building in Wells, shown here, now serves as a court, library, and health center.

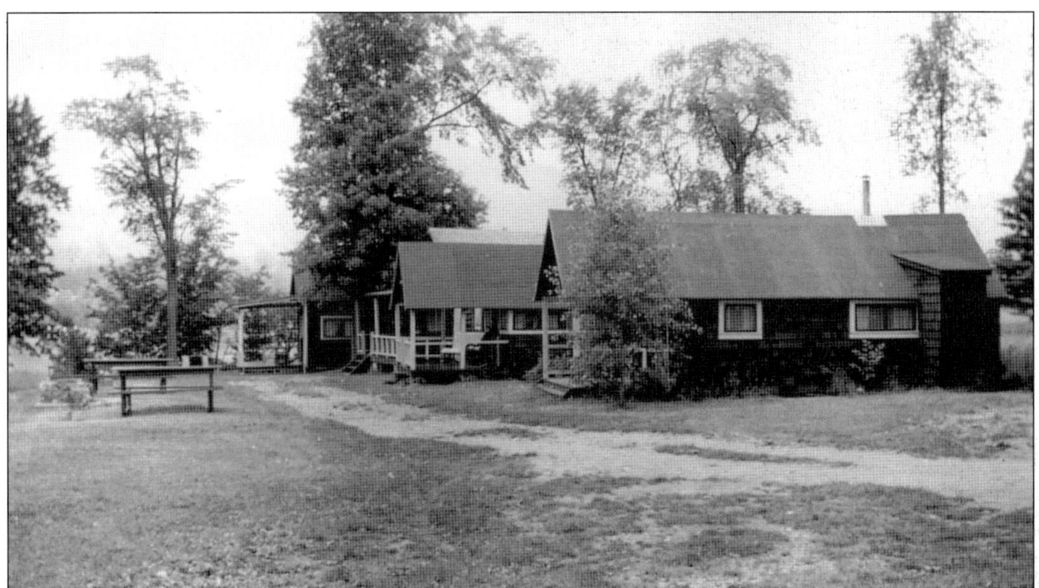

Brown's Cottages, on Lake Algonquin at Wells, represent the residences of choice for those who toured the Adirondacks or came to stay for the summer. Cabin colonies became popular when the automobile found the Adirondacks and continued in popularity until motels began to take away the business. Many of the cabins enjoyed repeat business, year after year, and cabin users often bought and settled in the Adirondacks in later years.

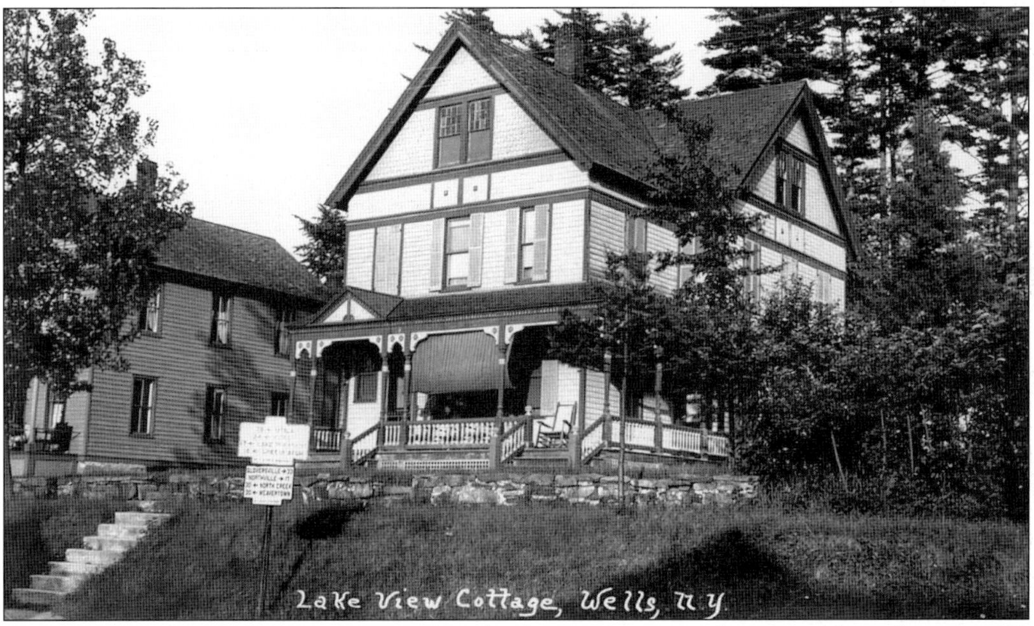

Settlements along the Adirondack Trail evolved from the original scattered log cabins to well-built cottages and homes. Many provided a good view of the lake or were on lakefront property. In the early years, the valuable land was across the road from the river or lake, away from the cold winds of winter. Lakefront houses were hard to heat. Note the road sign in the front of this Wells cottage, with mileages north to Utica, Piseco, Lake Pleasant, Speculator, Weavertown, and North Creek and south to Gloversville and Northville.

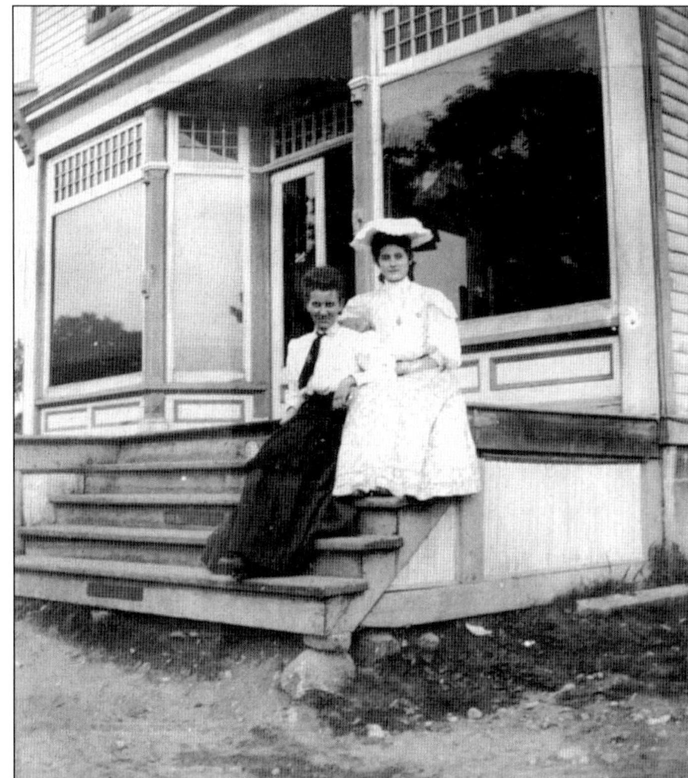

When the Adirondack Trail was straightened and improved in the 1920s and 1930s, it required some disruption of the roadsides. In some cases, concrete walls were built to hold back the dirt banks. Where the road was lowered, steps were built up to the buildings. Martha Babcock and Cora Buyce are seated on the steps of the Hosley Store in Wells before the building was removed to make way for the road.

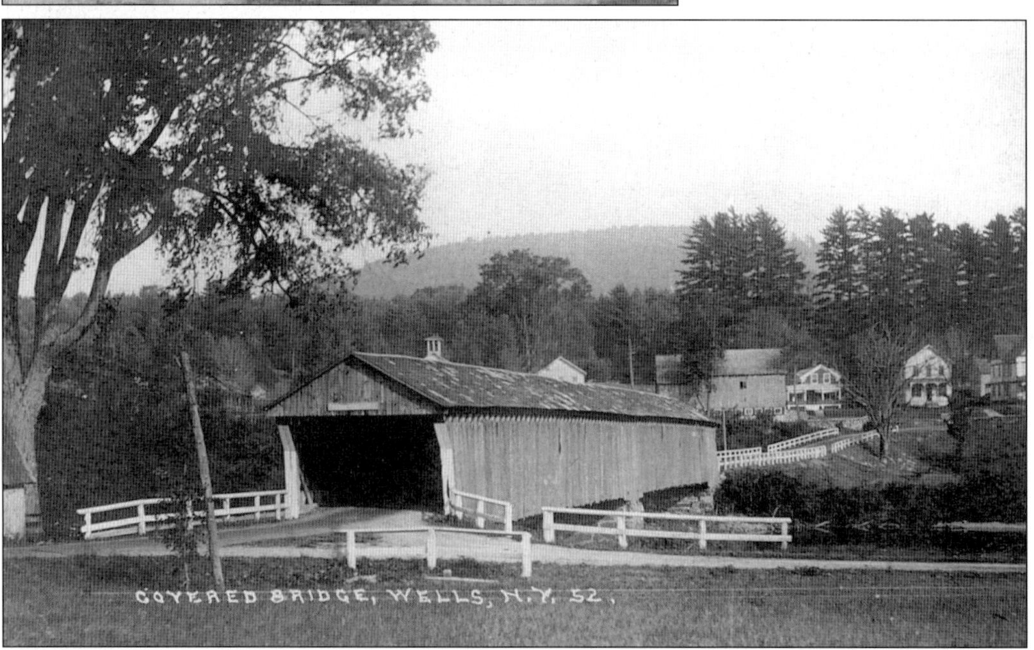

This 1913 view looks from west to east at the old covered bridge over the Sacandaga River, now the site of the Wells public beach. Shown are the old Hosley barn, which housed stagecoach horses; some early homes; and above the bridge, the top of one of the early schoolhouses, which today is the American Legion Hall.

Auger Falls is a popular hiking destination on the Sacandaga River between Wells and Speculator on the Adirondack Trail. From the top of the hill beyond the intersection of Routes 8 and 30, it is a short and easy hike to the chasm, where the Sacandaga has cut through the rock for generations. Named Olger Falls on early maps, it was once the site of a power dam. The photograph, taken during a dry season, shows many rocks that are usually under water.

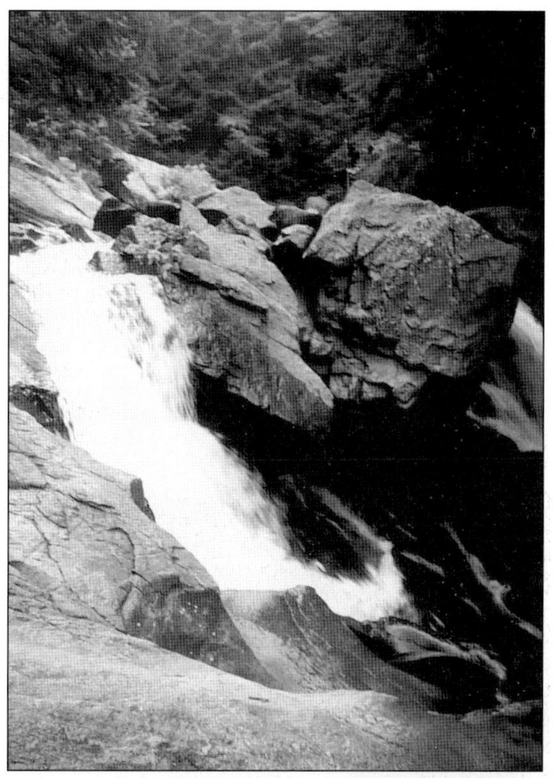

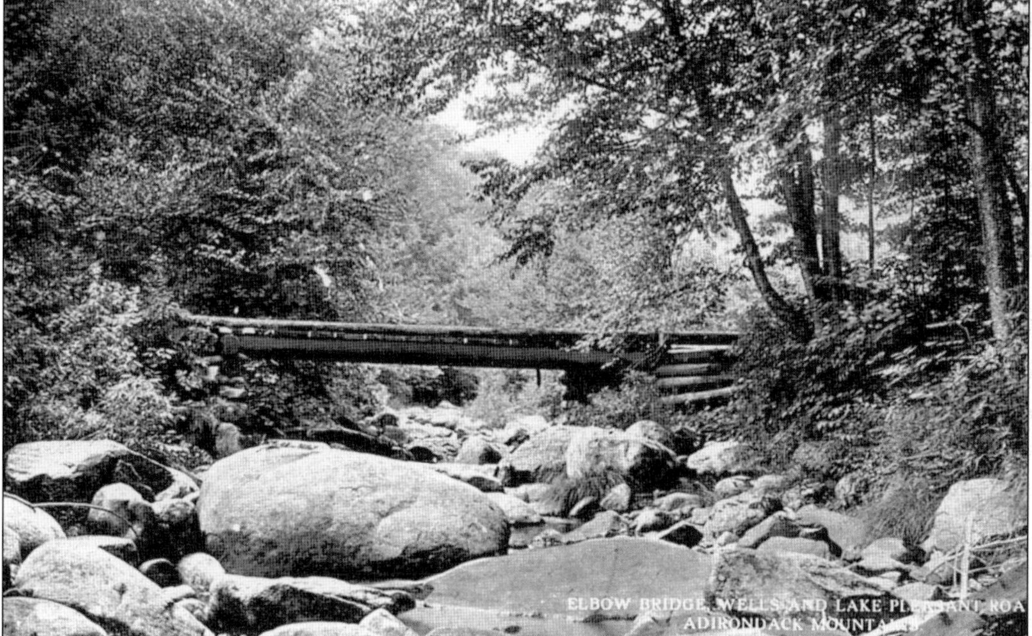

Elbow Creek was followed as the main route to Canada when a military road was constructed during the War of 1812. Elbow Bridge was once on the main road north through the Adirondacks between Wells and Lake Pleasant. Today, it is on an alternate route, the Gilmantown Road. The bridge was reconstructed in 1927, after it was damaged by an automobile.

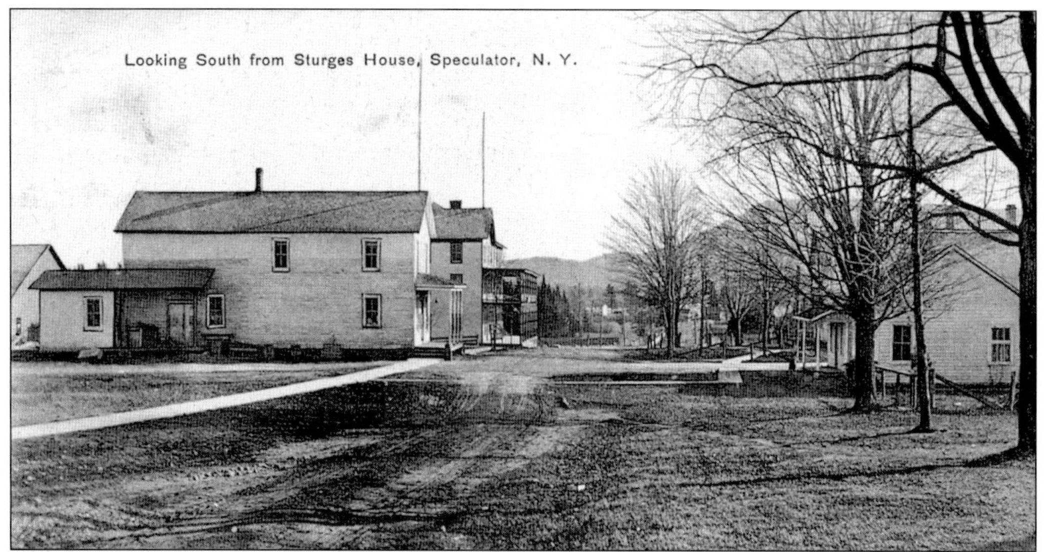

The Adirondack Trail was a dirt highway during its formative years, and those who lived in the hamlets found ways to cope with the sometimes dusty and muddy roads. Entrepreneurs, such as Ellery Schoolcraft in Northville, became the town sprinkler and watered the dusty streets in front of the homes of his customers to "lay the dust." In this scene at Speculator, plank sidewalks can be seen along the side of the road, with one going across the road to connect at the other side. Pedestrians could cross without getting in the mud. When dust bunnies (small clumps of dust) formed under beds and chairs, homemakers would said they came from the dusty roads.

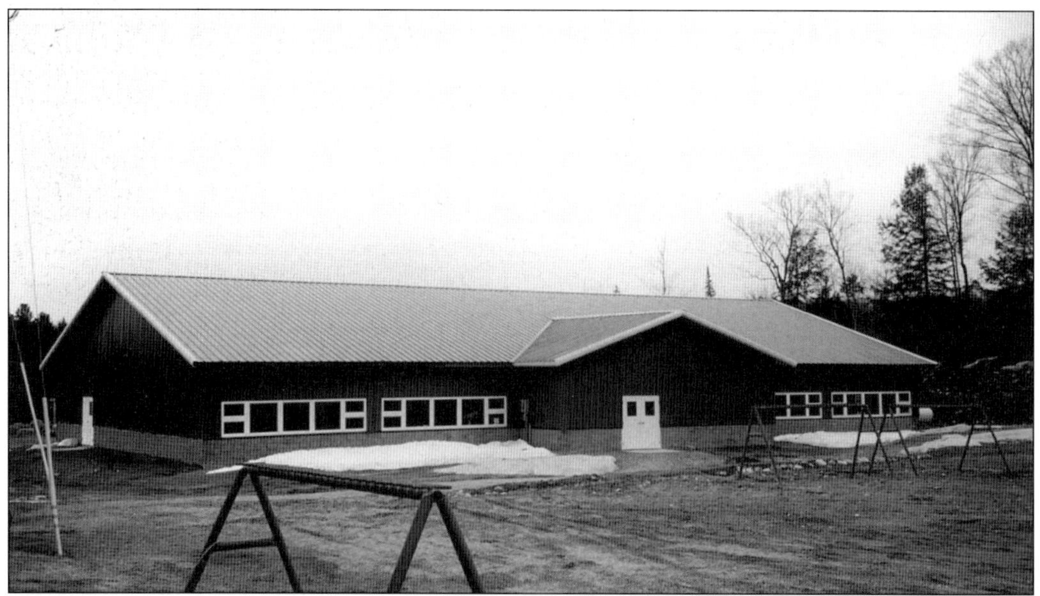

Speculator, an incorporated village, attracts summer residents and tourists, as well as skiers and snowmobilers who visit Oak Mountain Ski Center. It was first known as Newton Corners after postmaster Newton, who served from 1843 to 1870. In 1898, it became Speculator after nearby Speculator Mountain, named by early land speculators. This new building, at the Oak Mountain Ski Center, is designed as a restaurant, with seating for 300 and a warming hut for skiers.

The Sacandaga River Community Park on the Adirondack Trail at Speculator is a moderately handicapped-accessible area along the Sacandaga River. The mile-and-a-half-long walking trail makes the Adirondack wetlands and forest available to all. It includes educational displays, picnic areas with grills, and wooden walkways. Native Americans, loggers, guides, settlers, and the naturally occurring flora are featured along the trail.

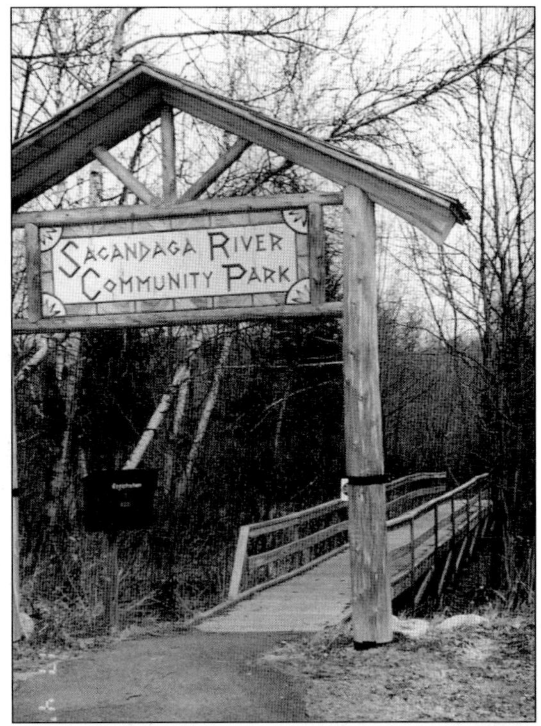

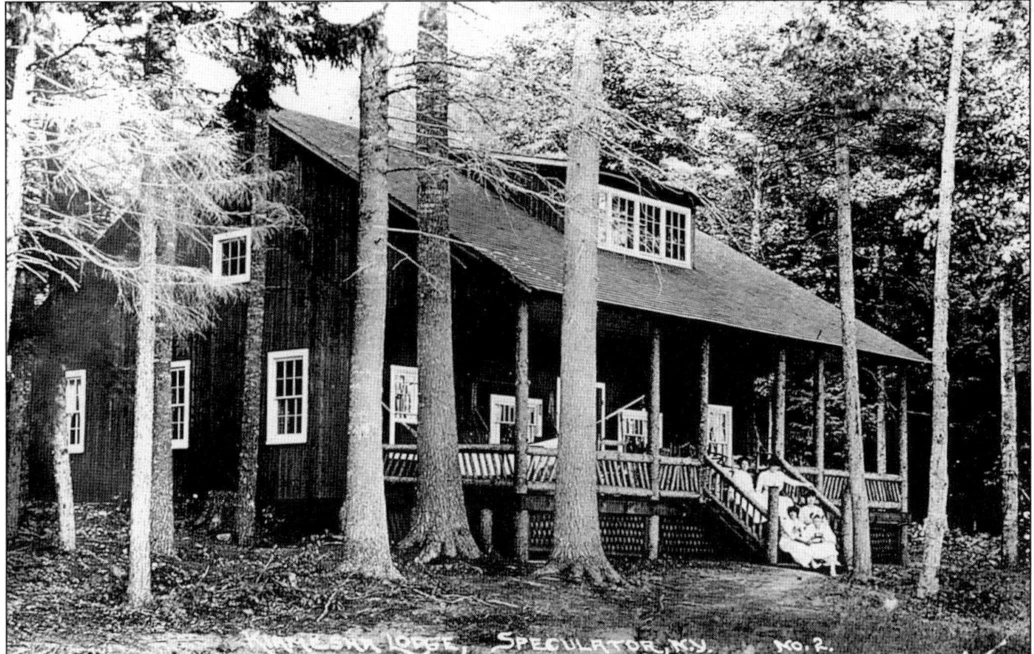

Kiamesha Lodge, near Speculator, is typical of thousands of private camps that grew up in the Adirondacks during the first half of the 1900s. Once transportation to the Adirondacks became more available with the use of the automobile, vacationers deserted the hotels for ownership of private camps. Many camps were built in the rustic style with native materials and were only used during the warm weather. They were often passed down to children and grandchildren.

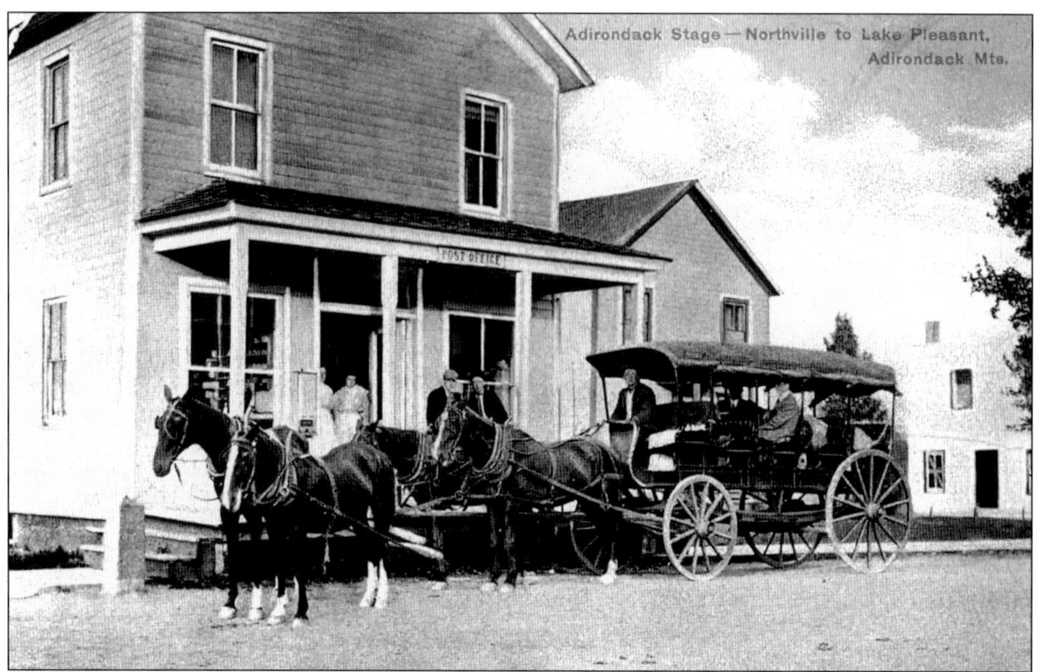

The Adirondack Trail was busy in the days before automobiles, with the tallyho stagecoach from Northville and the taxis that supplemented the limited capacity of the stage. A taxi is pictured in front of the Henry B. Slacks store, which for some 70 years also housed the post office at Newtons Corners (later Speculator). Note the side curtains that could be rolled down in wet weather.

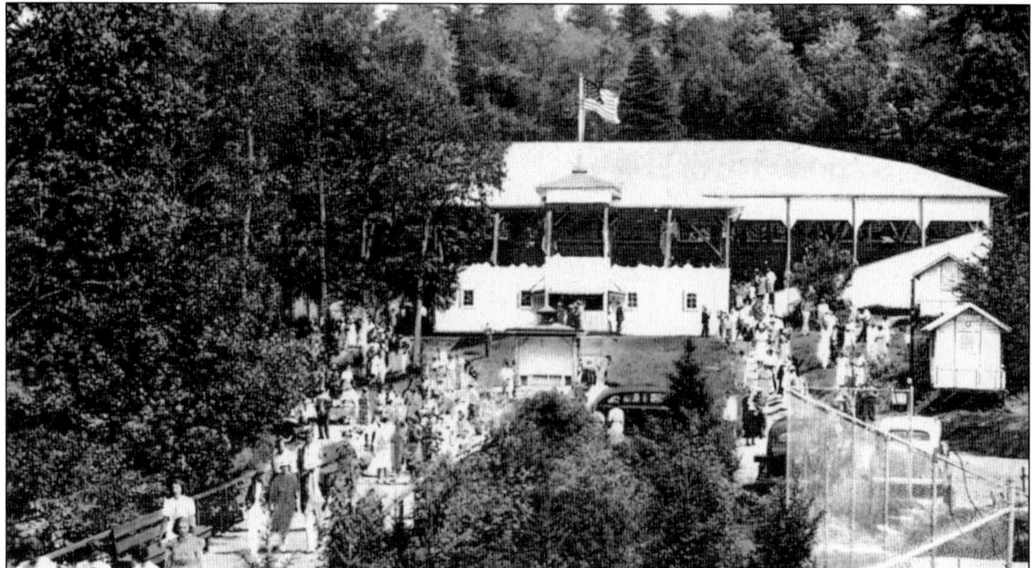

The Adirondacks became the home of several religious camps and retreats, to which hundreds came for rest and relaxation in a religious environment. Camp-of-the-Woods, at Speculator, was founded by George "Pop" Tibbitts in 1917. Gordon Purdy carried on the camp through a period of growth after the death of Tibbitts in 1948. Today, it presents programs in a 1,200-seat auditorium and has housing for hundreds.

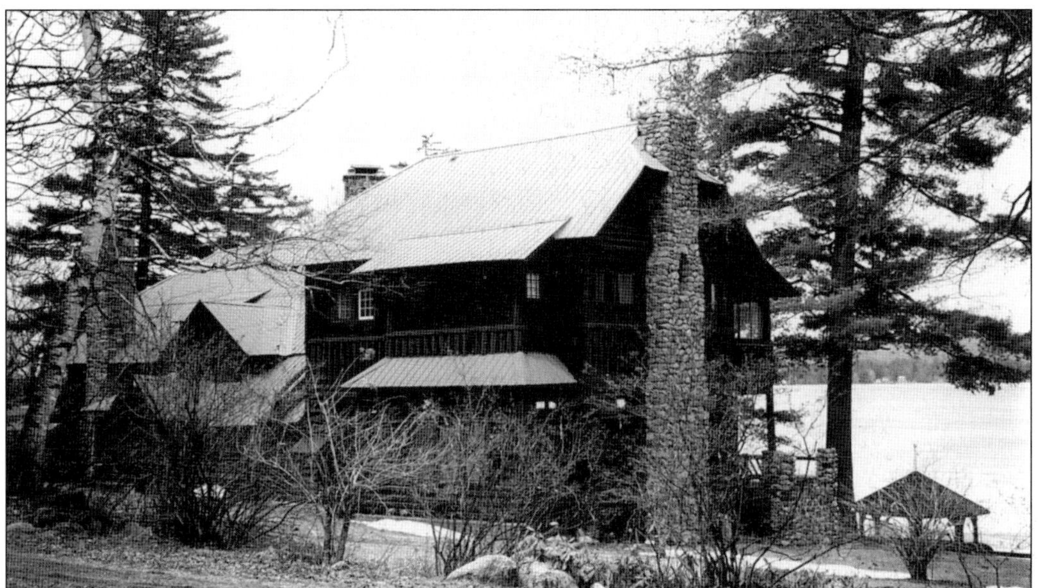

The Adirondack Trail has a history of wealthy summer visitors building palatial summer camps on the Adirondack lakes. Bearhurst, on Lake Pleasant, was built in 1895 by New York businessman Emil Meyrowitz. The massive native stonework and the rustic log buildings are open today for those seeking the forested Adirondacks. Guests can enjoy the same clear lakes and fresh mountain that the wealthy who built the camps did. Even the icehouse has been turned into a cottage for two at Bearhurst.

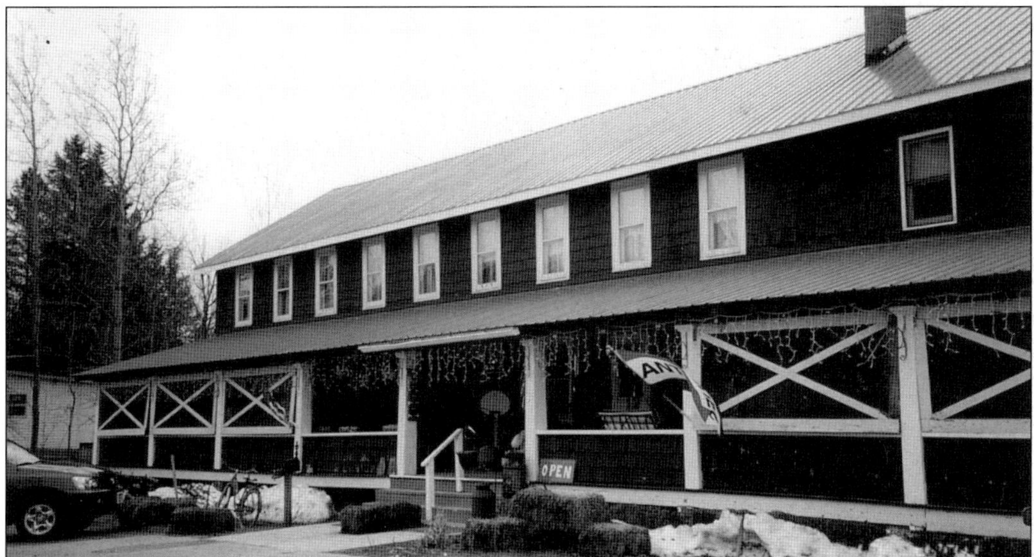

Speculator's Grahams Hotel was built in 1923 by DeWitt Graham to serve the tourists and travelers finding their way up the Adirondack Trail to the mountains. It was moved from its original location across the street and some distance from today's location by Chet Rudes in a day when moving buildings made more sense than tearing them down. The hotel also contained a dance hall, a barbershop, and a bar. It went through a series of owners over the years. Today, it has been reborn as an antiques and gift shop with a coffee bar known as the Family Tree.

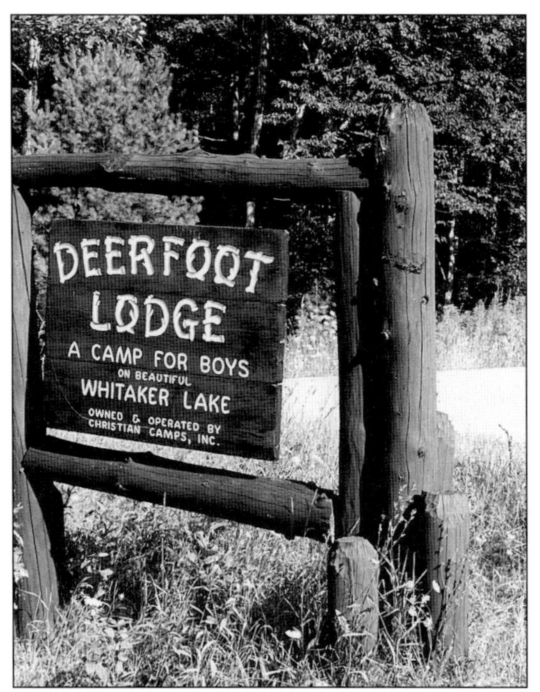

Deerfoot Lodge began in the Kunjamuk camp of Cal Wilber in 1929. It was founded by YMCA worker Alfred Kunz and his wife, Florence, as a Christian camp to help boys bridge the gap from boyhood to manhood. In 1933, Deerfoot moved to a site on Whitaker Lake in a cooperative lease with guide Halsey Page and the International Paper Company. In 1939, Deerfoot was incorporated under Christian Camps Inc., and the paper company sold the corporation 50 acres of land on Whitaker Lake, including 2,000 feet of shoreline, for $17,000. Deerfoot celebrated 75 years in 2004.

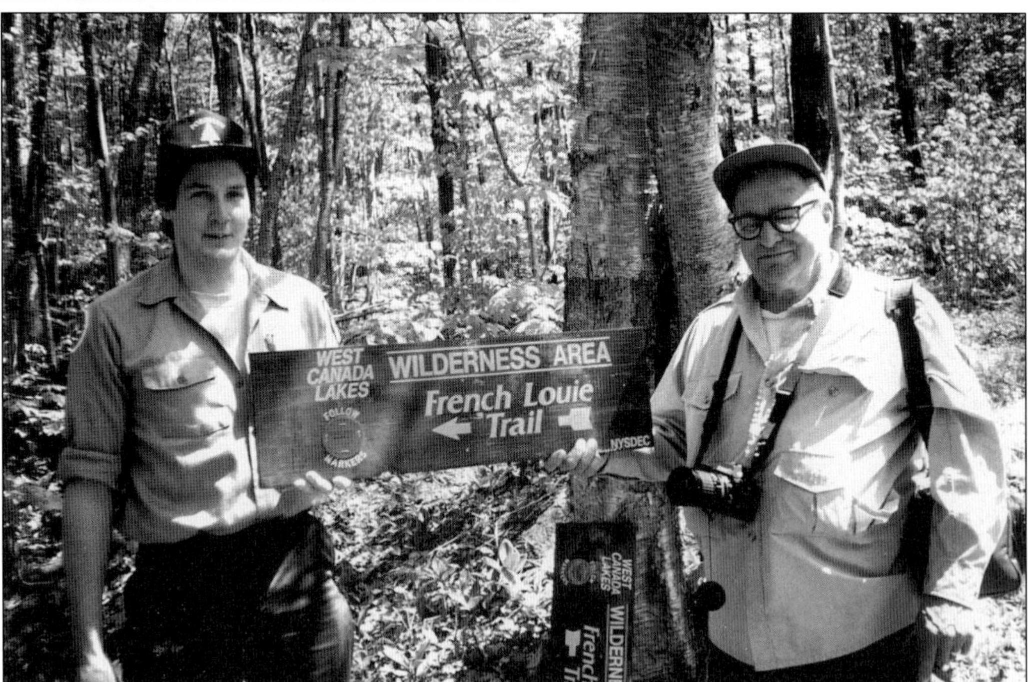

In June 1996, Louis "French Louie" Seymour, a well-known Adirondack hermit and guide, was immortalized when a trail was named after him. Signs with his name were posted for the West Canada Lakes Wilderness Area trail from Sled Harbor in the Perkins Clearing area to the Northville-Lake Placid Trail. He moved into the mountains in 1870 and opened a sporting lodge 25 miles back in the woods. He made good use of the Adirondack Trail to haul his furs to Speculator for sale. He passed away at age 83 in 1915. His grave is in the Speculator Cemetery.

Five

INDIAN LAKE AND LONG LAKE

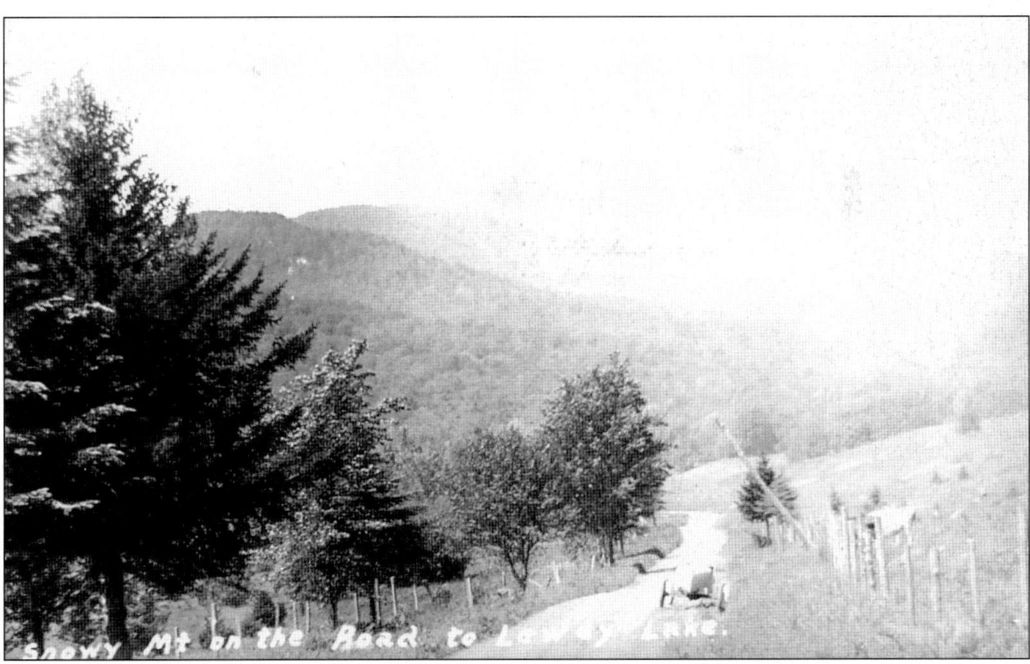

The Adirondack Trail provides easy access to several fire tower trails. With its fire tower restored, Snowy Mountain, at 3,900 feet high, is the highest mountain in the southern Adirondacks. It is 5 miles north of Lewey Lake and 6.5 miles south of Indian Lake. The 3.9-mile trail offers 1 mile of moderate hiking, followed by a continuous climb to the top, which offers a view of Indian Lake, Speculator, Piseco, the Blue Ridge Wilderness, and Blue Mountain Lake.

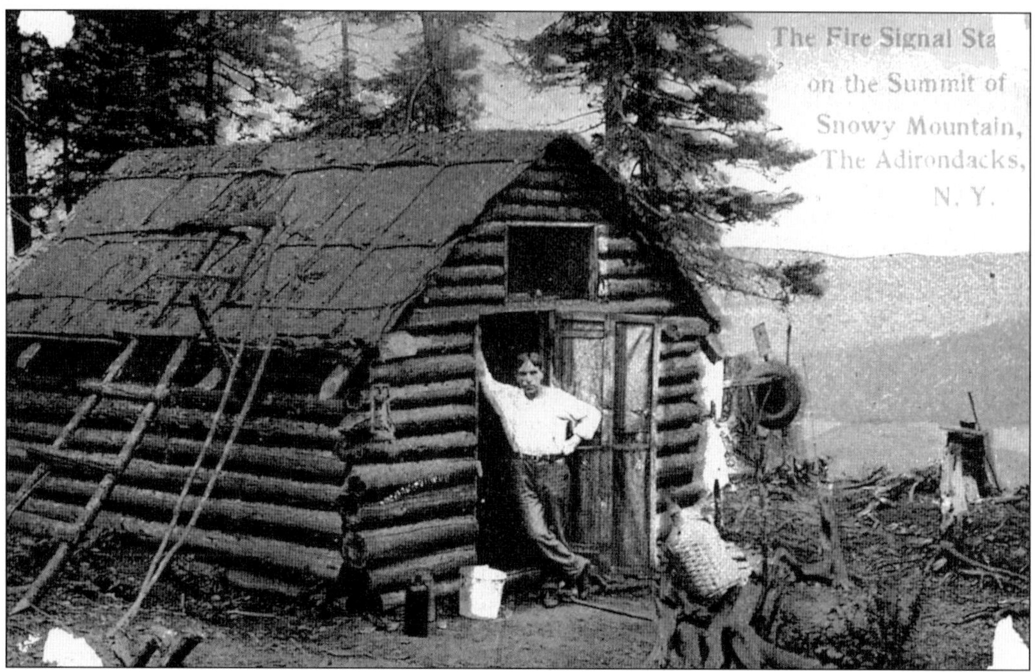

With its vast vista of the southern Adirondacks, Snowy Mountain was a good location for one of the early Adirondack fire towers. Rangers who worked on the mountaintop during the fire season lived in a small cabin. They carried their food and water up the mountain during their tour of duty. Fire observation was often a lonely job. Snowy Mountain was first called Squaw's Bonnet after the Indian Sabael's wife.

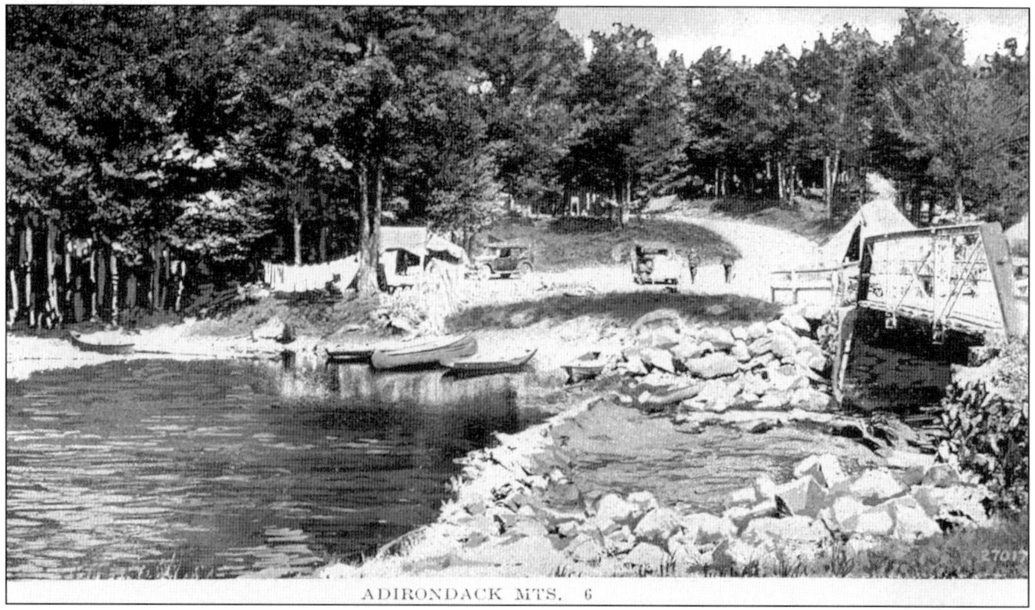

Camping at the bridge between Lewey Lake and Indian Lake began well before the construction of the Lewey Lake Campsite and Indian Lake Island Campsite in the 1920s. The Adirondack Trail was primitive at the time, but the automobiles pictured here made it over the dirt road. Here, the Adirondack Trail crosses over the bridge and leads into the woods.

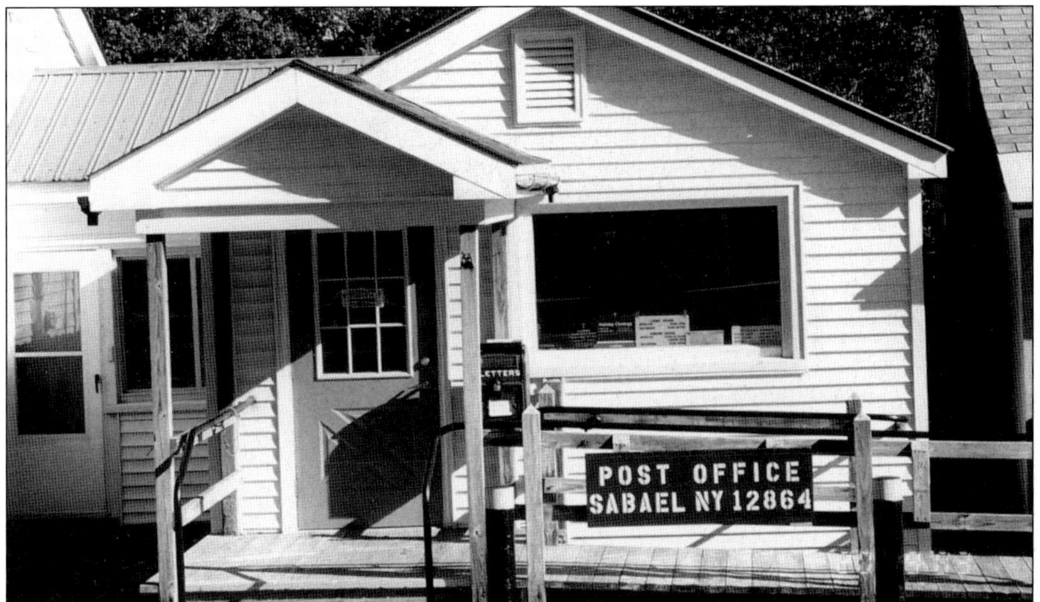

The Sabael Post Office and surrounding lands along Indian Lake are named after the first settler, a Native American from the Penobscot tribe named Sabael. Originally from Maine, he joined the Abenakis in Canada, where as a young boy he helped supply the British army at the Battle of Quebec. He built his wigwam at Sabael c. 1762 and settled in Adirondack country. Squaw Brook was named for his wife. Later, he chose Benedict as his last name. He went off in the woods at the age of 105 and never returned.

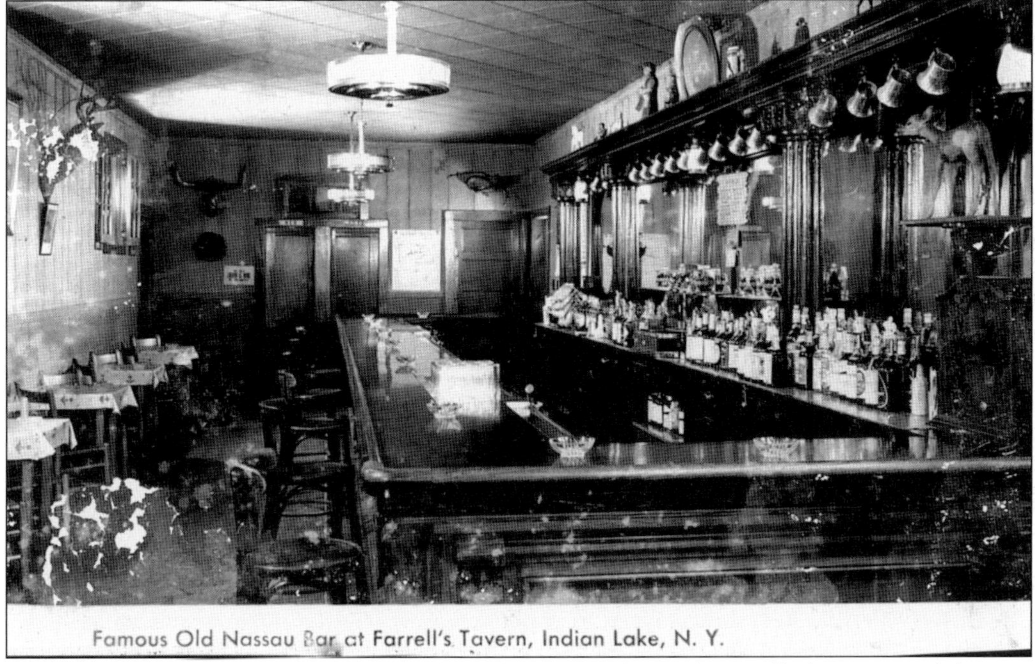
Famous Old Nassau Bar at Farrell's Tavern, Indian Lake, N. Y.

Farrell's Hotel, in Indian Lake Village (now known as the Oak Barrel), has a special feature. The well-known bar itself was transported from the old Nassau Inn in Princeton, New Jersey. It came complete with the inscribed pewter mugs used by Ivy League college students.

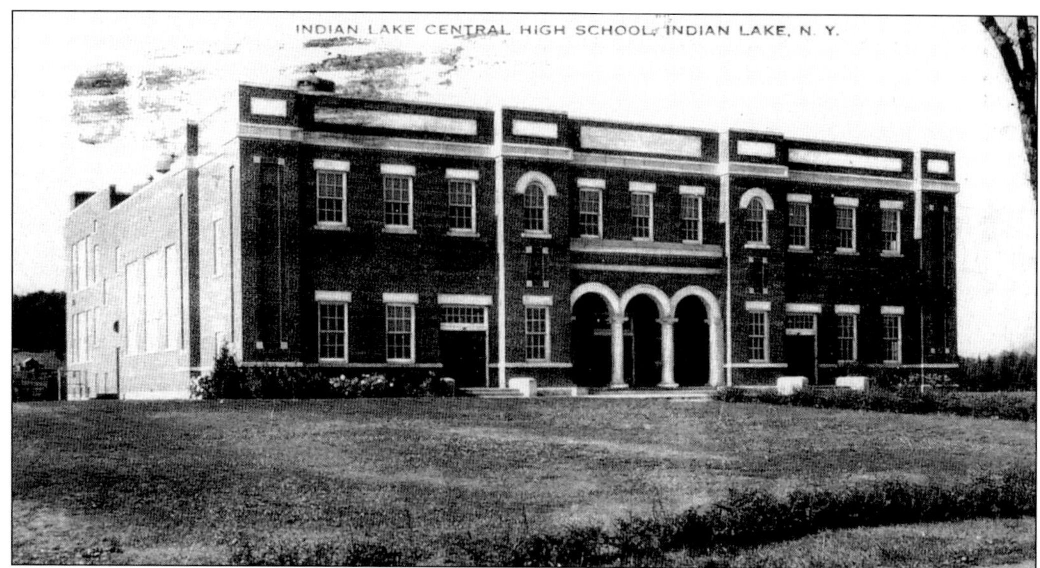

The Indian Lake Central School, pictured in 1937, was built in 1929 and, with a sizeable addition, is still in use today. School buildings were important to the Adirondack Trail settlements. Without extensive bus routes, they provided an education for children, became community centers for many activities and events, and employed many townspeople. Teachers often chose the Adirondacks because of its healthy lifestyle and the forested mountains and lakes.

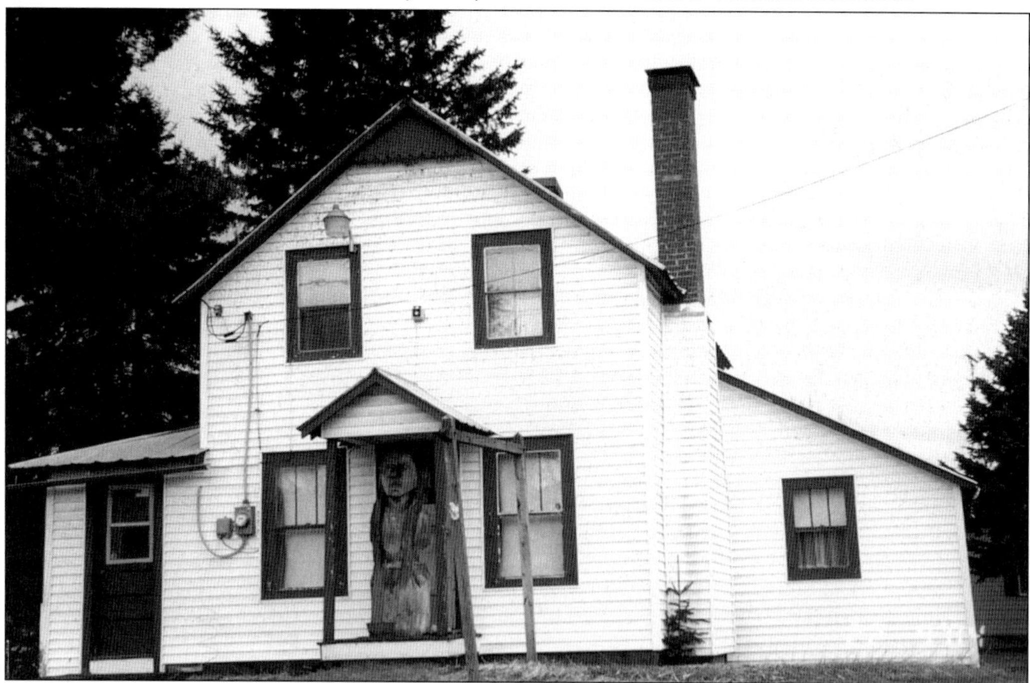

One of the oldest houses in the village of Indian Lake became the home of the Indian Lake Museum. Standing next to the public school, it was built in 1865 by Allen Brooks on his return from the Civil War. He and his wife, Annis Smith, raised eight children on what was, at that time, a farm. The museum collection contains rare and interesting relics from the old times in Indian Lake.

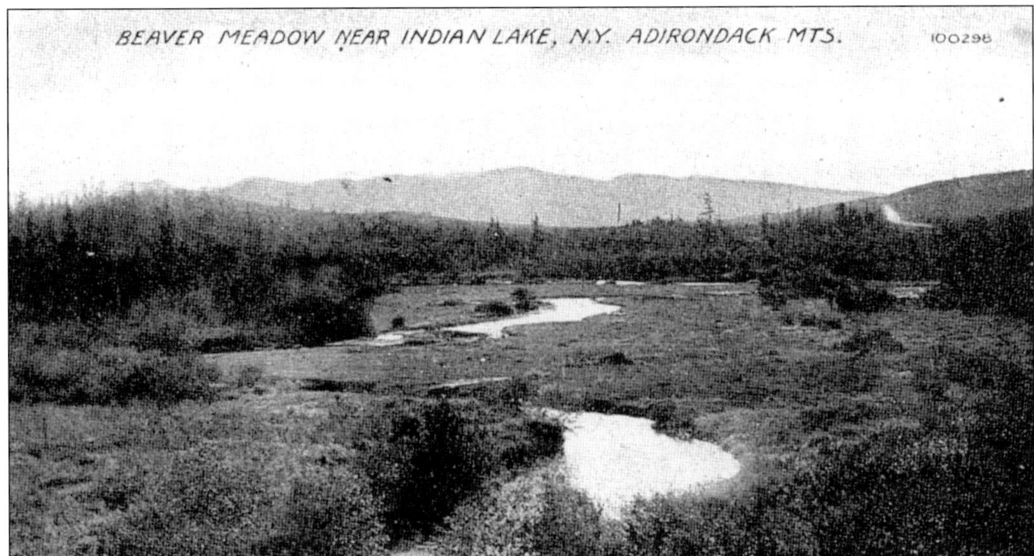

Ghost stories abound in the Adirondacks. Beaver Meadow, on the road from Indian Lake to North Creek, has some widely known ghosts. The rough lumberjacks did not like the looks of an old wild-looking peddler with white beard and hair who visited them. So, they dragged him out in the night and killed him. He and his horse and wagon were put in a cellar hole and burned to hide the evidence. Since that time, the ghost of the old peddler, his horse, and his wagon have been seen and heard bounding through Beaver Meadow.

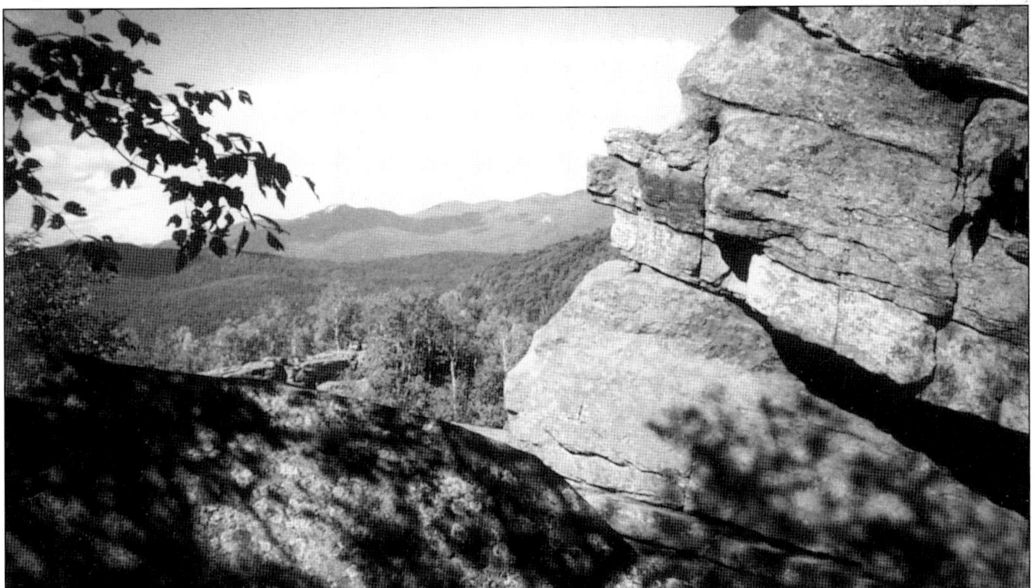

Chimney Mountain, near Indian Lake, is one of the Adirondack mysteries. It offers a complete Adirondack experience: an auto tour, a hike up a mountain, a walk in the woods, a majestic view of forested lands and rolling mountains and silvery waters, and a settlement, along with unmatched geological features. The mystery lies in the mountain's formation; no one knows how the mixed rock "chimneys" and caves, discovered in the 1930s, came to be. Chimney rock rises some 35 feet above the cliff, which from its base has a total height of 80 feet. The caves have their own cliffs, zig-zag tunnels, and great rooms.

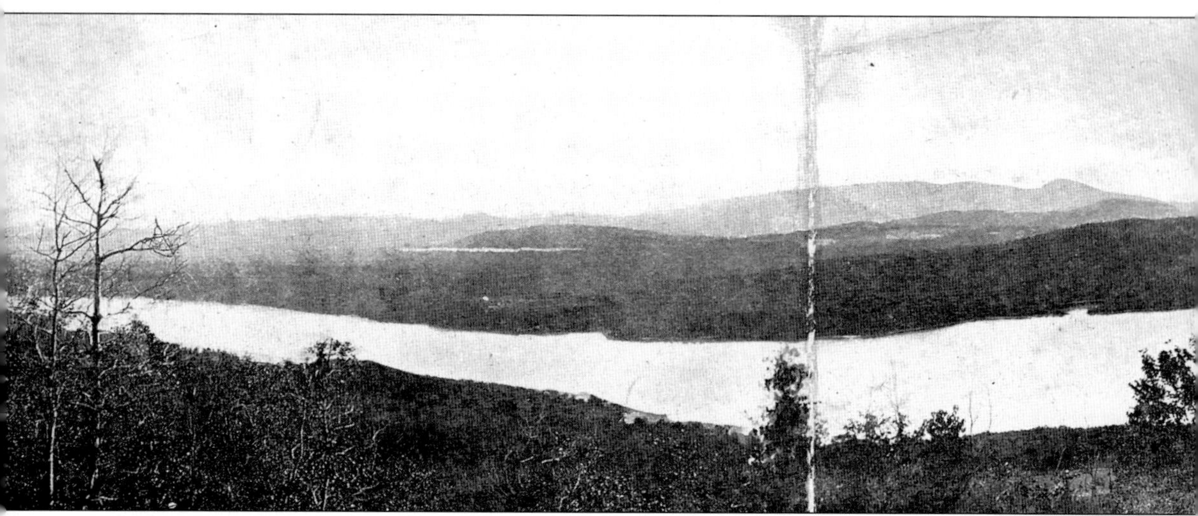

Lumbermen came to Indian Lake country in the 1840s to harvest the virgin timber. They built a wooden dam at the foot of Indian Lake in 1845 to raise the water 5 feet for easier floating of the logs. With an 11-foot dam installed in the 1860s, the lake became 9 miles long. The present 1898 dam raises the original water level more than 33 feet, lengthening the lake to 14 miles. Later, the lumbermen built a woods road through what is today's Indian Lake Village to carry out the heavy loads of logs pulled by oxen to get to the sawmill on the Cedar River. The dam

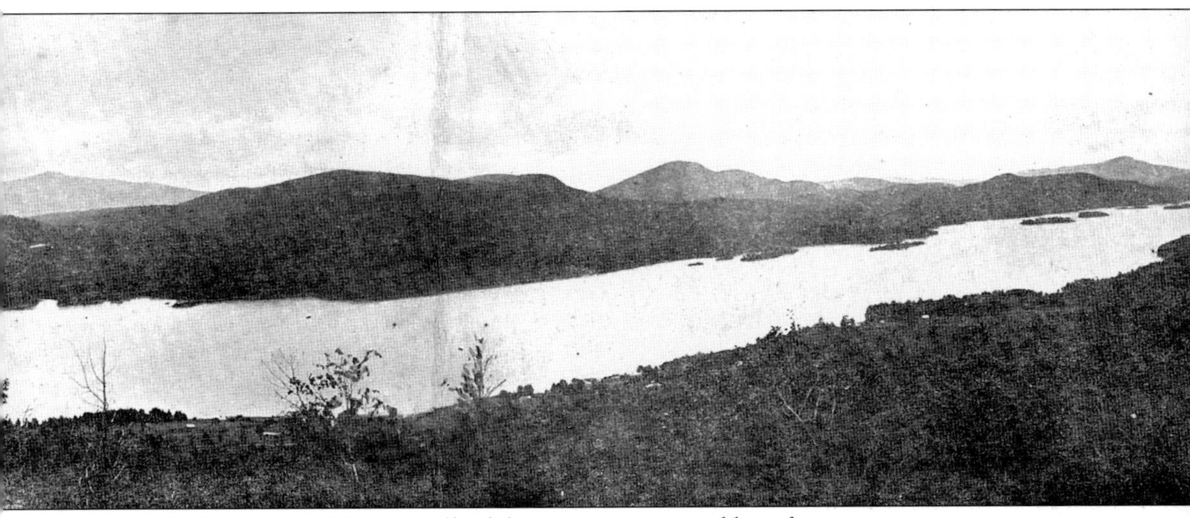

holds back the waters of three smaller lakes, once connected by a fast-moving stream, to create Indian Lake. It also controls flooding downstream. It became newsworthy a few years ago when consideration was begin given to selling the dam. New York City was interested in acquiring it for the water supply. Home to some 18 species of fish, including record game fish, Indian Lake offers island camping to summer visitors.

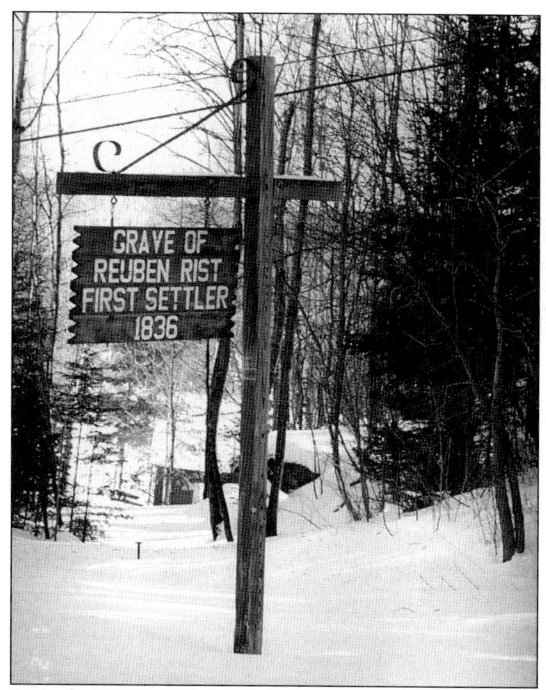

Indian Lake's first permanent white settler arrived just ahead of the lumbermen. Reuben Rist and his wife from Massachusetts came to Indian Lake in an ox-drawn cart in 1836. Three helpers came along to cut a roadway and clear the land; it was a tough trip through the roadless wilderness. In 1850, Truman Brown made his way along the future Adirondack Trail from Wells to Indian Lake. By 1860, the settlement consisted of a total of 38 log cabins.

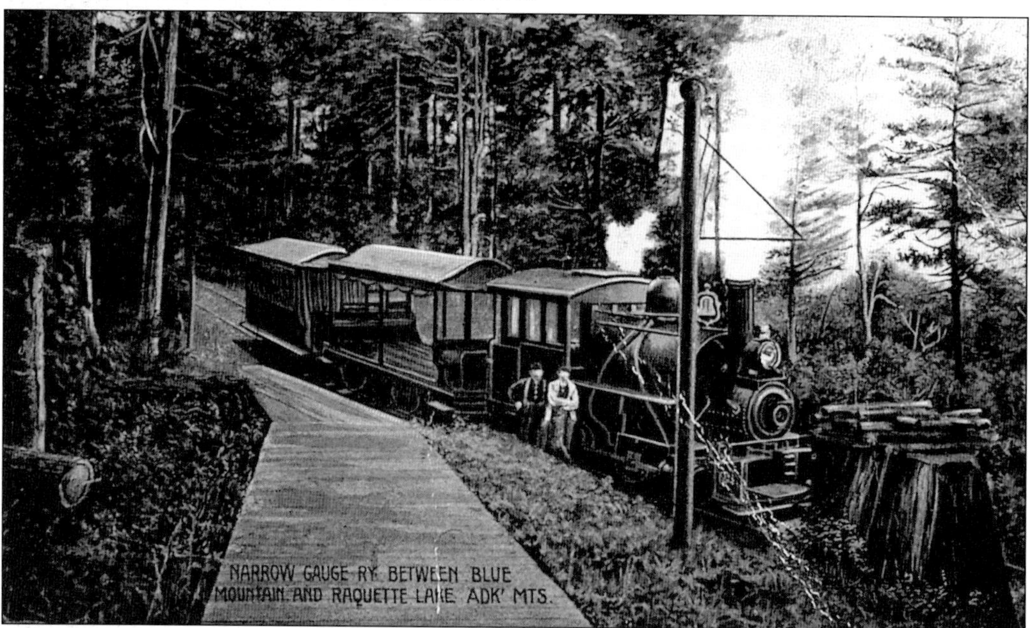

The less-than-a-mile-long Marion River Carry Railroad, from Marion River to Utowana Lake, was the smallest standard-gauge rail line in the world with the most prominent board of directors. Wealthy industrial barons directing the small line included Chauncey Depew, Collis Huntington, J. P. Morgan, Harry Whitney, Alfred Vanderbilt, William Whitney, and John Dix. The railroad served passengers traveling from the New York Central Station at Raquette Lake to the hotels and cottages on Blue Mountain Lake. The engine and a car are preserved at the Adirondack Museum, and a proposed reactivation of the Marion River Carry Railroad is under consideration.

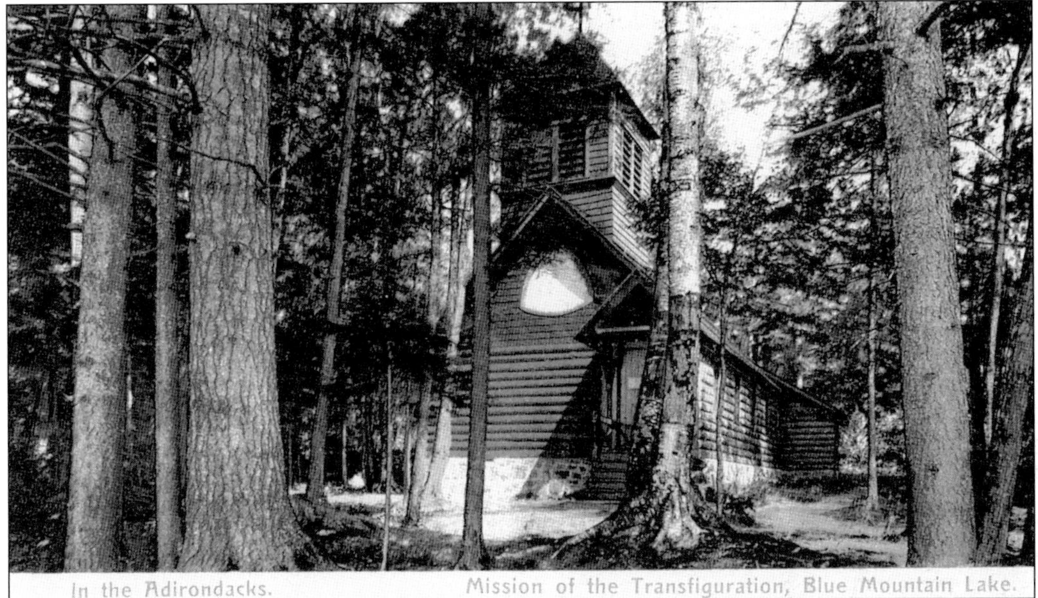

The Mission of the Transfiguration Church, now the Church of the Transfiguration, stands on the Adirondack Trail on the shore of Blue Mountain Lake. The historic 1885 log structure has been designated a national historic site. Holy eucharist ecumenical services are offered by the Episcopal church from June through September. The location makes it possible to attend church by boat or land transportation.

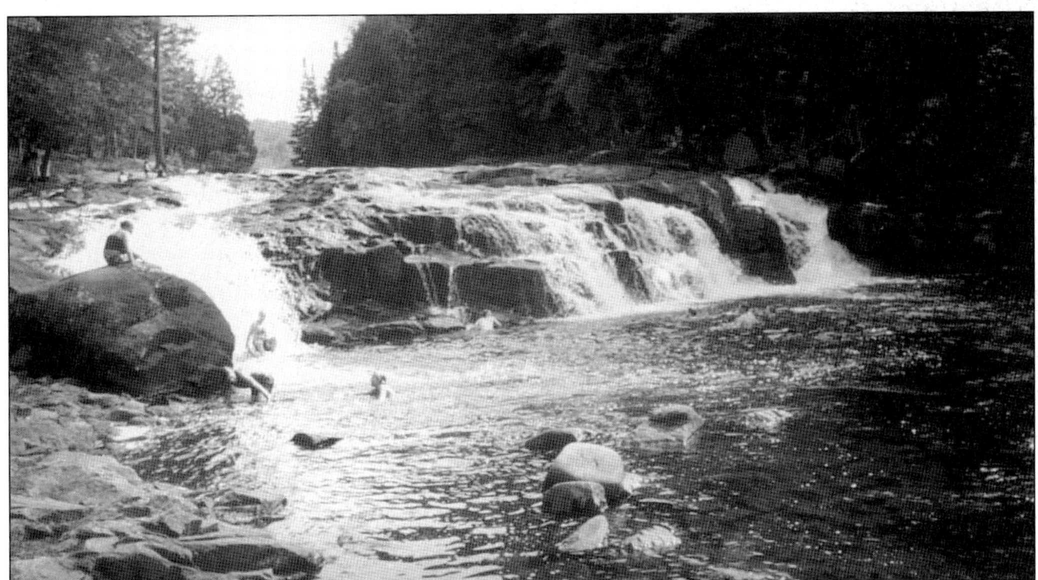

Off Route 30 near Long Lake, Buttermilk Falls offers a breathtaking sight on the Raquette River at North Point Road. The state maintains the picnic area, with tables and fireplaces. As early as the 1860s, Adirondack Murray was writing stories about Buttermilk Falls.

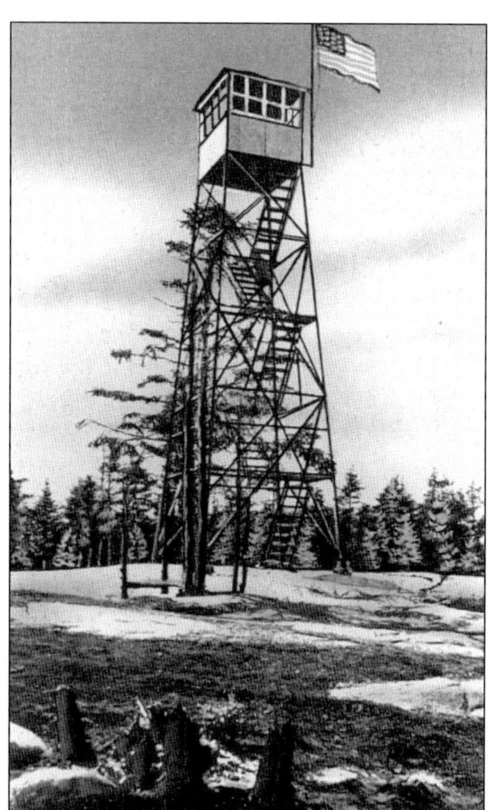

The Blue Mountain fire tower is one of the most popular tower hikes in the Adirondacks; thousands take the two-mile hike to visit the tower and see the view from the 3,759-foot peak each year. Built in 1917 to replace the 1911 wooden tower, the Blue Mountain tower was slated to be demolished in the 1990s. Public outcry and support saved it, and through the cooperation of many interested parties, the tower was restored.

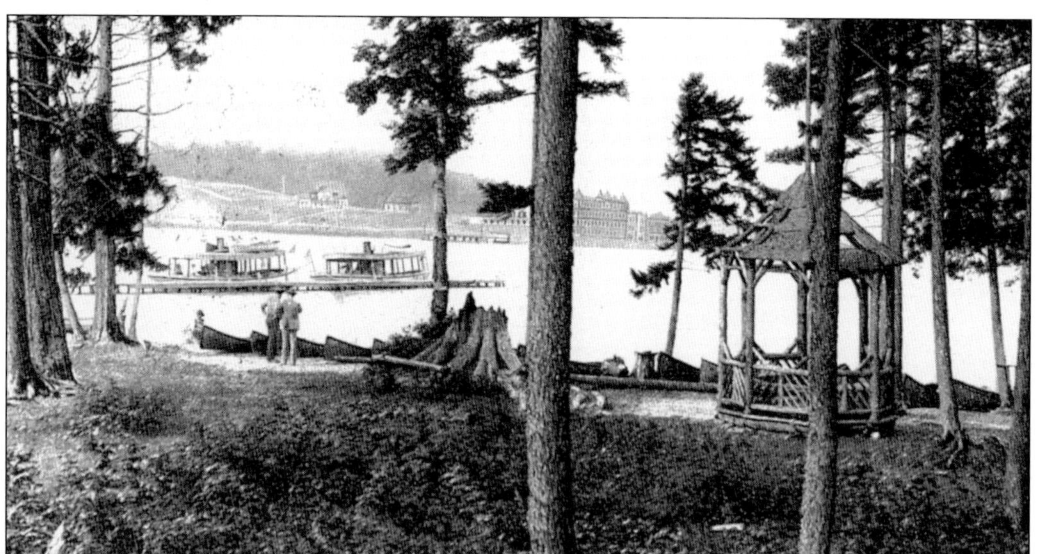

Gazebos, guideboats, passenger boats, and hotels were popular on the Adirondack lakes, and Blue Mountain Lake was no exception. The giant Adirondack hotels attracted thousands who wanted to escape the city heat and grime and to spend long vacations in the mountains. Boating was a popular pastime for both the ladies and the gentlemen who enjoyed the Adirondacks. Gazebos, also called summerhouses, were ideal places to relax, have some tea, and read a book.

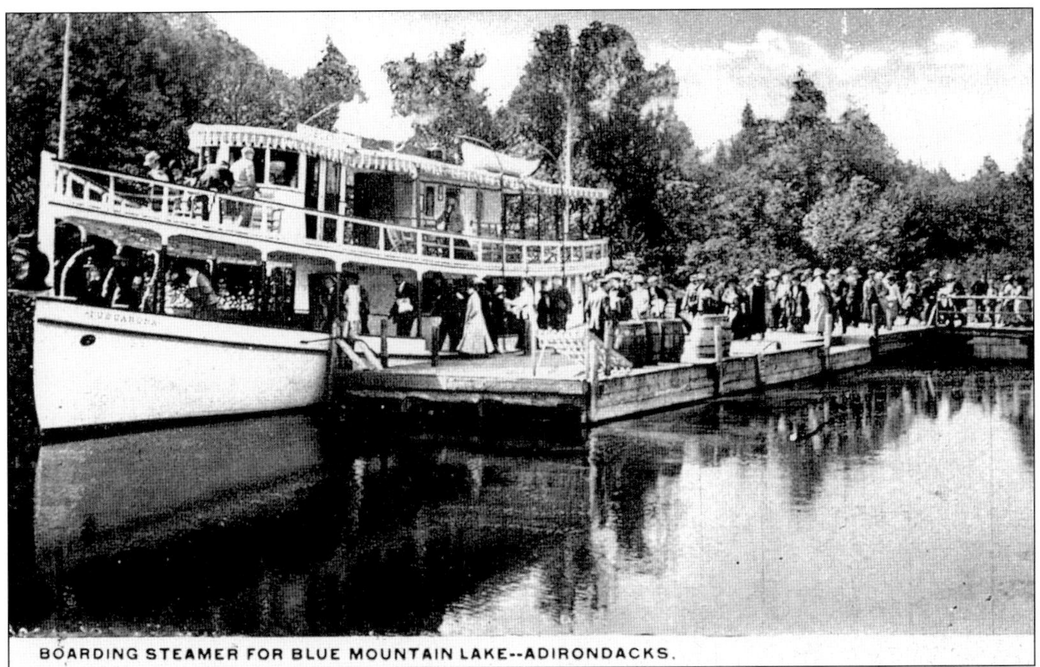

BOARDING STEAMER FOR BLUE MOUNTAIN LAKE--ADIRONDACKS.

Thousands were able to enjoy the Adirondacks because of the transportation provided by the waterways. The Adirondack Trail was undeveloped for many years, and long trips from the North Creek Railroad Station by stagecoach and buckboard were not too comfortable. The steamers *Tuscarora* and *Adirondack*, shown here, transported those who came by train to Raquette Lake to enjoy the accommodations at Blue Mountain Lake. The trip involved travel through Utowana Lake, the Marion River, Eagle Lake, and Blue Mountain Lake. Beginning in 1900, the Marion River Carry Railroad transported passengers between the waterways. From 1878 to 1900, Blue Mountain was the most fashionable resort in the Northeast.

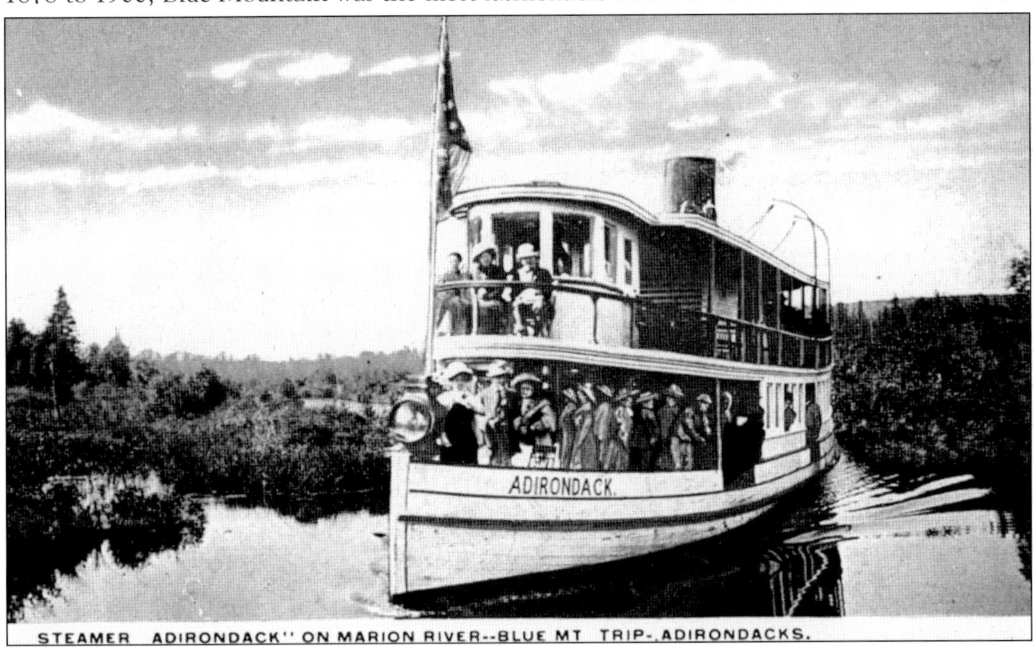

STEAMER ADIRONDACK'' ON MARION RIVER--BLUE MT TRIP-.ADIRONDACKS.

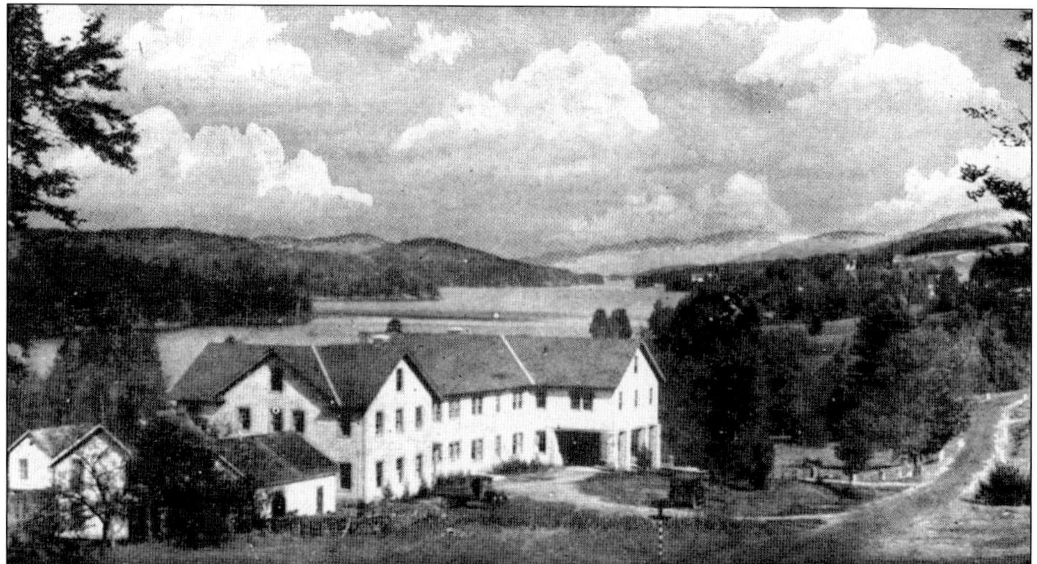

New and Modern. Long View Hotel, Long Lake, N. Y. Facing Long Lake. W. F. Emerson, Prop. Adirondack Mountains—Route 28 and 10. Under same management 30 years. Officially Inspected and Approved by Publicity Bureau.

A 1920s newspaper item reported that Wallace F. Emerson was taking 40 guests at his Long View Cottages for $25 per week. Four generations of the Emerson family took guests at Long View Lodge and Cottages, on Routes 28 and 10 (today's Route 30, the Adirondack Trail) on Long Lake. The 14-room inn and cottages, with a restaurant, a swimming beach, and a marina, was, and is, a good example of Adirondack accommodations.

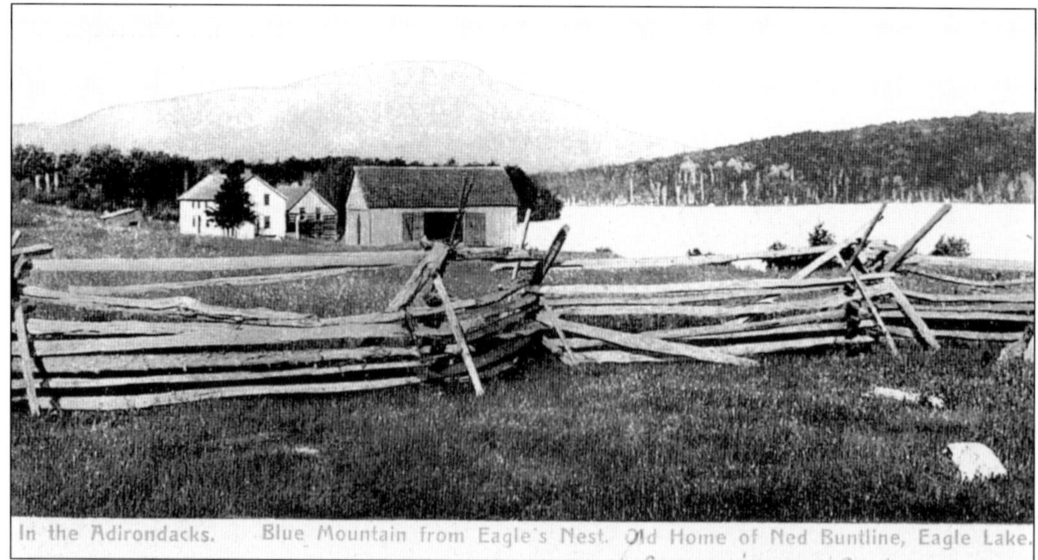

In the Adirondacks. Blue Mountain from Eagle's Nest. Old Home of Ned Buntline, Eagle Lake.

In 1856, Edward Zane Carroll arrived in the Adirondacks from New York City to hunt and fish at Piseco Lake. He journeyed on to the town of Indian Lake for some more fishing and decided to stay. Carroll, a writer of the early dime novels, was better known by his pen name, Ned Buntline. He named his Adirondack home Eagles Nest, and the lake, Eagle Lake, after some nearby nesting eagles. He got his own post office in 1860 so that he would not have to travel long distances to mail his manuscripts.

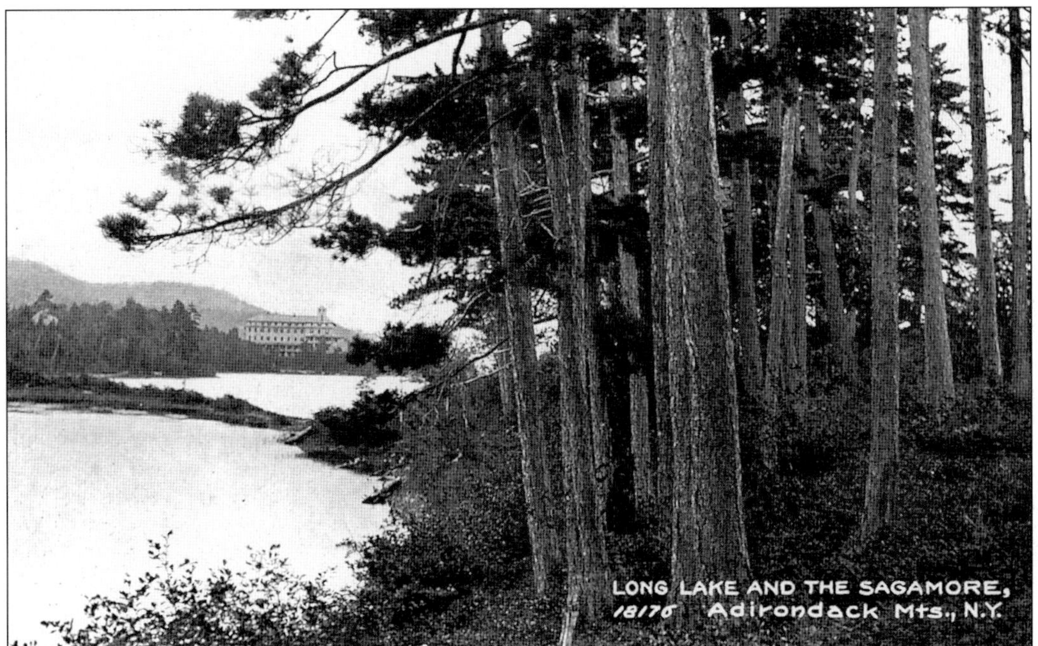

Long Lake, created at a wide section of the Raquette River, is some 14 miles long and 1 1/2 miles wide. The shoreline ranges from sandy beaches to rugged cliffs. It is dotted with camps and homes. The Sagamore Hotel (a popular name for Adirondack hotels), shown here, served the Long Lake community beginning in 1883. The hotel offered telegraph and mail service, both desirable in the remote Adirondack communities to maintain contact with the outside world. It was taken down in 1960.

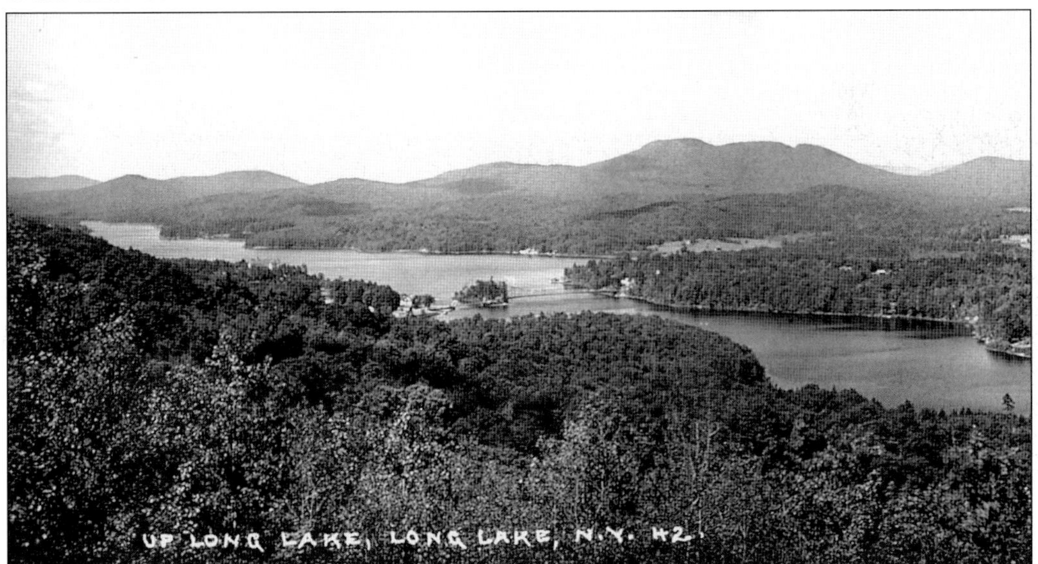

Long Lake was first settled in 1830. By 1836, E. H. St. John was sawing lumber at his mill—a sign of growth. Long Lake has the distinction of having had the earliest summer resident in the Adirondack heartlands. Theophilus Anthony built a summer home here before the first permanent resident, Native American Peter Sabattis, arrived. By 1844, there were 100 residents in the wilderness community of Long Lake. The Adirondack Trail bridge is visible in the center.

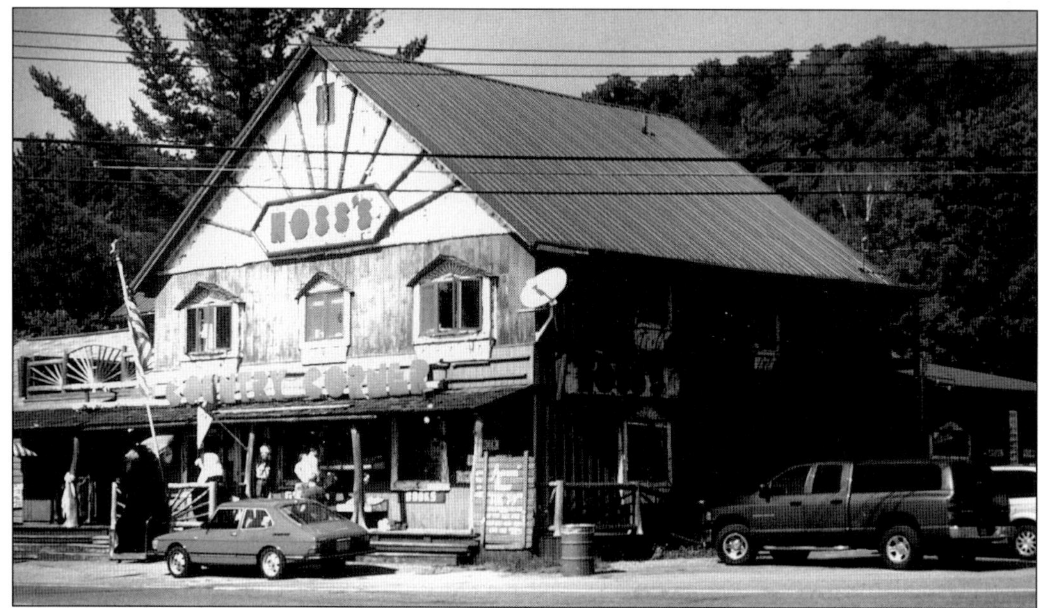

Hoss's Country Corner, owned and operated for many years by John and Lorie Hosley, has become a landmark in Long Lake. The store has now been passed down to their daughter, Jules Hosley-Pierce and manager Ali Hamdan. The Hosley family has a long history in the Adirondacks, with connections to the early industries in forest products, surveying, and hotel keeping. John Hosley served several terms as town supervisor, and his father, Dr. Morris Hosley, practiced medicine in town for many years.

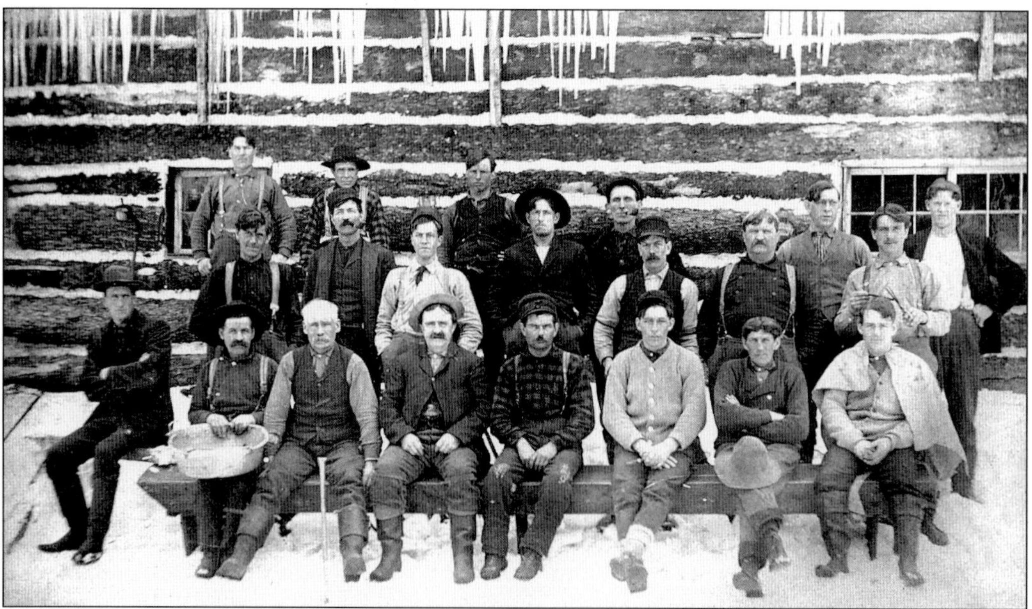

Shown in 1920 are the loggers at Abrams Camp, near Little Tupper Lake on the Adirondack Trail north of Long Lake. The man on the left with his arms crossed is the boss, D. B. Abrams. Loggers came from the Adirondack settlements to stay in the lumber camp during the winter season, when the logs are cut and piled along the waterways to be transported by water to the mills in the spring.

Six

TUPPER LAKE AND SANTA CLARA

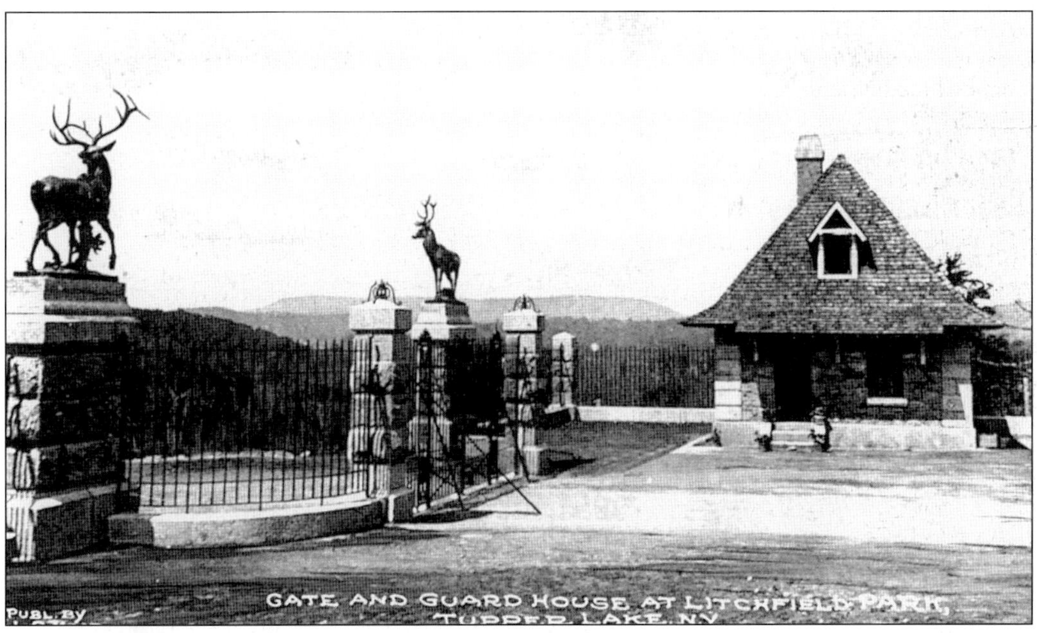

Litchfield Park, on the Adirondack Trail between Long Lake and Tupper Lake, is the camp of the Litchfield family. Edward H. Litchfield, a lawyer from Brooklyn, first came to the Adirondacks in 1866 to camp and hunt. In 1893, he bought 8,600 acres; by 1913, he had built a massive chateau estate. The stone chateau has walls from three to six feet thick. The entrance gate and guard house, shown here, were designed by a French architect and made of native Adirondack granite. The 12-foot-high towers are surmounted by an American elk and an English stag, both animals that Litchfield tried to restock *c.* 1900. The Litchfields, good stewards of the land, are still maintaining the vast "summer retreat."

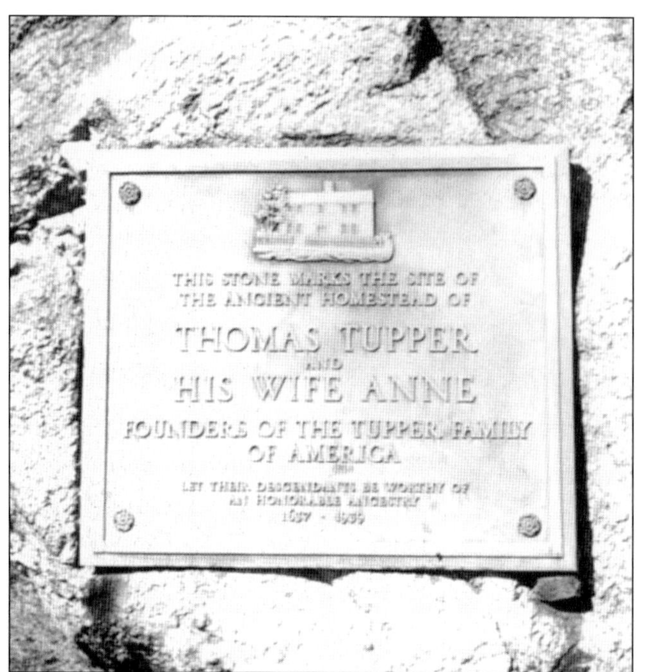

A large stone is located on a side road in a small well-kept park near Sandwich, Massachusetts, on Cape Cod, that has an Adirondack connection. The metal plaque reads, "This stone marks the site of the ancient homestead of Thomas Tupper and his wife Anne, founders of the Tupper Family of America." One of America's oldest families, the Tuppers gave their name to the Adirondack lakes and village through Ansel Tupper, a surveyor who was born in 1799. He was drowned in an Adirondack lake that afterward became known as Tupper's Lake.

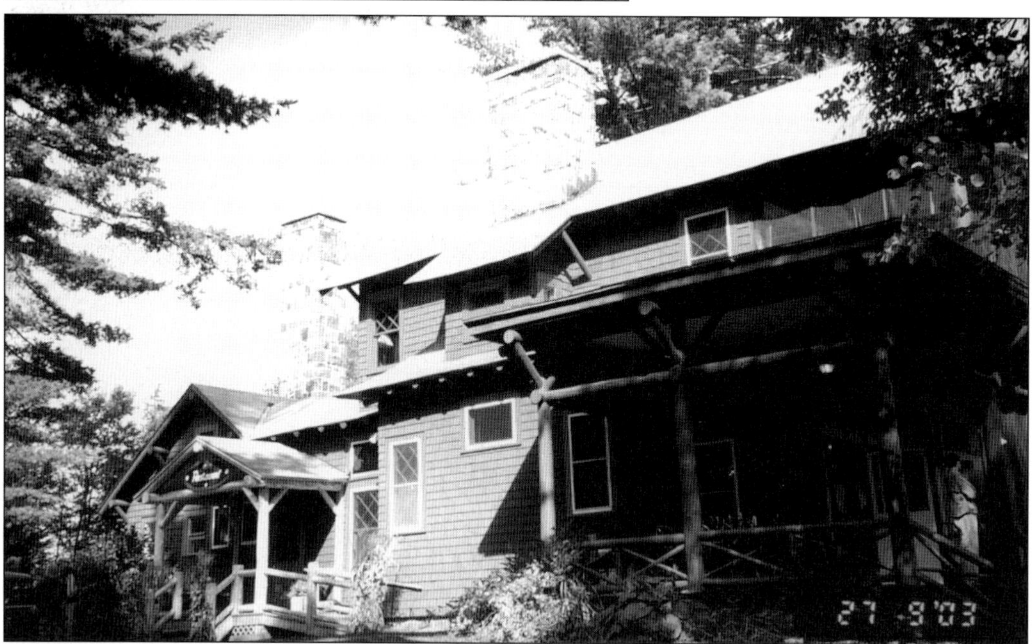

Wawbeck, on the Adirondack Trail between Tupper Lake and Paul Smiths, has an interesting story to tell. The Native American word *wawbeck* means "big rock" and refers to the big boulders left by the glaciers. The location on the Upper Saranac Lake has been occupied by well-known Adirondack guide O. A. Coville and his wife, two different hotels, a private great Adirondack camp, a boys' camp, and today's restaurant and resort. It has unique double stairway chimneys. The first hotel was constructed in 1880 and was reached by boat or a nine-mile stagecoach ride from Tupper Lake's railroad station. The second hotel, built in 1930, burned during the 1980 Olympics.

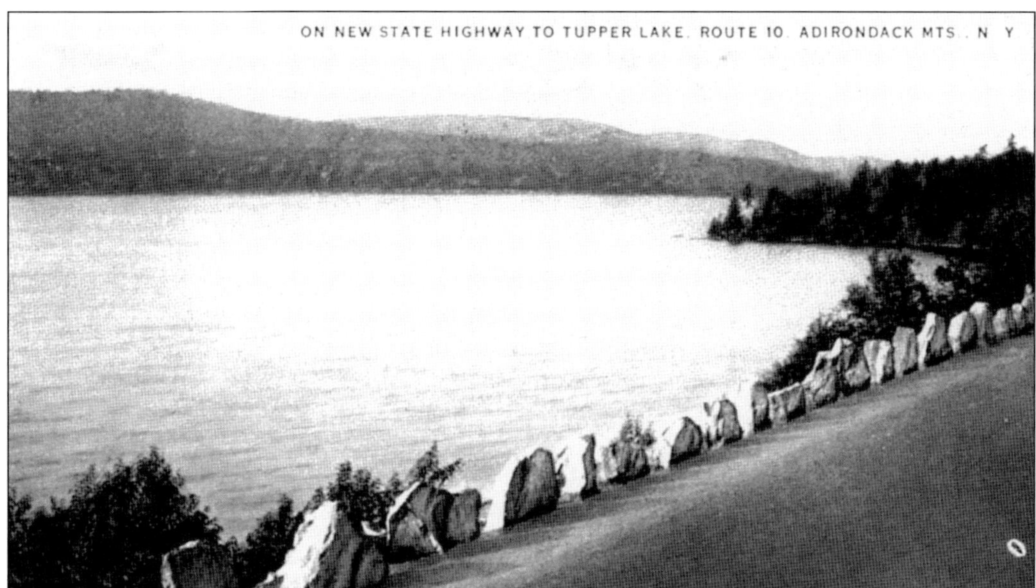

In the 1920s and 1930s, guardrails made of solid rock were placed along the Adirondack highways to keep cars from running off the road. On the "new state highway," then Route 10, the rocks protect the Adirondack Trail to Tupper Lake along the lakeshore. When it was proposed to remove the rock guardrails in Warren County a few years ago, public outcry saved them. The view of them today, however, has been blocked by the new steel guardrails.

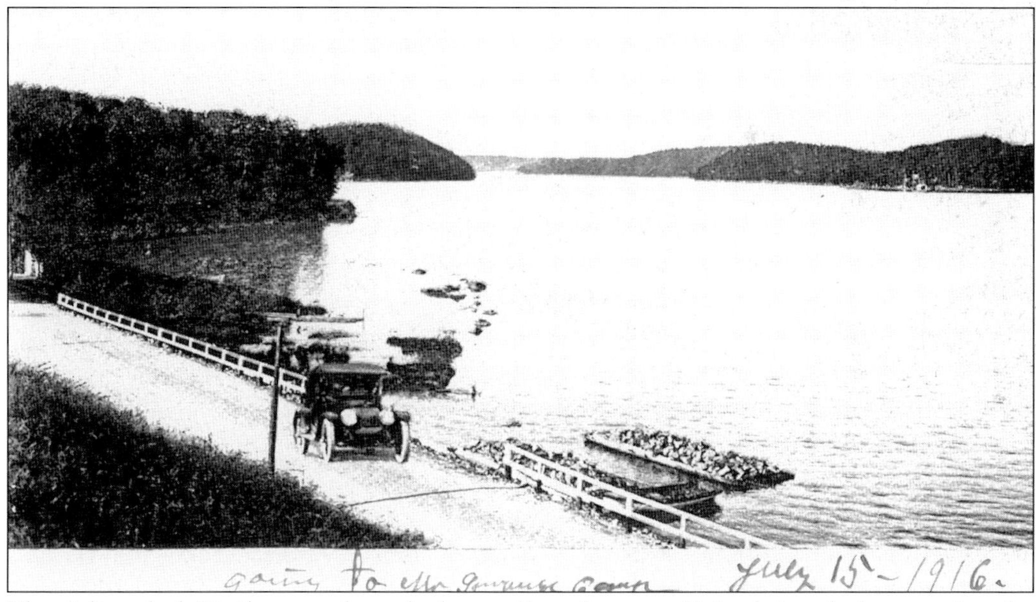

The Adirondack Trail passes through the small settlement of Moody just before crossing the causeway into Tupper Lake. Moody got its name from Adirondack guide-storyteller-hotelkeeper Martin "Uncle Mart" Moody, whose sportsman's hotel, on the northeast end of the lake, was called Moody. Moody guided many of the famous people of the late 1800s. While guiding Pres. Chester Arthur, he asked for a post office and got it. He became postmaster and retained his job regardless of which political party was in power because he also guided Pres. Grover Cleveland.

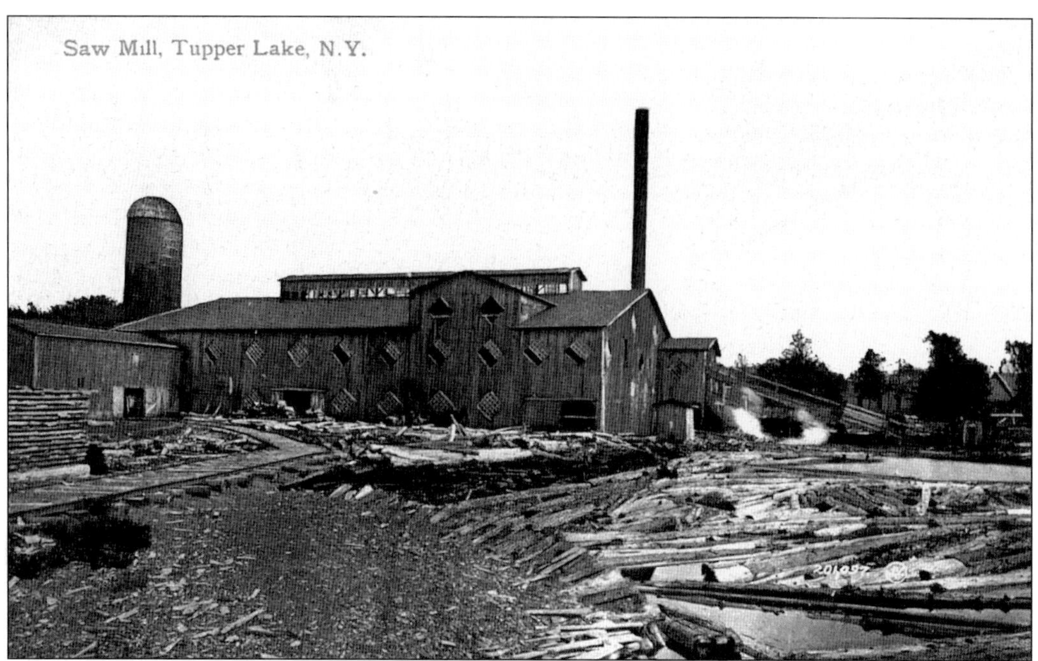

Tupper Lake was once a major center for the Adirondack lumbering industry. In 1890, the town of Altamont had few settlers, but by 1900, the population had grown to over 3,000. Major logging and sawmill operations brought in the workers who settled in Adirondack country. At one point, they out-produced high-ranking Glens Falls with lumber and were tops in the state. The annual Woodsman's Field Day became centered at Tupper Lake and is shared with Boonville.

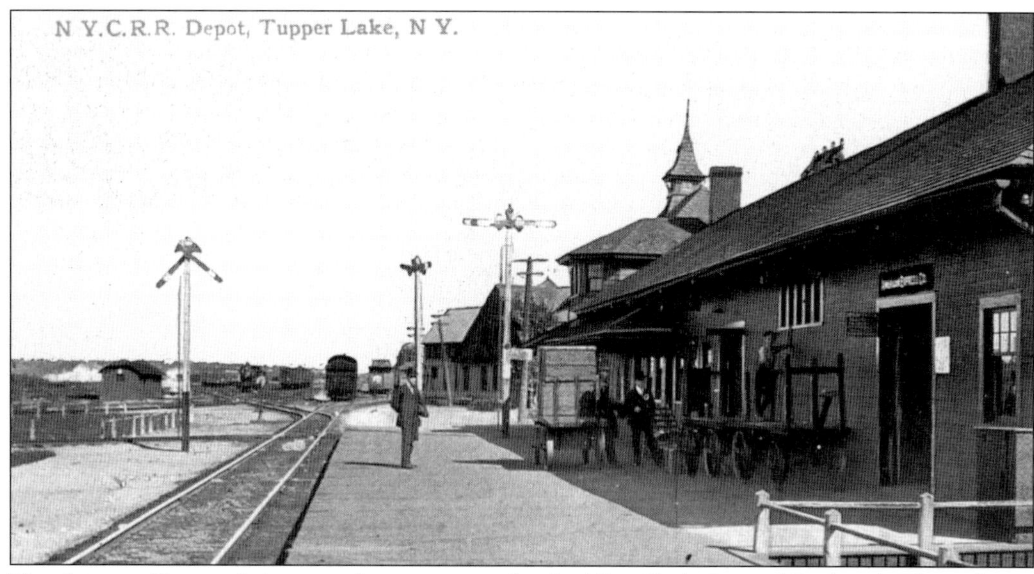

The depot at Tupper Lake was a busy stopover for the New York Central Railroad. The railways opened by John Hurd and Dr. William Seward Webb served the logging and sawmill operations that were Tupper Lake's major industries. Hurd's line became part of New York Central in 1906 and operated for another 30 years. Webb's Adirondack line, completed in 1892, lasted until the 1960s. The depot was torn down in 1975.

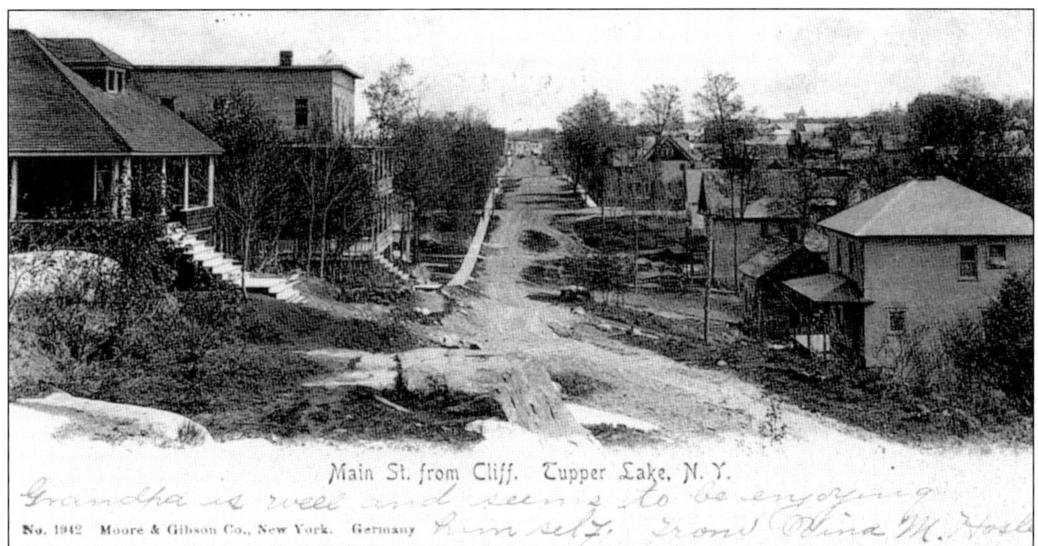

In the first decade of the 20th century, Main Street in Tupper Lake was still just a narrow dirt road. In 1913, St. Lawrence County ceded a strip of land to the town of Altamont so that the north–south road could be built between Long Lake and Tupper Lake. When the first settler, Michael Cole, arrived in 1840, Tupper Lake was a trackless wilderness. Within 10 years, the Pomeroy Lumber Company logged the Tupper Lake forest and left a clearing where the village soon developed.

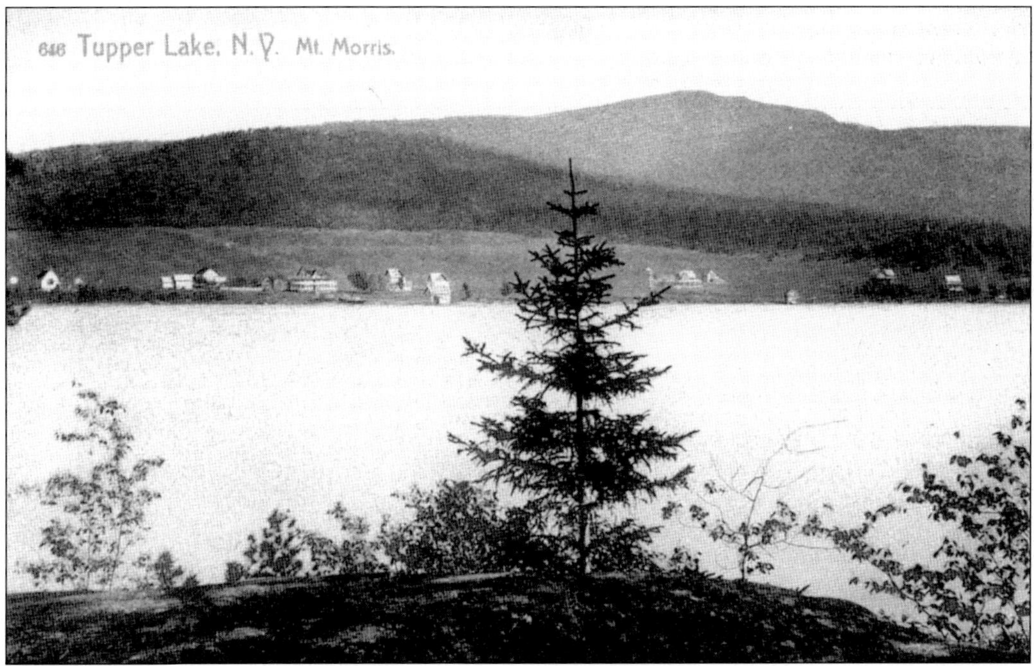

Mount Morris, a little over 3,100 feet high, is seen overlooking Tupper Lake. The wide vista made Mount Morris a choice location for the first fire observation tower in New York State, erected in June 1909. After devastating fires in 1903 and 1908, fire commissioner James S. Whipple convened a meeting of prominent citizens and recommended building observation towers to report fires, many of which were caused by the trains.

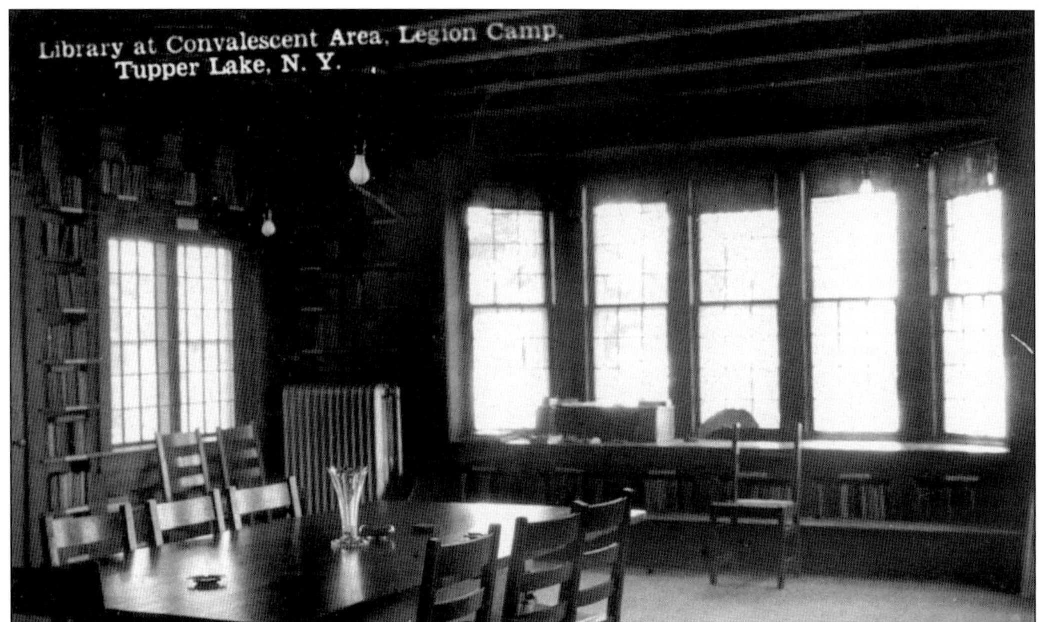

In April 1918, New York State purchased more than 13,000 acres of land on Big Tupper Lake from millionaire William Barbour. The land formed the beginning of the American Legion Mountain Camp. In 1921, the American Legion decided to establish a camp in the Adirondacks to care for disabled veterans of World War I. An additional 1,260 acres were purchased, and the first patient was admitted in 1923. In the beginning, the camp cared for tuberculosis patients. Then, in 1925, it became a veterans convalescence and rest camp, without a fee of any kind.

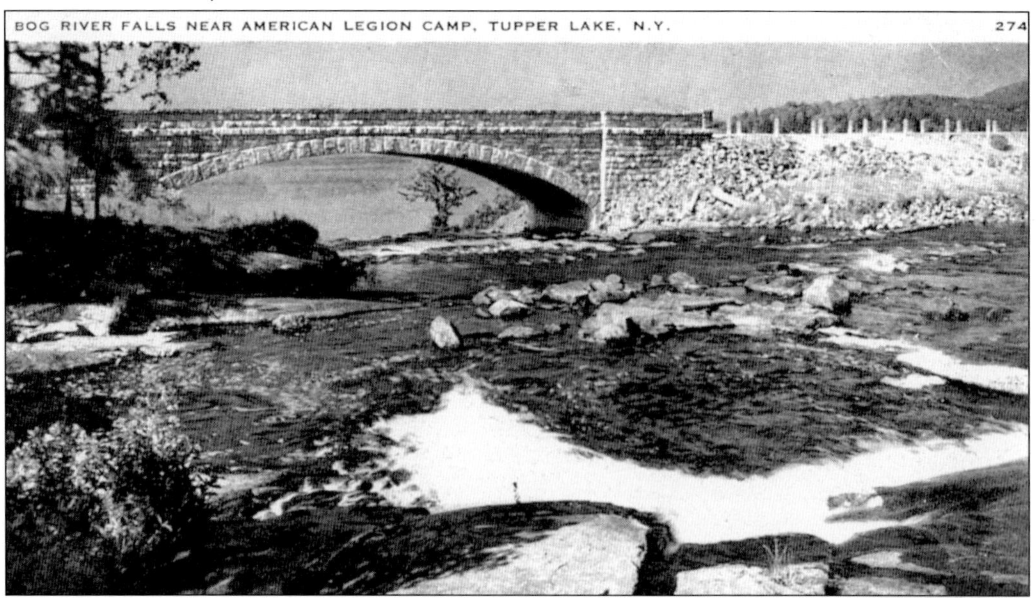

The original access to the American Legion Camp at Tupper Lake was by water from Tupper Lake or a five-mile dirt road from the Horseshoe railroad station. The state legislature passed a special act to build a two-mile macadam road from the Adirondack Trail to the camp. To get to the camp, a graceful stone span arching above Bog River Falls had to be built.

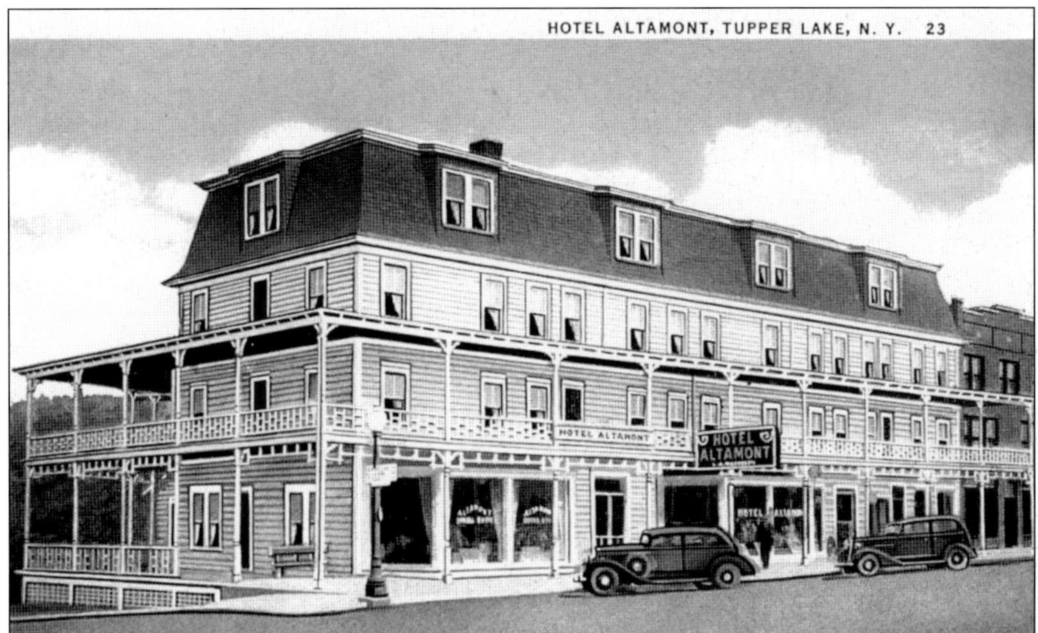

The Hotel Altamont is no more. It was the second hotel built at Tupper Lake. The hotel opened on New Year's Day in 1891 and served the community until the 1950s. Over the years, it had six owners, including John H. and Thomas Weir, Warren Alfred, Edward Alfred, Larry Rafferty, Hugh Beaton, and William Snider. The hotel was slated to be torn down in the 1930s and a new six-story hotel built to replace it, but the Depression killed the project. The Grand Union Company razed the building in 1957 to erect a supermarket on the site.

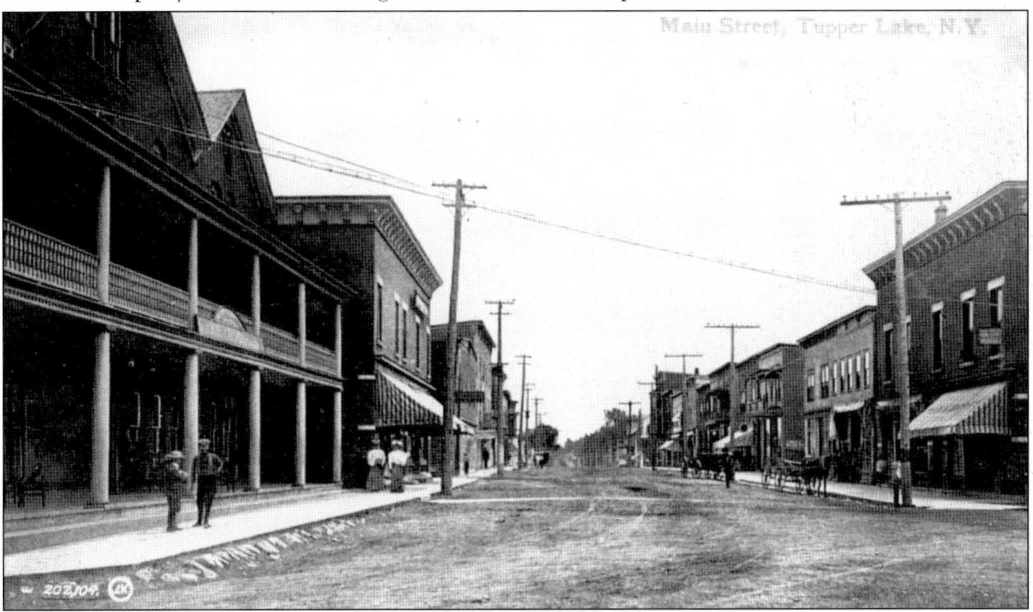

A 56-room hotel was built on Tupper Lake's Main Street in 1902 by Frederick LaDuke. The site, on the left, had been left vacant by the 1897 burning of the Commercial House. In 1927, a fourth story was added. The hotel closed in 1973 after 71 years of operation under some 16 different owners. The Adirondack Trail was still a dirt road through the village in 1900.

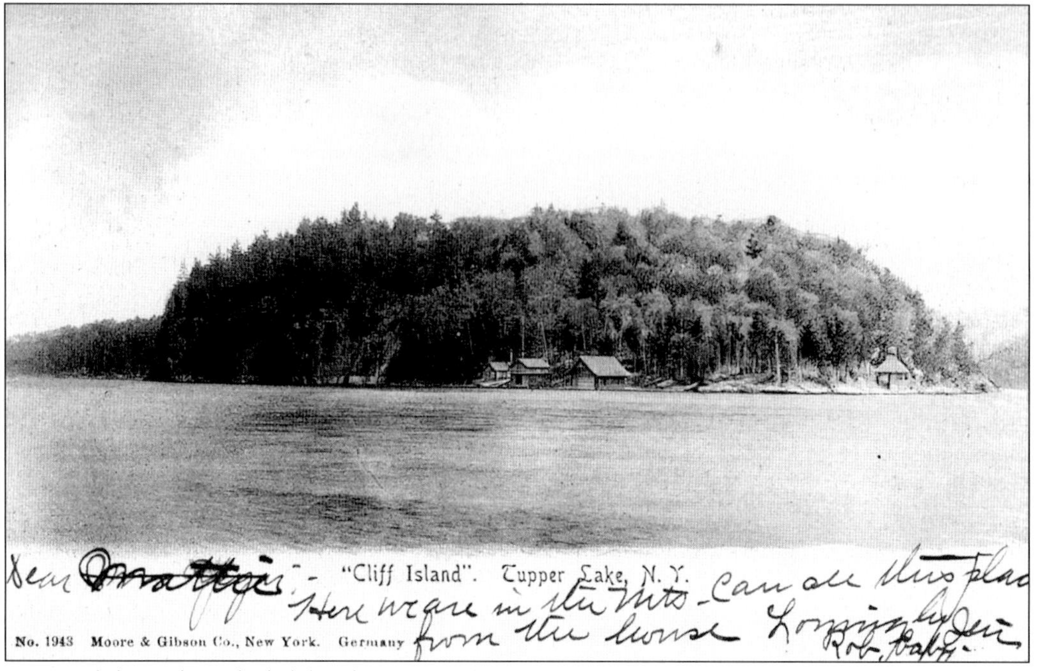

Many of the Adirondack lakes have islands big enough for primitive camping or permanent cottages. By 1906, Cliff Island, in Tupper Lake, had several buildings, including a boathouse, cottages, and a gazebo. Living on an island often required the purchase of a piece of property on the mainland shore for a boathouse, dock, and parking space. Deliveries of heavy items and construction materials were often taken across the ice by horse and sleigh in the wintertime.

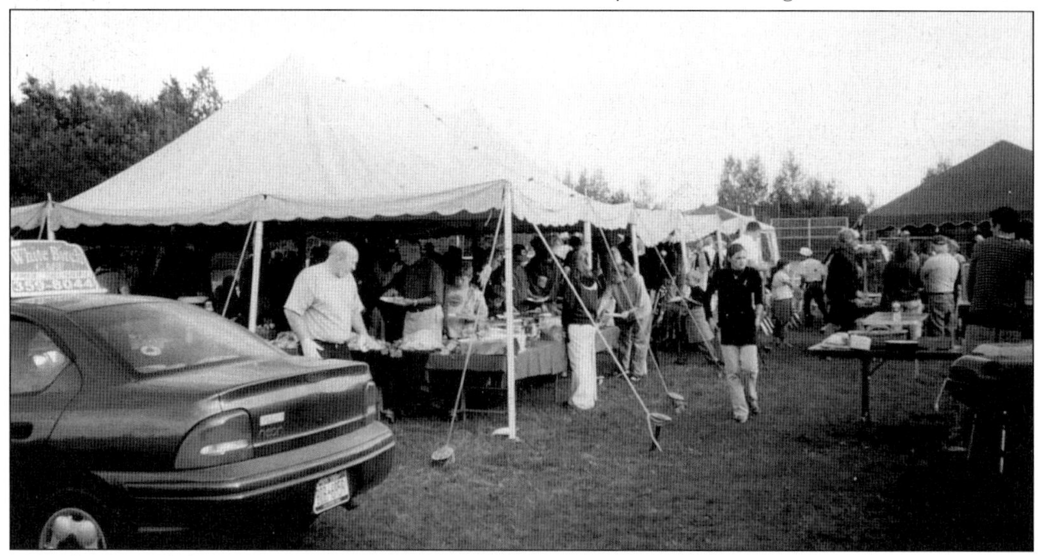

A gathering of those interested in the planned Natural History Museum of the Adirondacks (NHMA) was held on the proposed site of the new museum, adjacent to the Tupper Lake's school property, in August 2003. Trails and boardwalks are under construction, with buildings soon to follow. The Adirondack-style museum building will feature two wings and one great hall with a 20-foot waterfall and otter pond. More than $11.5 million has been collected, with some $3.5 million to go.

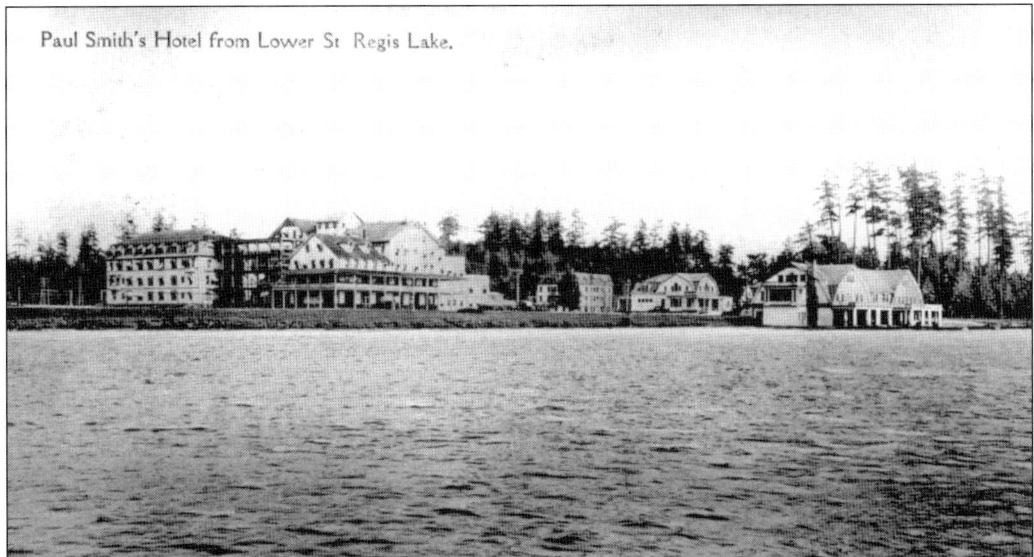

Paul Smith came to the Adirondacks in the 1840s to hunt and fish. He soon became an Adirondack guide and opened a tourist home. His business grew and, with the help of his wife, Lydia, he opened a 100-room hotel, a railroad, a real estate company, a lumber company, a stage line, and his own post office. Honoring him today is the four-year Adirondack college, Paul Smiths College, established by his son, Phelps Smith.

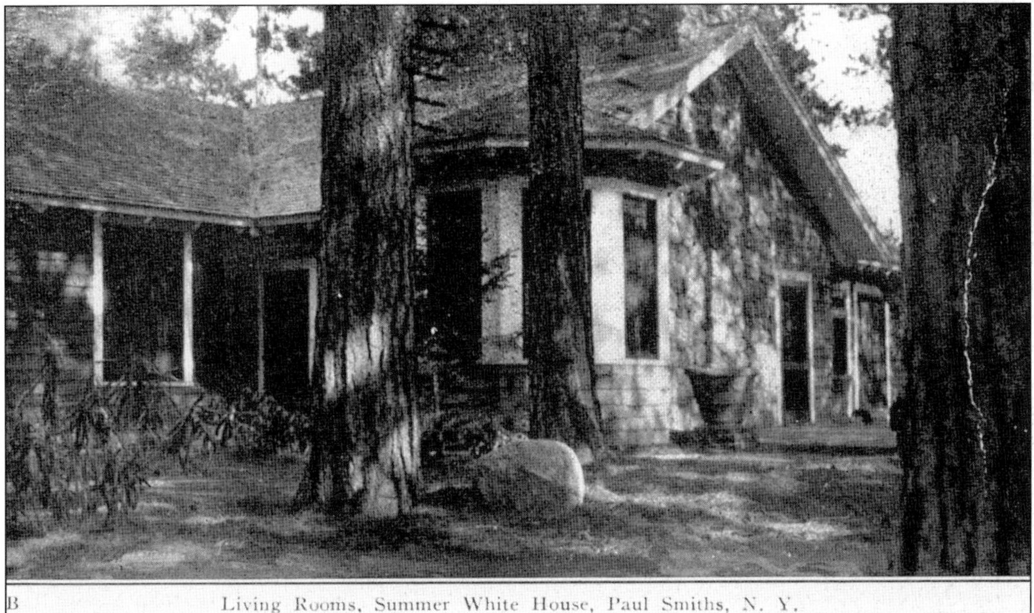

Restored and open to the public is the summer white house of Pres. Calvin Coolidge, located near Paul Smiths. Coolidge spent his 10-week vacation at the White Pine Camp on Osgood Pond in 1926. At the time of the president's stay in the Adirondacks, a Paul Smiths promotional brochure boasted, "New State highways in all directions make motoring delightful!" The president provided a real challenge for the Secret Service guards when he made good use of the Adirondack Trail to go to church and to visit Paul Smiths, the veterans hospital, and the American Legion Camp.

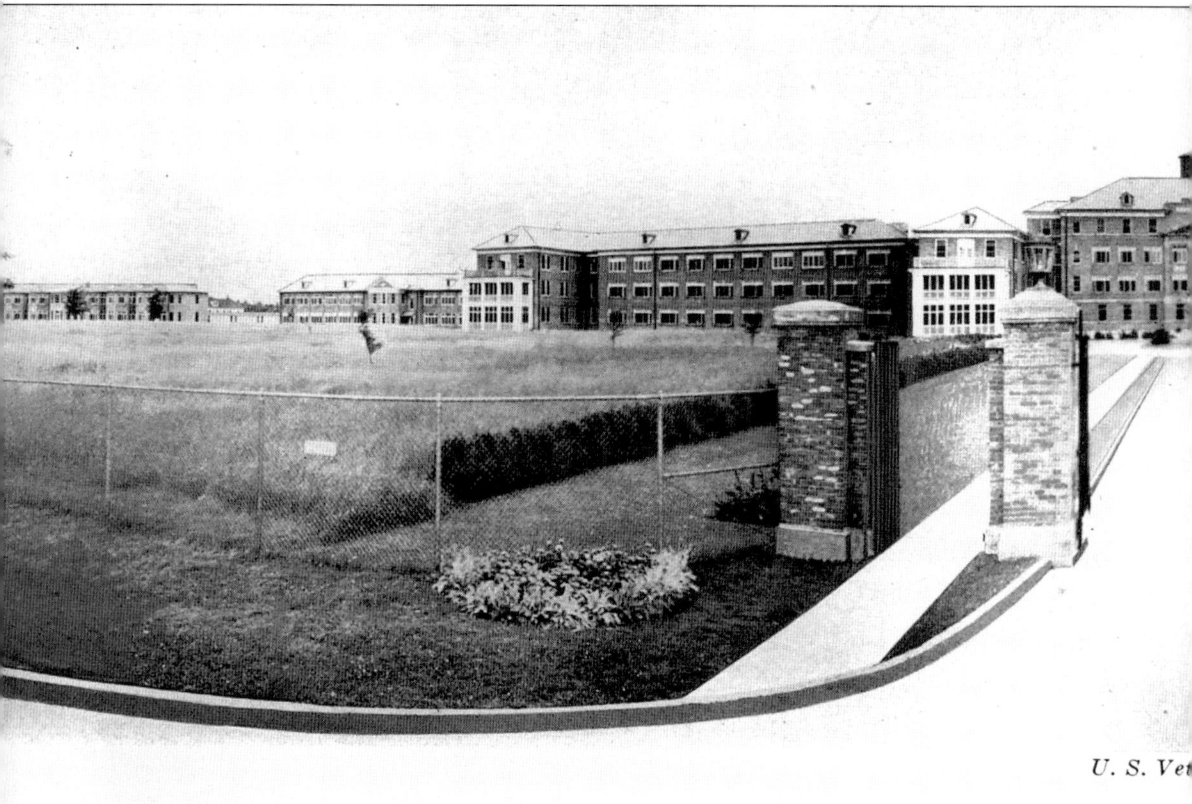

Sunmount Hospital, in Tupper Lake, took care of disabled American veterans for some 40 years. In 1922, when the United States was looking for a new hospital for World War I veterans, many suffering with tuberculosis, it turned to the health-giving Adirondacks. The village of Tupper Lake raised $20,000 to buy the 160-acre Albert Hosley farm and sold it to the government for $1. The hospital cared for thousands until August 1965, when the government phased out the facility in a cost-cutting measure. The state then took over the hospital and

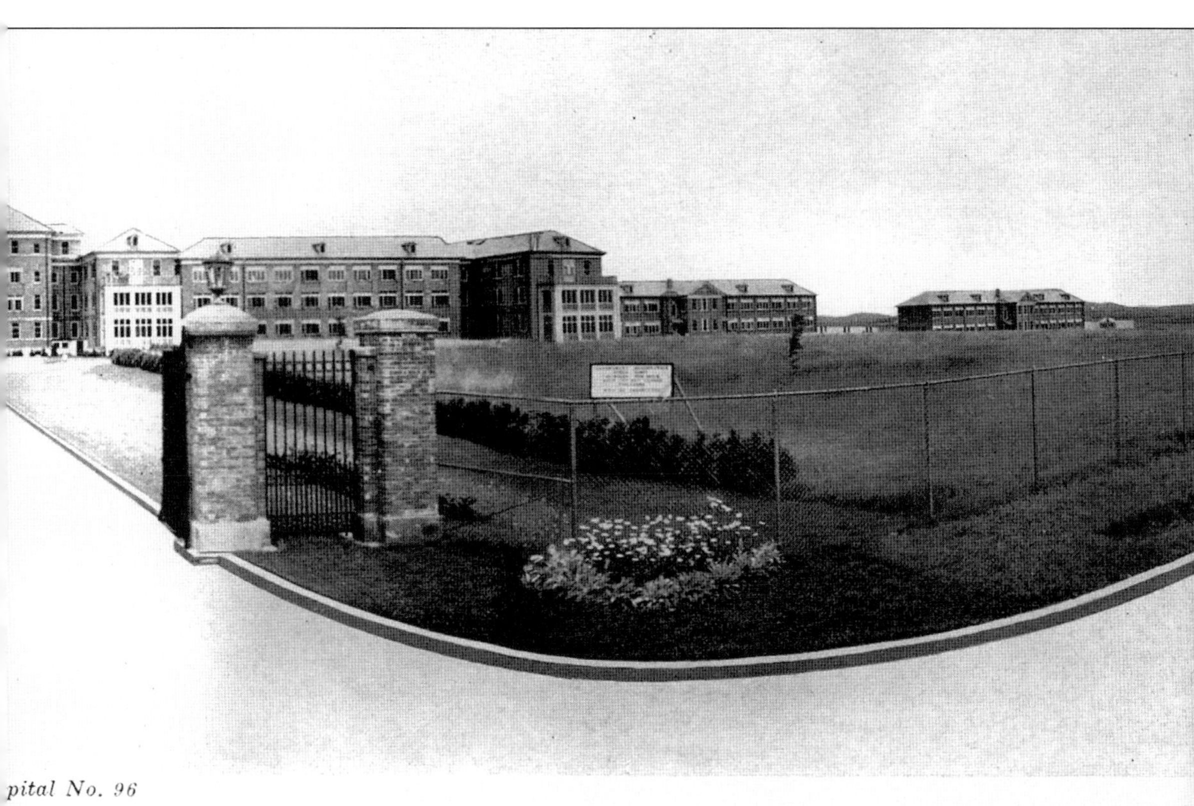

pital No. 96

opened a state mental hospital, renaming it the Sunmount Developmental Center. When the announcement was made for the closing of the veterans hospital, the community launched a huge campaign to save the hospital because the large payroll at the facility was vital to the economy of the Adirondack country. With a capacity for more than 500 patients, Sunmount employed a staff of 500, making it a major employer for the region.

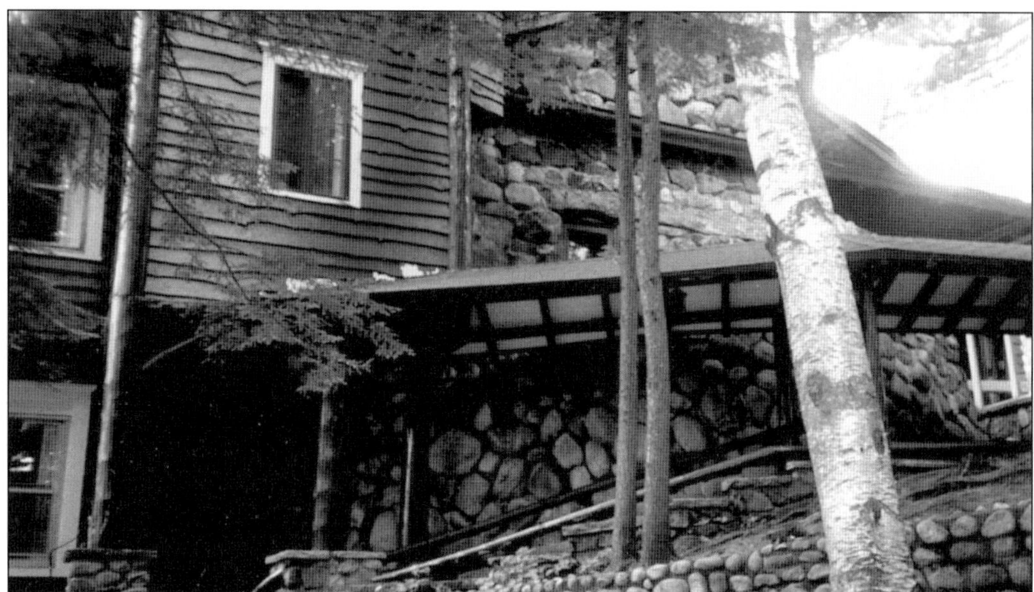

Camp Topridge, also known as Camp Hutridge, on the St. Regis Lake, was once the summer residence of heiress Majorie Merriweather Post. At Topridge, Post had a staff of 85, with a maid in each of the 18 guest cottages. Her four marriages produced three daughters, one of them actress Dina Merrill, who had her own cottage at Topridge. The complex was willed to New York State, which chose not to maintain it. Thus, it was sold to a private buyer.

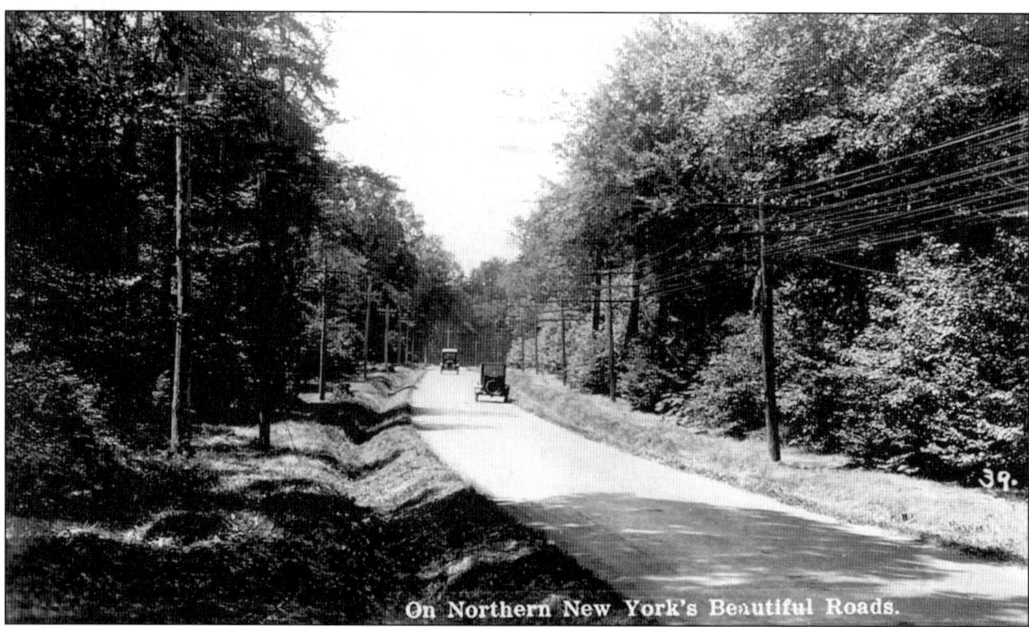

The caption on this 1920s photograph reads, "On Northern New York's Beautiful Roads." The road appears to be a level gravel road that is wide enough for two vintage automobiles to pass each other. It was a period in American history when road building became a priority, along with the electric lines, to meet the needs of the public. The written records of the Adirondack settlements include a multitude of road districts and the raising of funds to build and to improve roads.

Seven

BRIGHTON, DUANE, AND MALONE

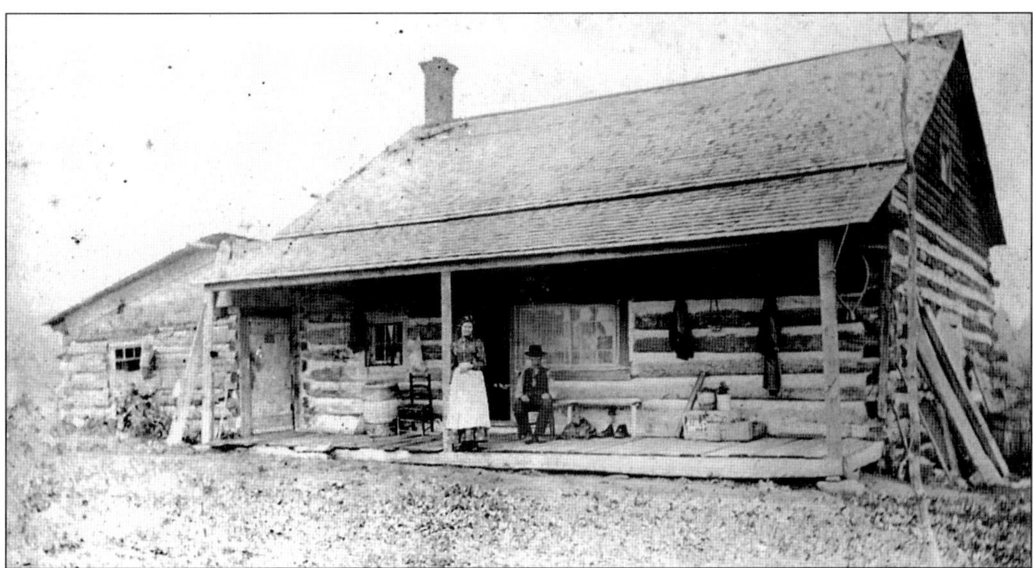

Log cabins were the home of choice for early Adirondack pioneers. Those who came to settle along the Adirondack Trail, from north to south, found that the available logs and sphagnum moss caulking made a warm, tight home. The history of each settlement includes the record of a group of log cabins constructed in the woods, creating a community. Griffin began with four log cabins. Long Lake had nine log cabins when Rev. John Todd visited there in 1841. Indian Lake began with 10 log cabins in 1850. As early as the 1790s, the settlement in Wells began with log cabin homes. Paul Smith built his first hotel, a log building, on the shores of St. Regis Lake, in Brighton, in 1850. Most of the Malone pioneers had homes of logs, some with a single room and split-log floor, heated by a fireplace with a hole in the roof for the smoke to go out.

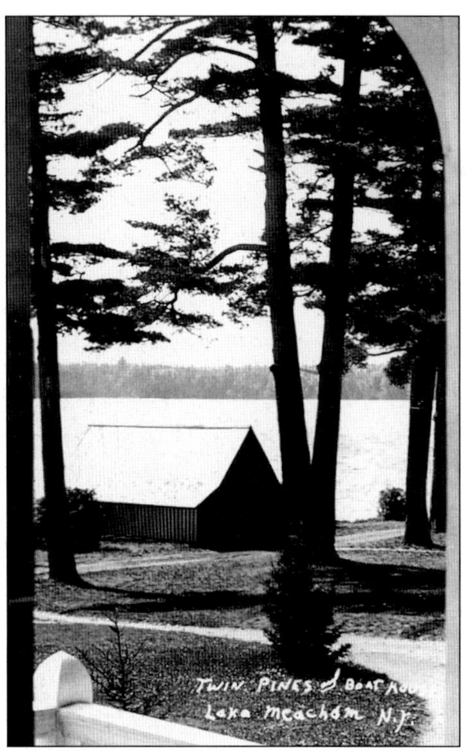

Meacham Lake, on the Adirondack Trail between Paul Smiths and Malone, has been a popular camping site since the first settlers arrived. The state campsite on Meacham provides boating, bathing, camping, fishing, picnicking, and other services. It has room for trailers and a trailer dumping station. Bathhouses and showers are included, along with lifeguards at the beach. It has boat-launching facilities for motorboats, rowboats, and canoes, along with rowboat and canoe rentals.

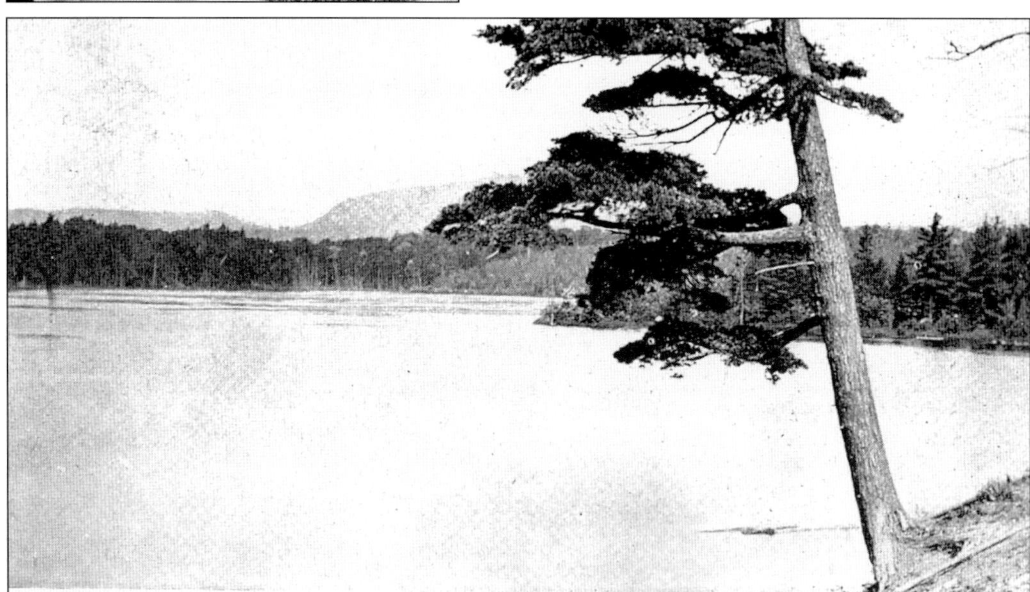

McColloms sits close to the northern border of the Adirondack Park, between Rice Lake and McColloms Pond. Rice Lake was once Rice Pond. In the Adirondacks, there is no size requirement; some ponds are bigger than lakes, and some lakes are smaller than ponds. In 1849, Amiel C. McCollom moved into a log cabin that was built by Amos Rice on some burnt land north of Paul Smiths. McCollom opened a sporting lodge for hunting and fishing, and later, he went into the hotel and hops-growing businesses.

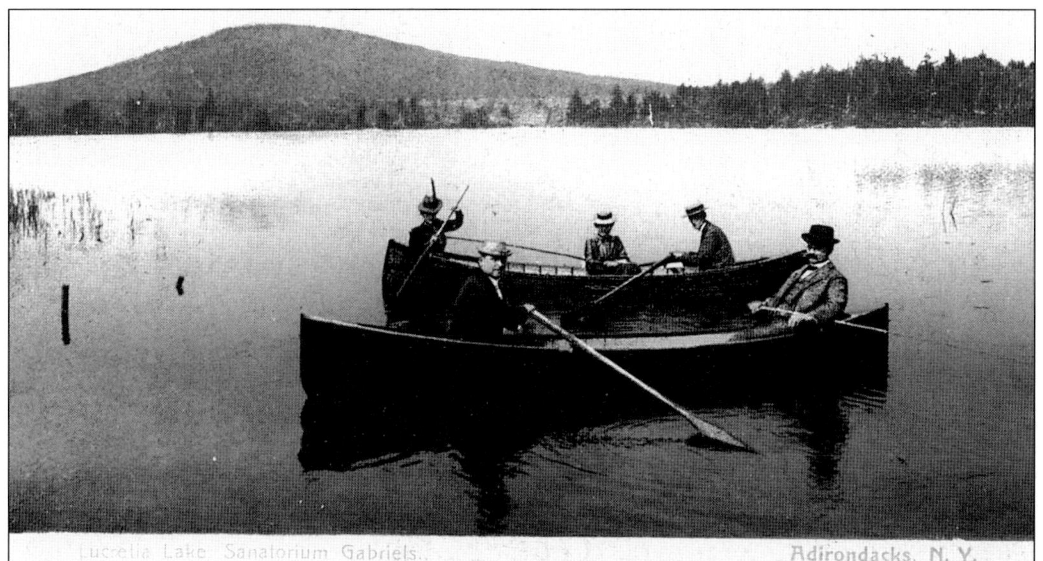

The community of Gabriels, just off the Adirondack Trail near Paul Smiths, was born when the Adirondack and St. Lawrence Railway was built in 1892. In 1910, Gabriels Sanatorium for tuberculosis patients was added to the growing community, which boasted stores, a hotel, saloons, and the railroad station for Paul Smiths guests. Eventually, Paul Smiths College purchased the lands and used the sanatorium buildings for dormitories until 1977. Today, Gabriels has become the site of a state prison.

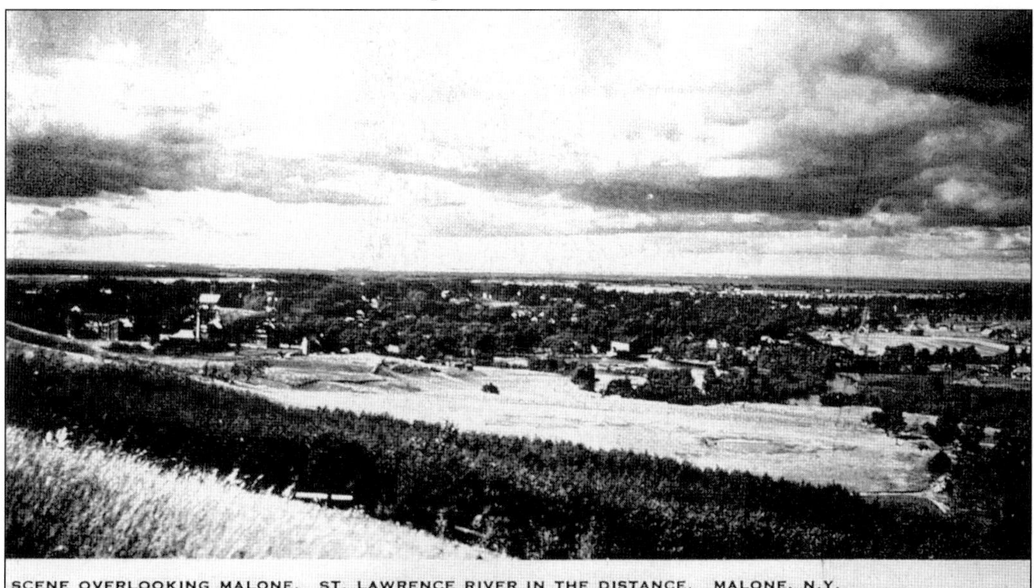

Malone, on the Salmon River, is an interior New York town that was settled by hardworking farmers from Vermont. Enos, Nathan, and John Wood came in 1802 and were the first to settle there. The healthy climate and fertile soils soon attracted others. Formed in 1805, the town of Harrison changed to Ezraville in 1808 and to Malone in 1812. In 1808, mills were going up on both sides of the Salmon River. A hotel appeared before 1809. Woolen mills came in 1825. Iron was discovered in 1828. Paper mills were in operation in 1872. The Adirondack Railroad from Herkimer to Malone was completed in 1892, and Malone's growth was assured.

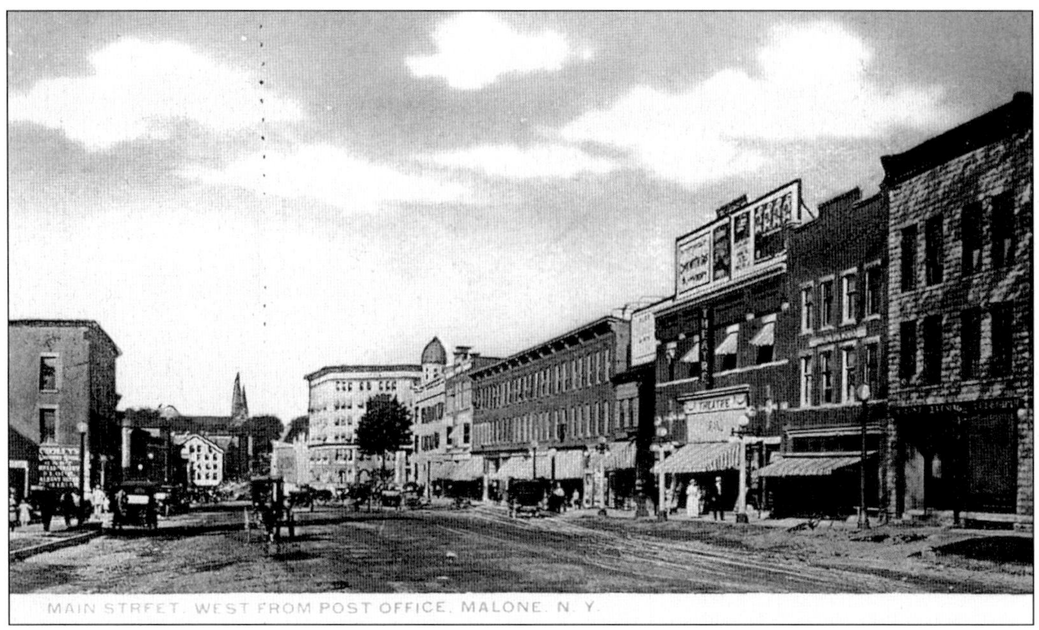

Richard Harison, Alexander Hamilton law partner and George Washington's friend, acquired Malone lands and envisioned a new community in the northern wilderness in 1801. He directed the early surveyors to lay out city lots along Main and Webster Streets. He first named the community Harison, changed it in 1808 to Ezraville after his friend Ezra L'Homedien, and finally, in 1812, settled on the name Malone to honor another friend, Edmund Malone, an Irish Shakespearean scholar.

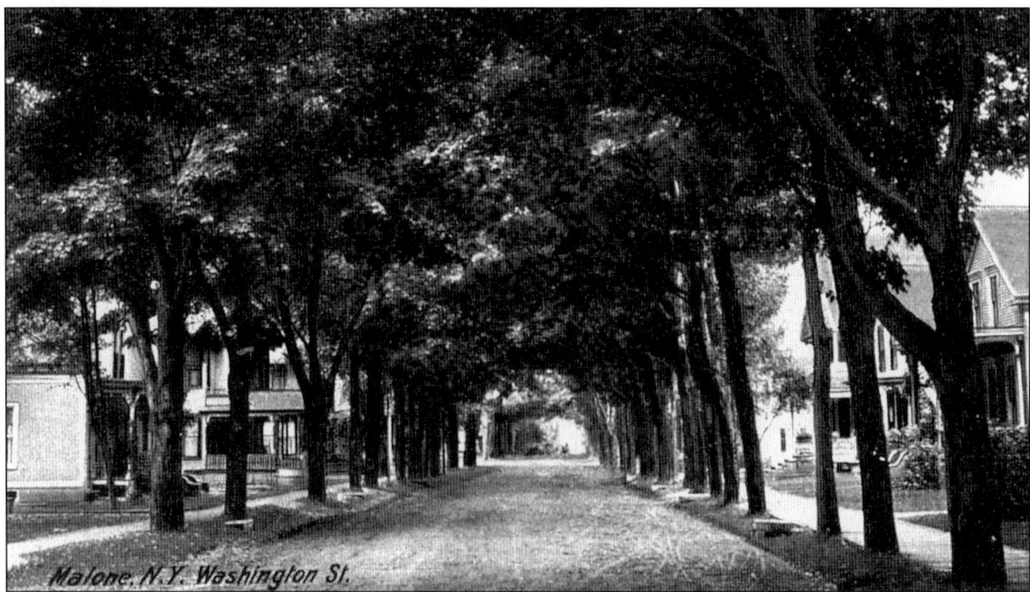

It is interesting to note that the town of Malone, at the northern end of the Adirondack Trail, was officially formed in 1805, the same time that the town of Wells was organized at the southern end. It appears that Washington Street in Malone was named after Pres. George Washington, a friend of the town's founder. In this 1905 view (created a century after the founding of the town), the tree-lined street is still a dirt road.

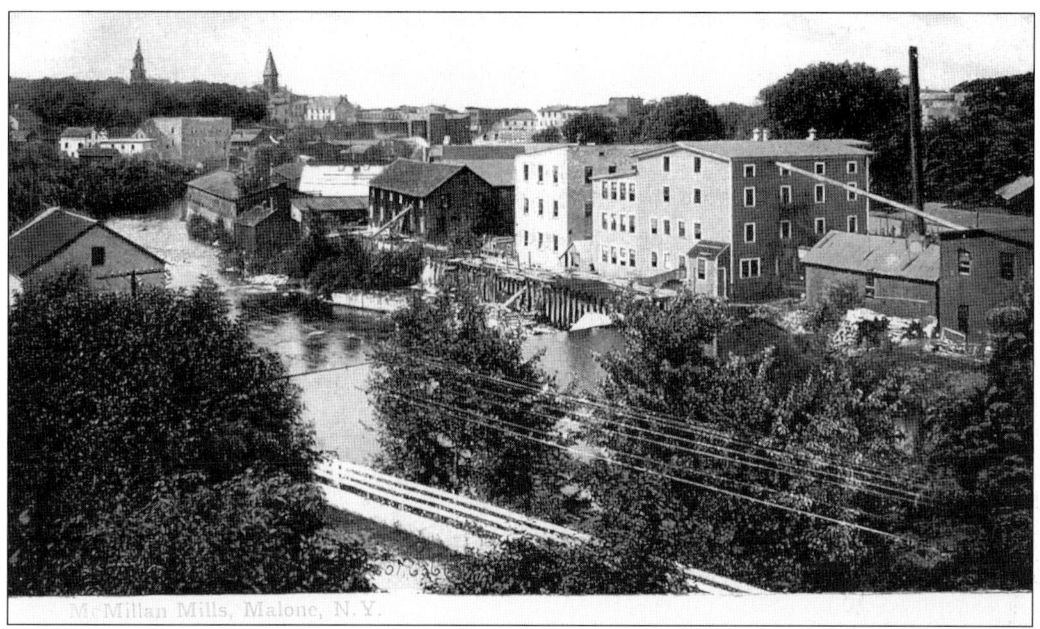

Woolen mills were among the major business interests in Malone in the 1800s. McMillan Mills, shown here, was one of a group that included Lawrence, Webster and Company, and the Malone Mills owned by John Stearns. The mills operated in the first half of the 1800s, closed, and then reopened in 1861 under C. C. Whittlesey. In the 1854 census, Malone had over 9,000 sheep and made over 21,000 pounds of wool, the highest producer in Franklin County.

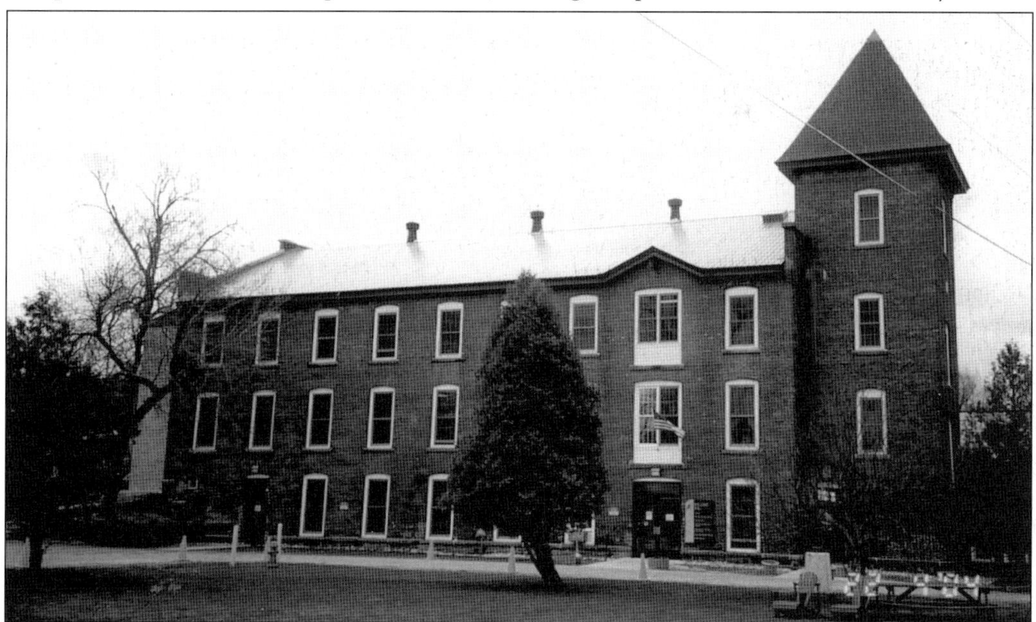

The Ballard Mill began manufacturing plaid wool cloth in Malone in 1901. After competition closed the mill in 1965, a portion of the building was opened as an art center. In the 1990s, when the abandoned building was on the way to ruin, the North Country Community College Foundation purchased it for a satellite campus. It houses classrooms, labs, offices, a library, and a center for 500 students.

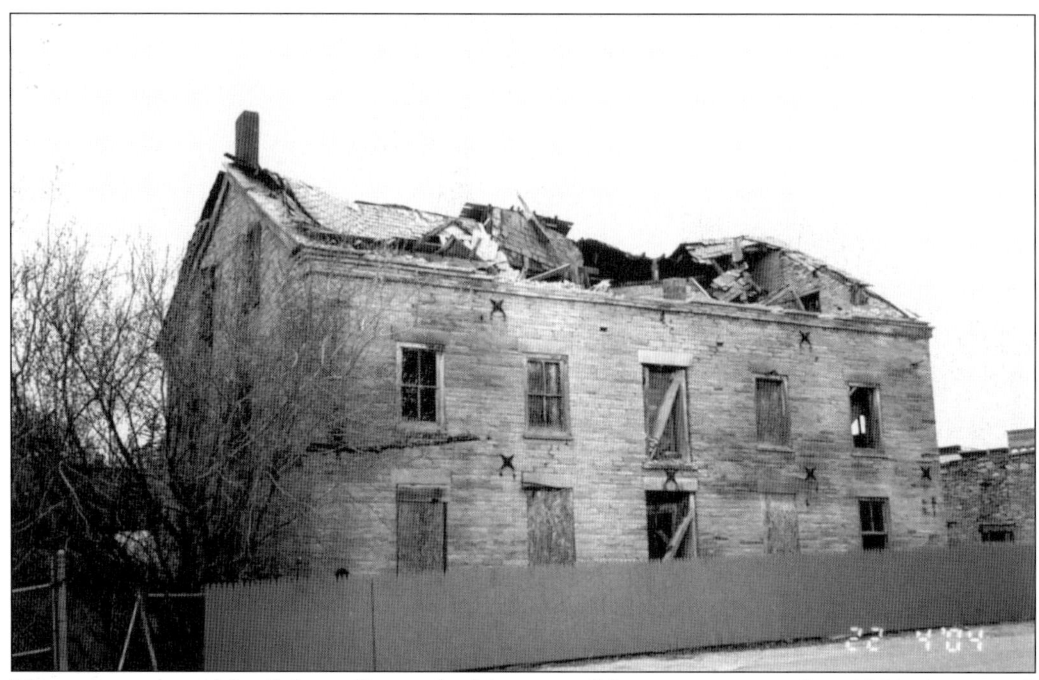

Using the power of the Salmon River, the Horton mill began as a sawmill in 1803. A gristmill was built on the old foundation in 1856. The building later became a hardware and lumber store. Today, it is being restored as the year-round home of the Malone Historical Society.

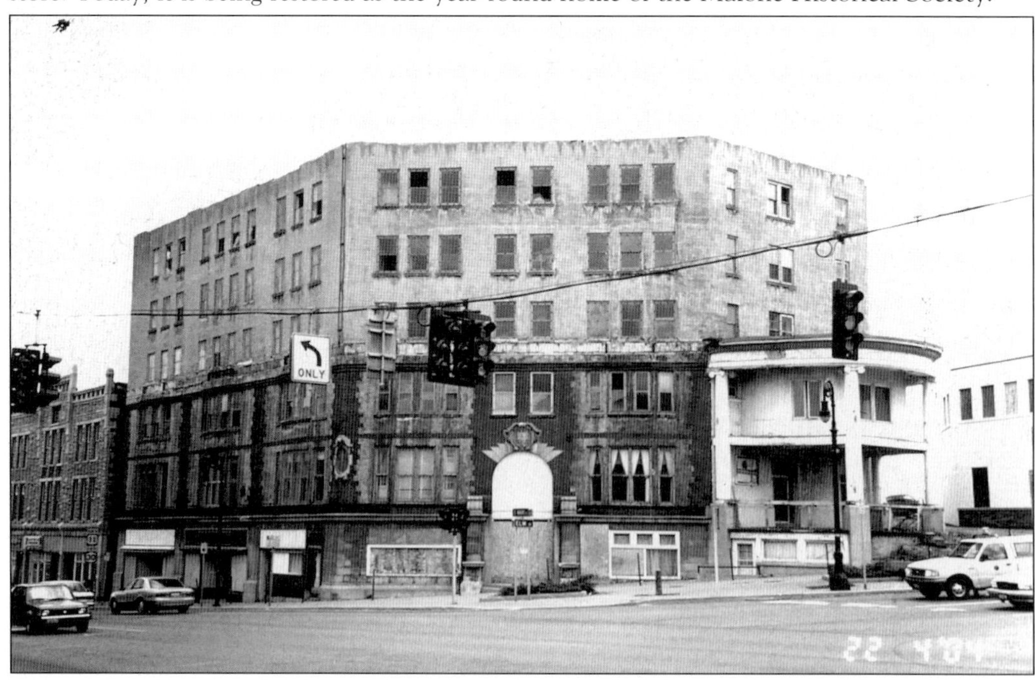

One of the most prominent buildings on Malone's Main Street is the old Flanigan Hotel. It stands abandoned today, having closed after a 1997 fire. It was once an elegant hotel catering to elderly residents and the general public. Plans are now under way to restore the hotel to its former grandeur and level of service.

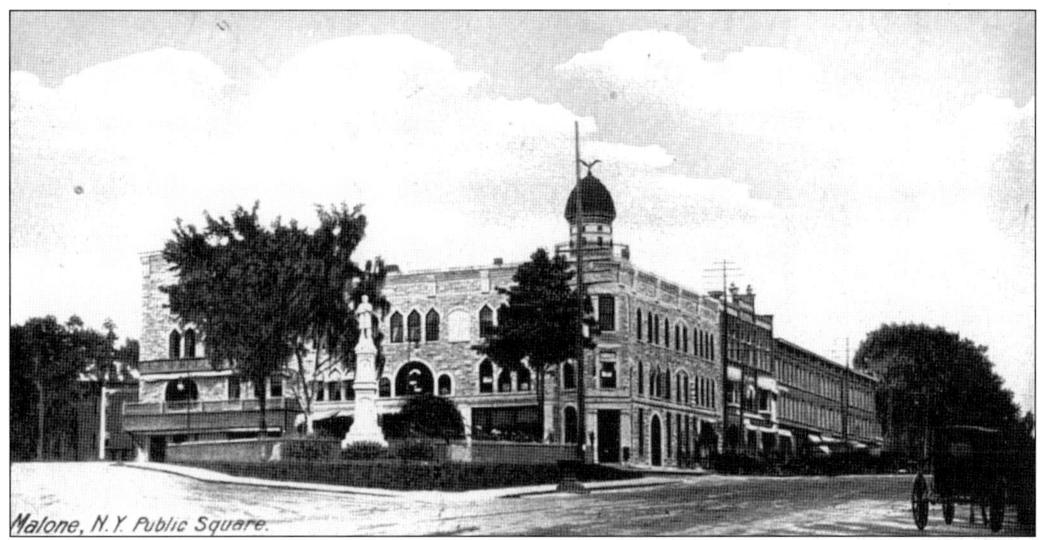

Malone, situated on the frontier, was once the headquarters of the Fenian Brotherhood, a group of Irish-Americans dedicated to the overthrow of the English authority in Ireland. The original Fenians in Ireland disbanded in 284 A.D., but a revival spread across America after the Irish famine of 1846. Malone became the headquarters of the Fenian raiders who wanted to invade Canada. In 1866, some 3,000 Fenians assembled in Malone's public square. In 1868, they invaded Canada, and in 1870, they made their headquarters in Malone. The Fenians dispersed after all their attempts were quashed.

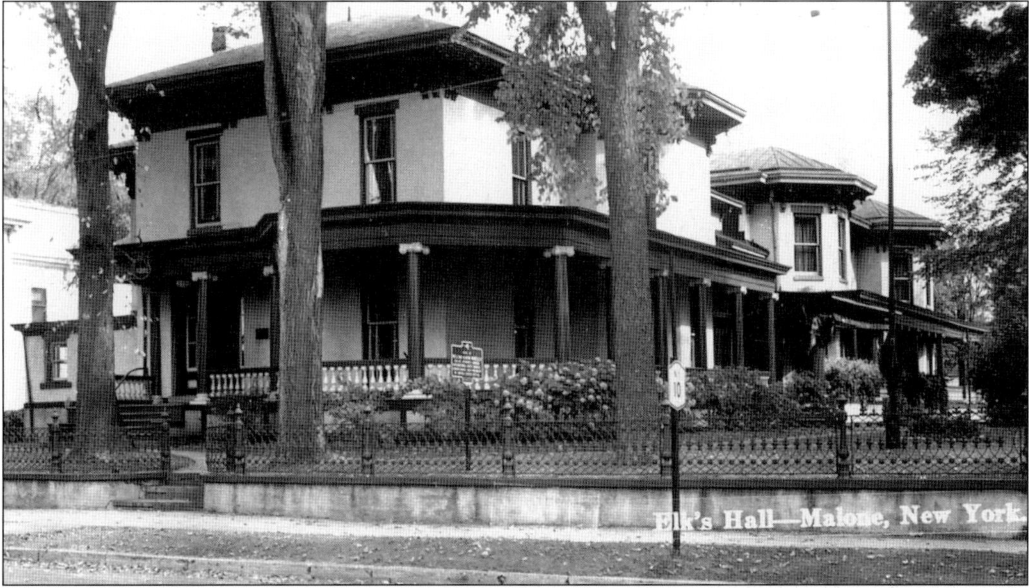

The Malone Lodge of Elks moved into the former residence of Vice Pres. William Almond Wheeler in 1913. Wheeler was elected in 1876 as the running mate of Pres. Rutherford B. Hayes. Born on June 30, 1819, he had risen from comparatively poor beginnings to serve in Congress. He attended Franklin Academy in Malone and the University of Vermont. He was a lawyer, a district attorney, a state assemblyman, and a state senator before going to Congress in 1863, where he served four terms. He returned in 1881 and died in Malone in 1887. His grave is in Morningside Cemetery.

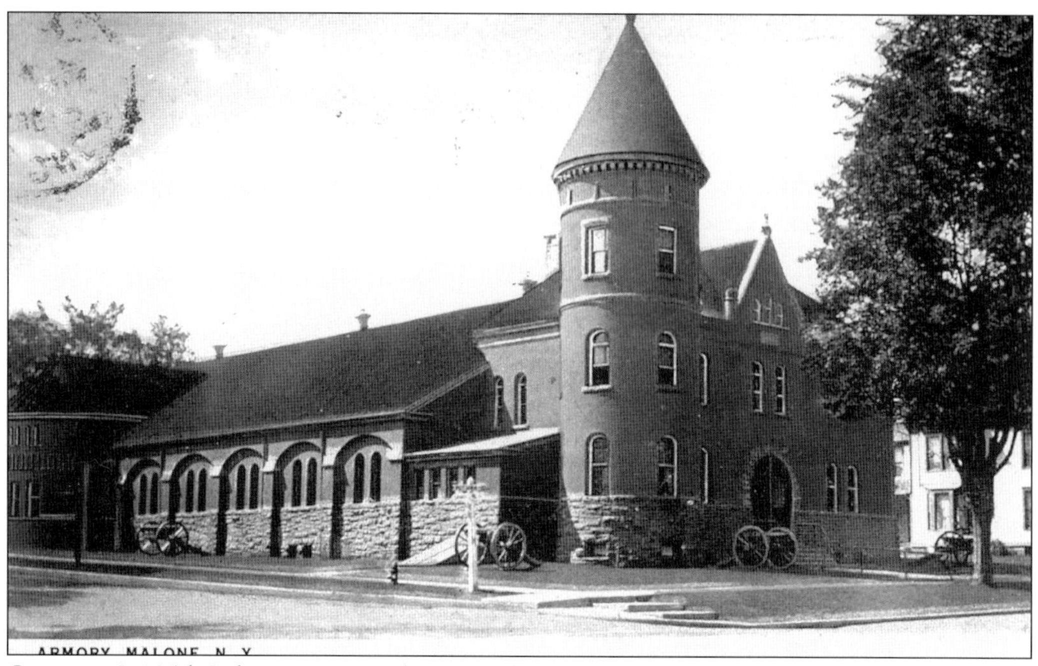

Company I, 105th Infantry, New York National Guard, is Malone's oldest military organization, dating back to 1878. The company served along the Mexican border in 1916, volunteered in 1898 for the Spanish-American War, fought in Europe in World War I, and served in the Pacific during World War II. The long-serving Malone Armory is now being converted into a YMCA.

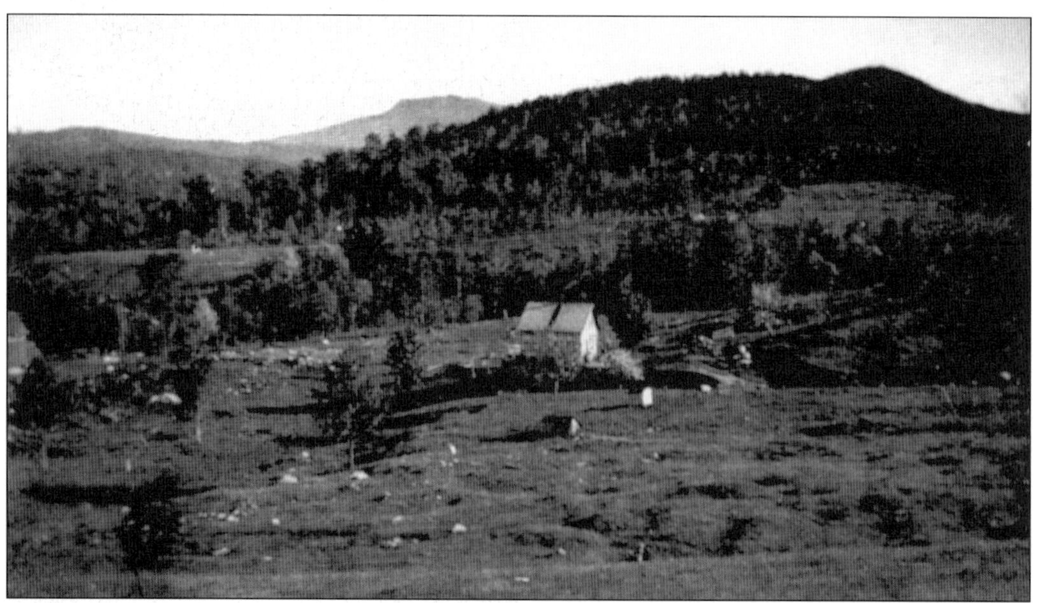

Malone and all the communities along the Adirondack Trail owe their existence to the hardy settlers who first cleared the forests and farmed the land with mixed success. Farming in the Adirondack soil, with its annual "rock crop" and short growing season, was marginal, and most of the farmland reverted back to forestland. Stone fences and abandoned farm machinery can often be seen in the woodlands along the Adirondack Trail.

Eight
Along the Trail

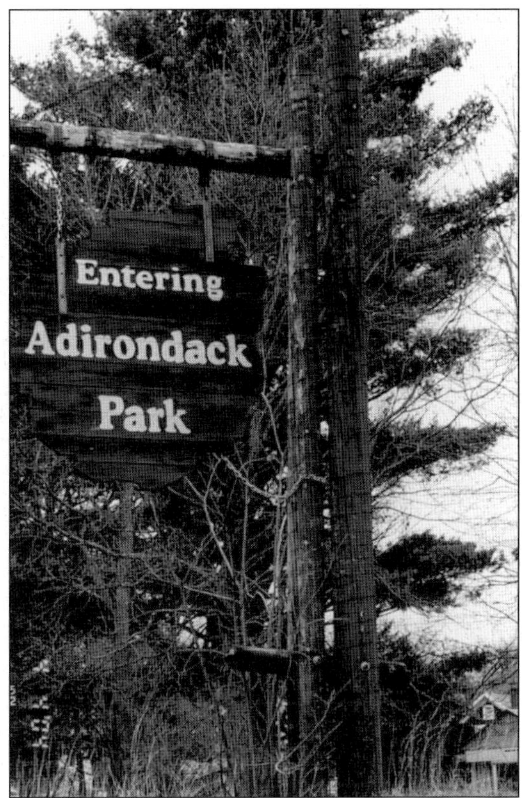

The Adirondack Trail crosses over the "blueline," or boundary, and enters the six-million-acre Adirondack Park at a point between Gloversville and Mayfield. Then, it exits the park about halfway between McColloms and Malone. Adirondack Park, established in 1892 with a patchwork of public and private lands, is larger than Yellowstone, Grand Canyon, Smokey Mountains, Yosemite, and Glacier national parks combined. The public lands within the park are forest preserve lands, created in 1885. They are open to widespread use as long as they are protected as forever wild.

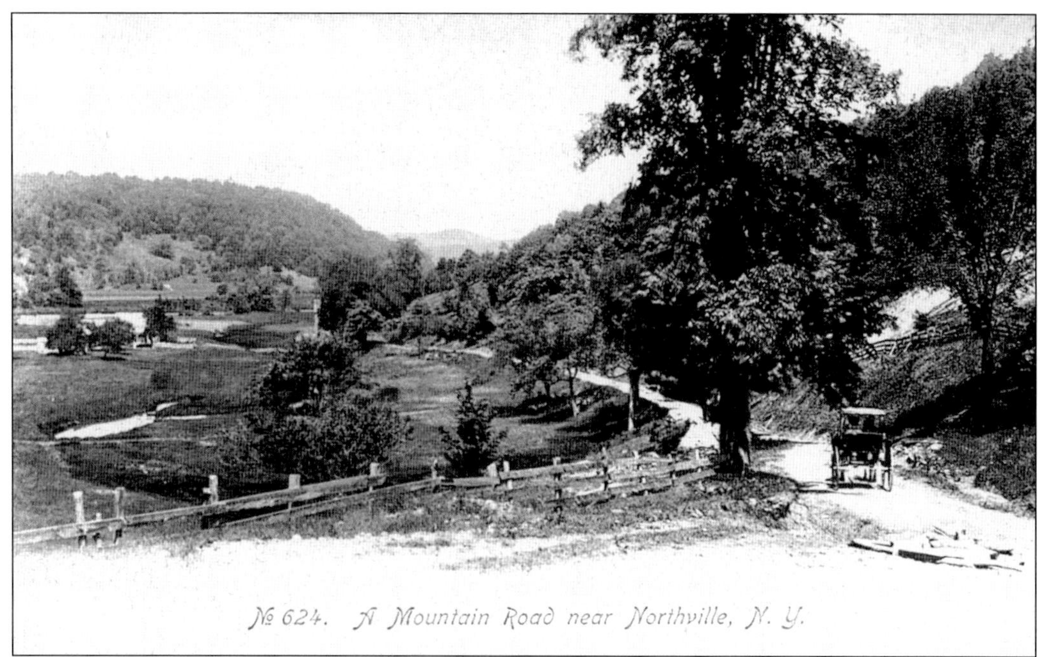

The southern portion of the Adirondack Trail followed the Sacandaga River and was first called the Sacandaga Trail. It meandered through flatlands and roadside cliffs, cleared farmlands and fenced pastures, offering a bucolic roadside scene for the traveler. The narrow roadways in the days of the horse and buggy often called for one conveyance to pull off the road to let the other pass.

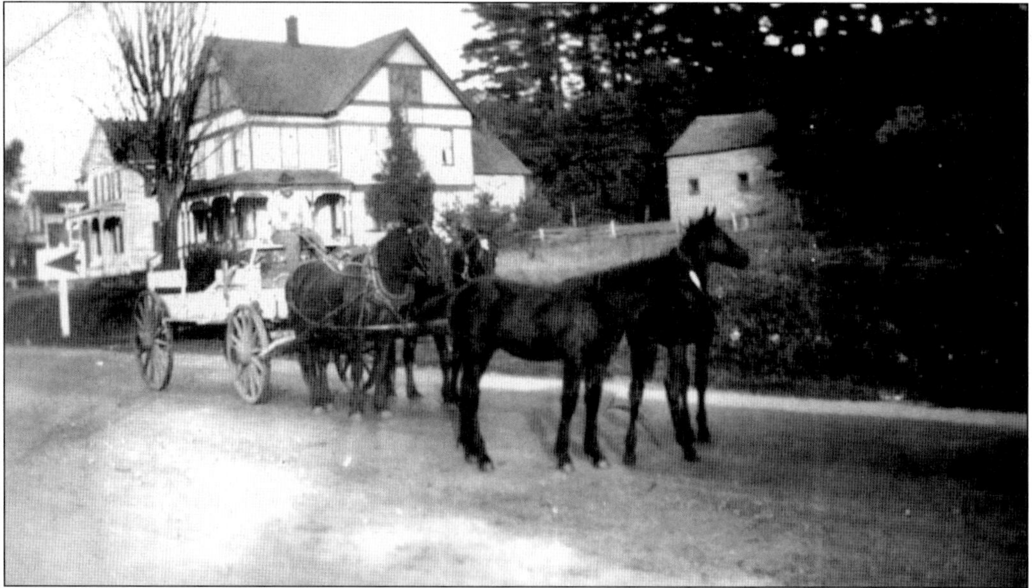

The Adirondack Trail was used by horses before the invention of the automobile, and it was a common sight to see the stagecoaches pass through the hamlets. Occasionally, peddlers with loaded wagons were observed, as well as the Adirondack residents who used their buggies, surreys, cutters, wagons, and buckboards for transportation. Shown are two loose horses, blocking the passage of a freight wagon.

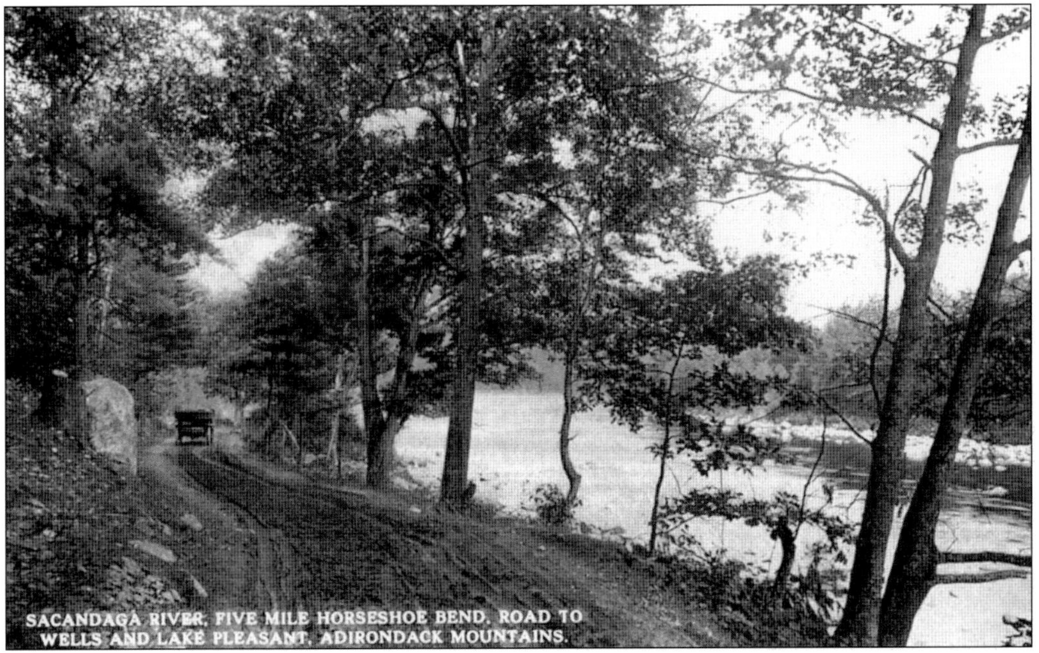
SACANDAGA RIVER, FIVE MILE HORSESHOE BEND, ROAD TO WELLS AND LAKE PLEASANT, ADIRONDACK MOUNTAINS.

The early Adirondack Trail followed the Sacandaga River closely. Trees and boulders lined the roadside banks, and the road surface was forest dirt. Shown is "five mile horseshoe bend." Little was done to straighten the early trail since vehicles moved at a slow speed.

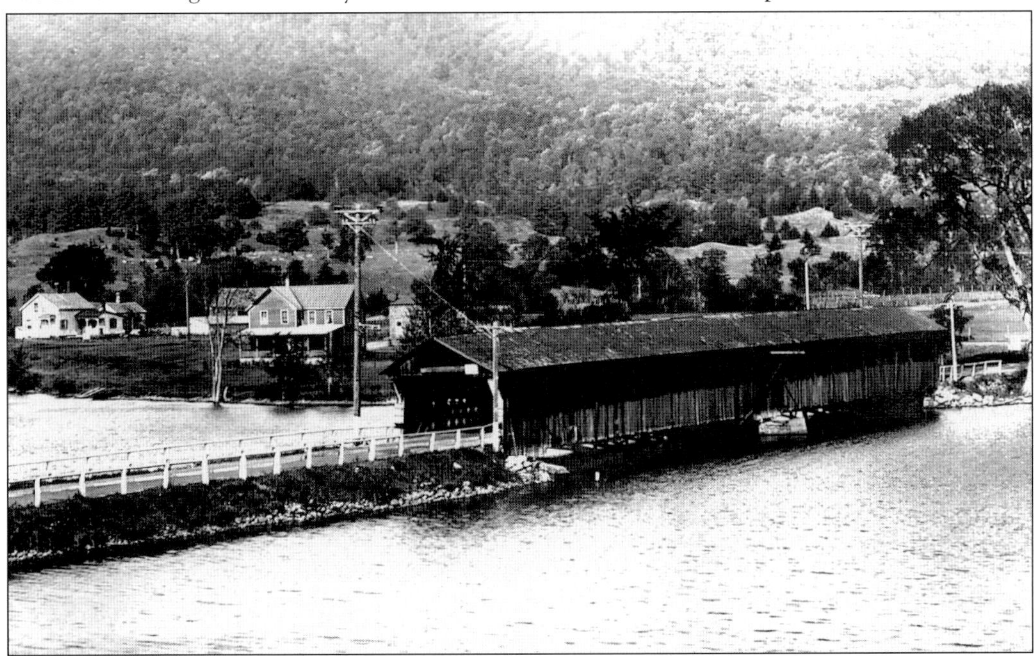

As the Adirondack Trail crossed many waterways, covered bridges were constructed to handle the traffic. Fording the river bottom often proved treacherous and fatal. Covering the bridge with a roof helped to preserve the road underneath and kept off the rain, snow, and ice. Restrictions on speed, weight, and vehicle type were often posted on the bridge, sometimes with a cost for crossing.

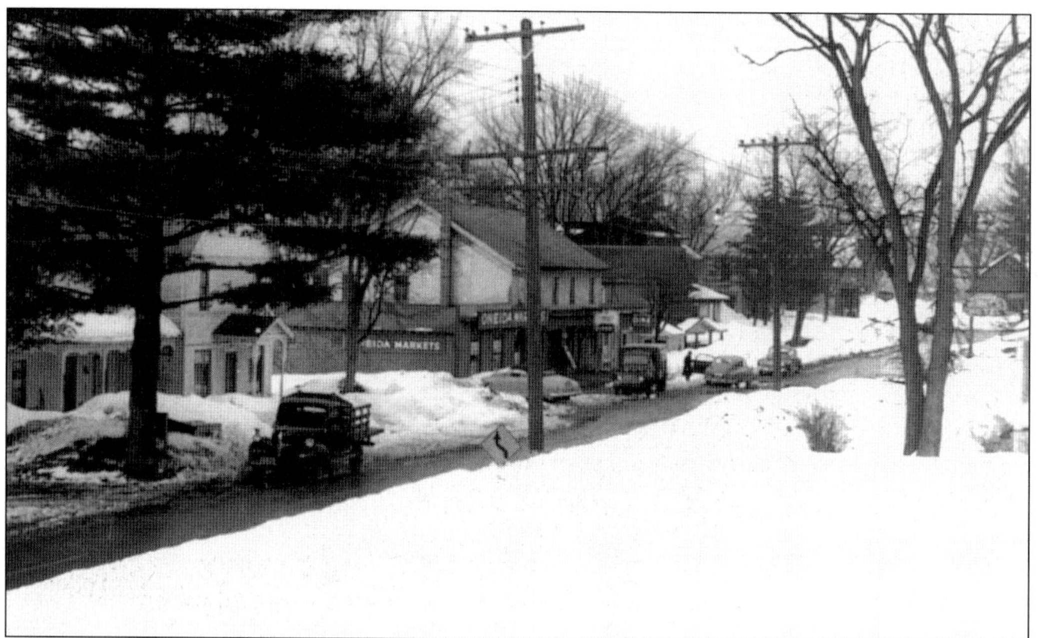

The task of keeping the Adirondack Trail open for traffic once automobiles became popular was a major enterprise. Highway departments, state and local, were established, and equipment was funded by taxpayers. Keeping the roads free of ice and snow, sanding, and salting, was costly. Those who plow the roads often worked long hours to keep the communities from isolation.

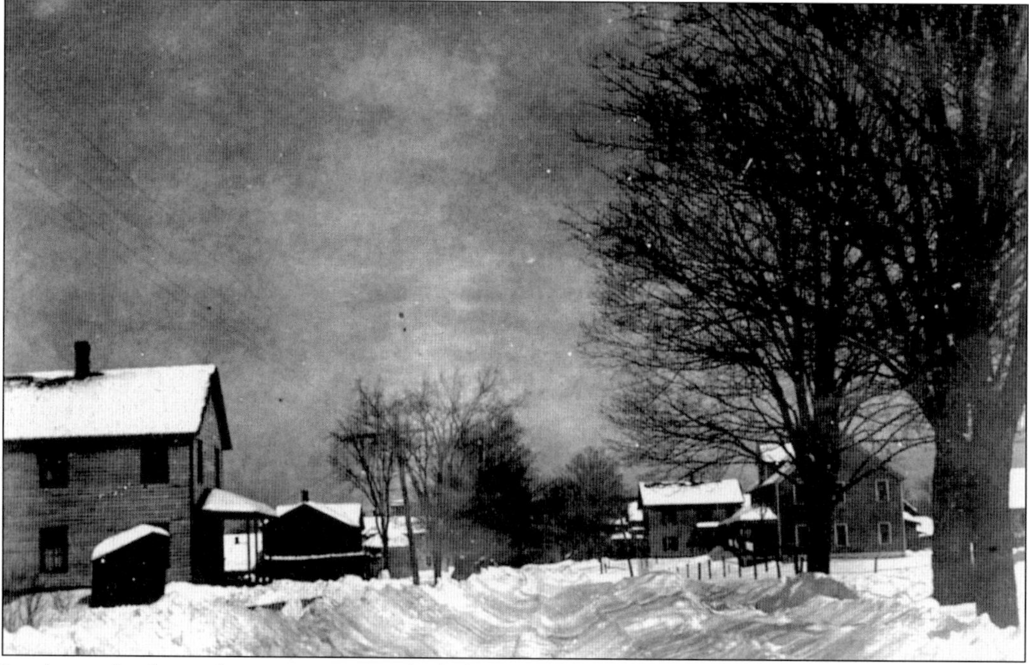

In the early days, the snow was packed down with rollers, as shown in this picture of the Adirondack Trail, rather than cleared by plow. The horses and sleighs formed the ruts in the snow and traveled in them throughout the winter months. When spring came, the snows melted and the mud season began. Schools were often closed during the mud season.

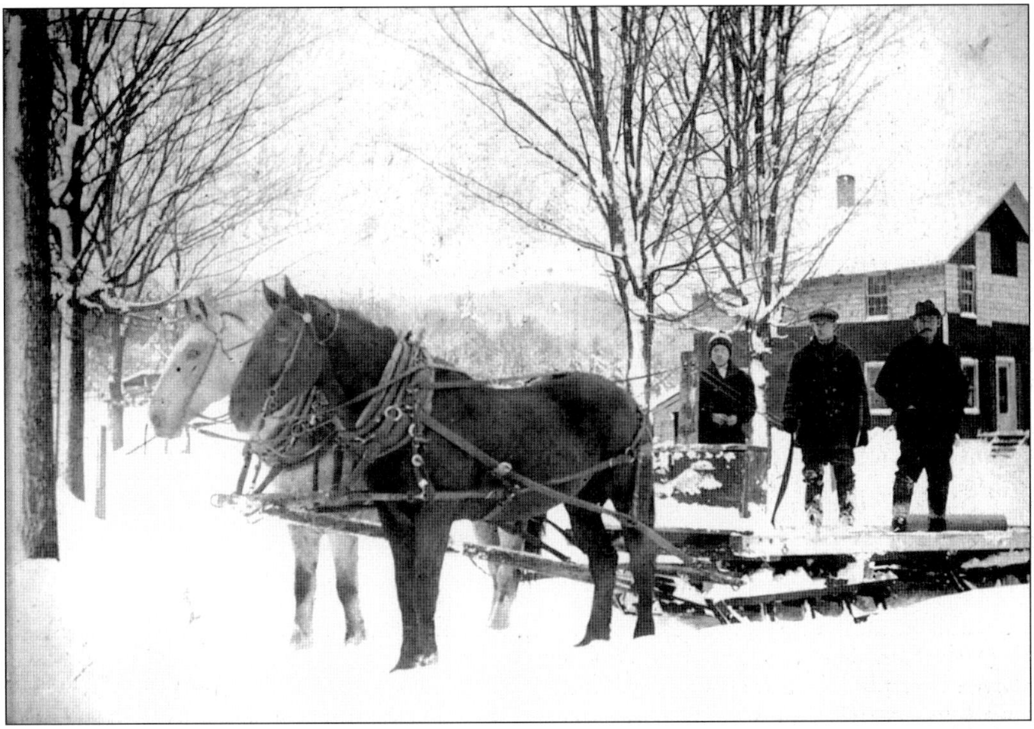

A good team of horses and a sleigh were the best transportation for the Adirondack Trail before the advent of the automobile. Horses required daily attention: feeding, brushing, and harnessing. Blacksmiths were kept busy shoeing the hardworking animals. Harness makers supplied miles of leather harnesses for driving the horses.

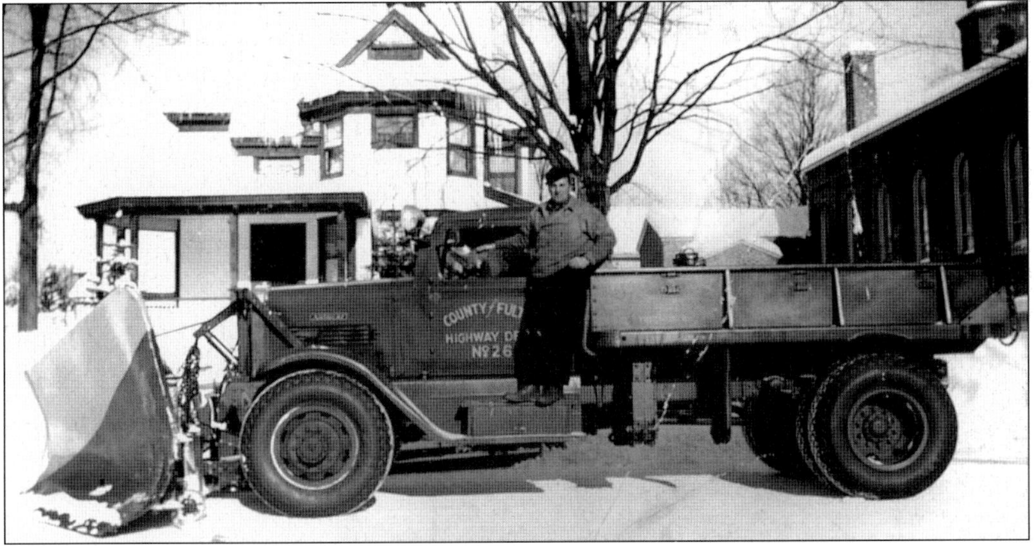

After automobiles replaced horses on the Adirondack Trail, plowing the road became essential. Keeping the way open for traffic fell on the shoulders of those who worked for the highway departments. Al Johnson, pictured in the 1940s, plowed the Fulton County highways in the southern Adirondacks for many years. The Adirondack Trail has a good reputation for being kept passable during winter storms.

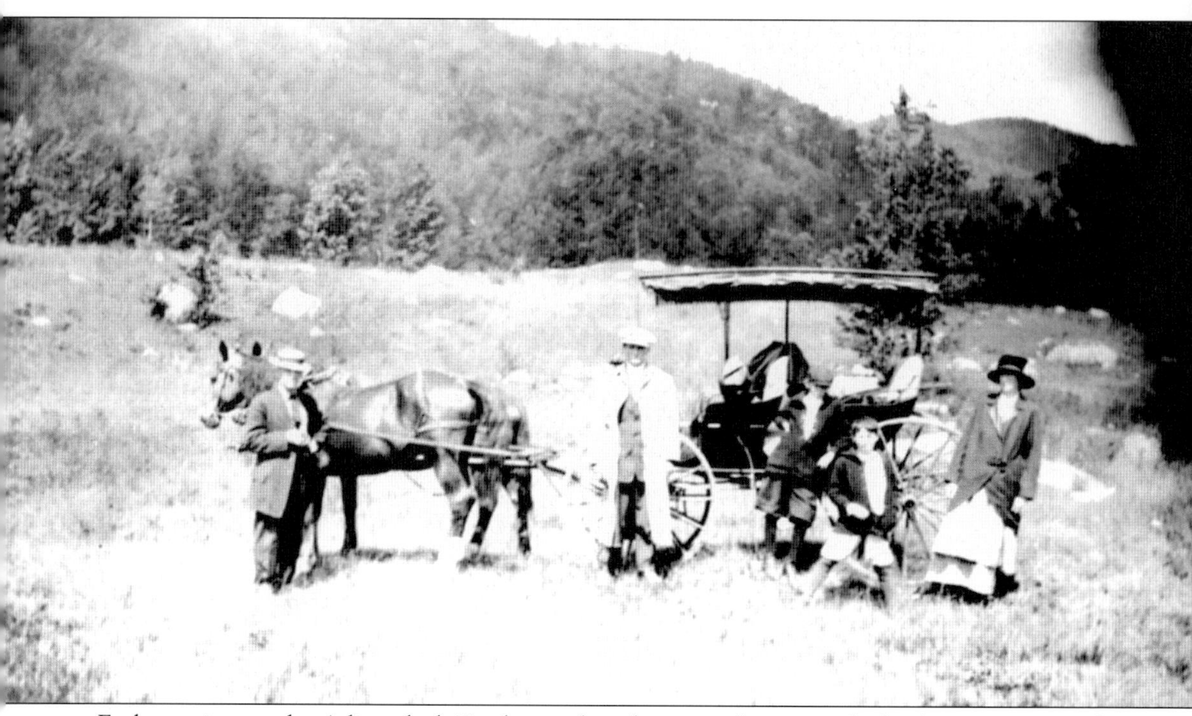

Early touring on the Adirondack Trail was often done in a "surrey with the fringe on top." The whole family could pile into the carriage, hook up the horses, and go. Stormy or cold weather required adjustments such as side curtains and lap robes. Heated stones were placed on the floor to keep feet from freezing. Dr. Edward Livingston Trudeau, the tuberculosis physician, and Paul Smith had a difficult winter trip. They went to Malone to pick up Mrs. Trudeau and got caught in a snowstorm returning down the Adirondack Trail. It took them two days to get home. They had to break the trail by riding the horses through it and then backtracking to get the load and passengers. They dug holes in the snowdrifts to keep the wife and children from freezing. They finally left the baggage at Barnam Pond and went on without it, reaching the hotel at midnight. It was a trip never to be forgotten. The horses used on the winter roads faced other hardships; when a horse slipped and fell, all its tangled harnesses had to be removed to get the animal up.

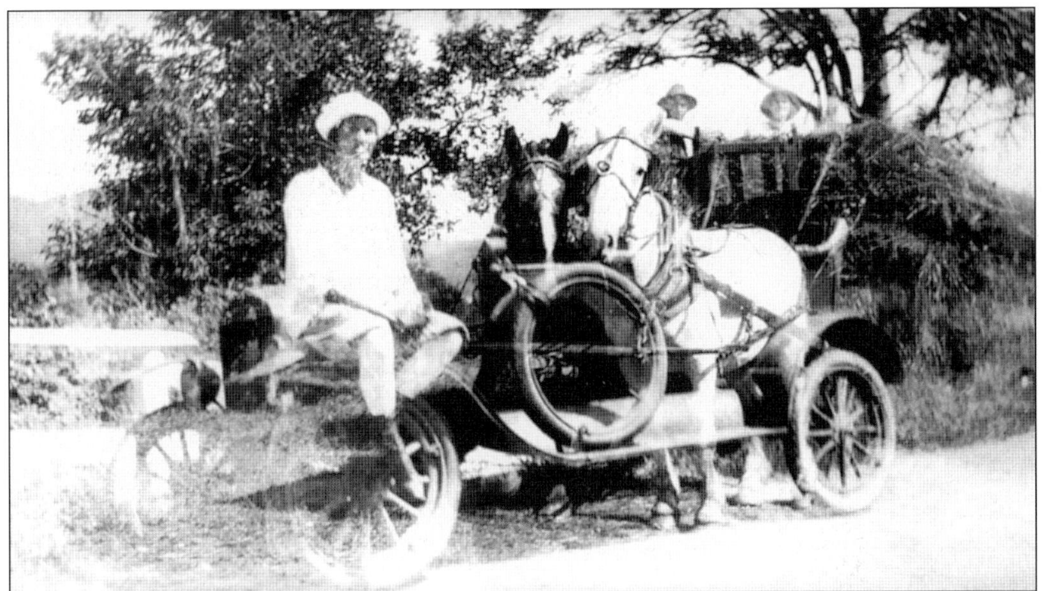

Anyone who took photographs in the early days had to remember to wind the film after each shot. Those who failed to do so ended up with a double exposure. This "prophetic" Adirondack Trail photograph, taken in the days between horse transportation and automobile transportation, is a double exposure with an automobile superimposed on a team of horses pulling a wagon. It symbolizes the days to come, when the automobile took over the highways and horses became transportation of the past.

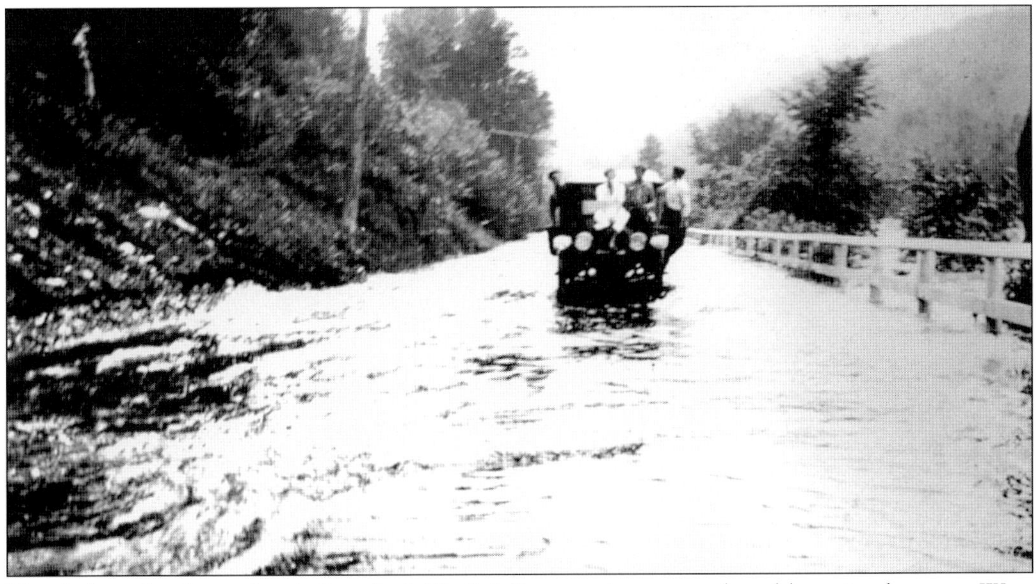

Flooded roads where the Adirondack Trail follows a river caused problems in the past. Wet, rainy springtimes and ice jams diverted the water into the roads, sometimes making them impassable. This automobile is either transporting passengers through the water or taking them on a sightseeing tour of the flooded road.

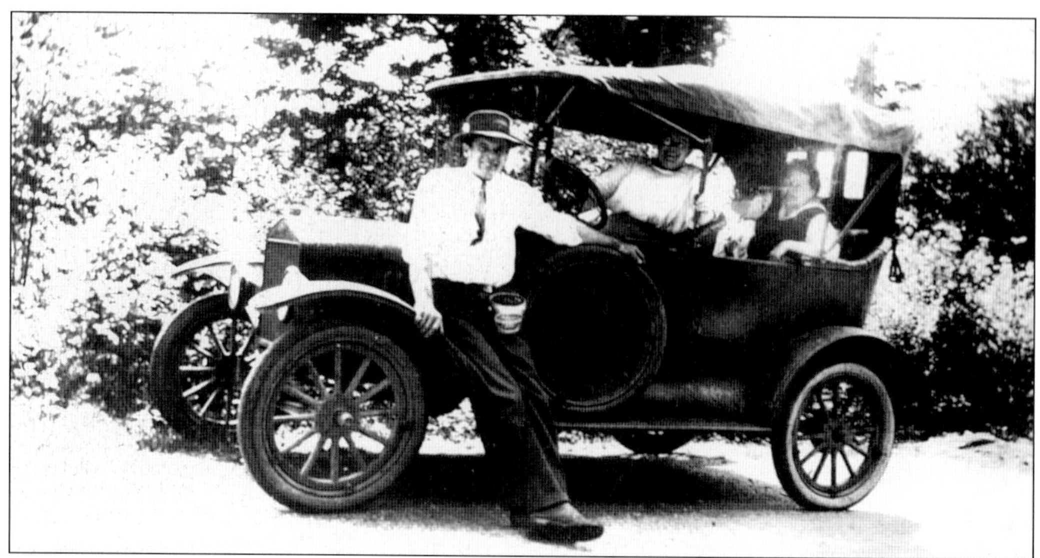

The Adirondack Trail was not constructed to serve as a thruway from New York to Canada. It was simply a series of roads connecting the hamlets of the Adirondack Mountain region. It allowed politicians to get to the county seats, friends and relatives to visit those in the next town, and hunters and fishermen to reach the woods and streams. When all its segments were connected to the outside world, it served the growing tourist trade to the Adirondack resorts.

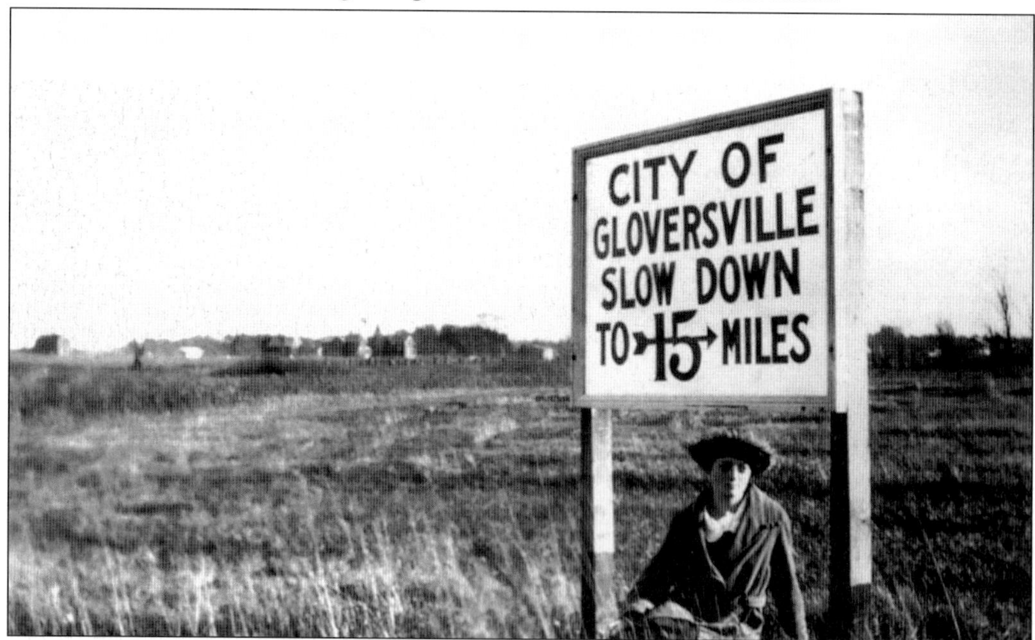

This sign on the Adirondack Trail near Gloversville was one of the early speed limit signs erected on the highway when automobiles came into use. Unfortunately, pedestrians were not accustomed to the fast-moving cars that reached speeds up to 20 and 30 miles per hour, and fatal accidents occurred when they did not get out of the road in time when a car approached. A prominent country doctor, Dr. Joseph Head, was killed on the Adirondack Trail on March 23, 1915, by a car going 15 to 20 miles per hour. Indian Lake set a speed limit of 10 miles per hour in 1912, and Lake Pleasant set its speed limit at 30 miles per hour.

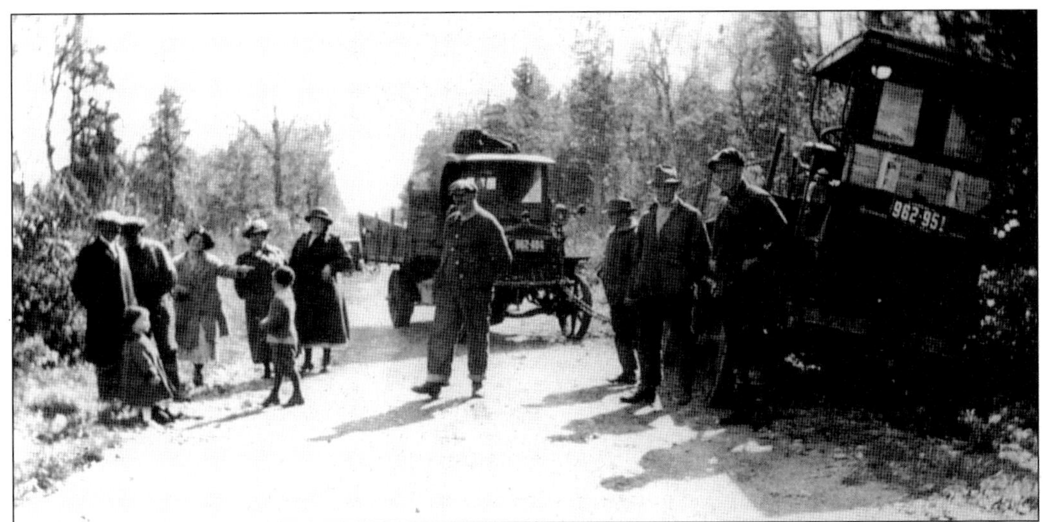

With motorized vehicles on the highways, new situations arose. The strange vehicle on the right apparently ran off the road and got stuck in the muddy ditch. The truck has a towrope attached to it and is trying to pull the vehicle out. The bystanders are dressed in their touring clothes and are waiting for the road to clear so they can go on. Their automobiles can be seen in the distance. Between flat tires, steep hills affecting the gravity-fed gas lines, overheating, and blocked roads, travel was much slower at the beginning of the 20th century.

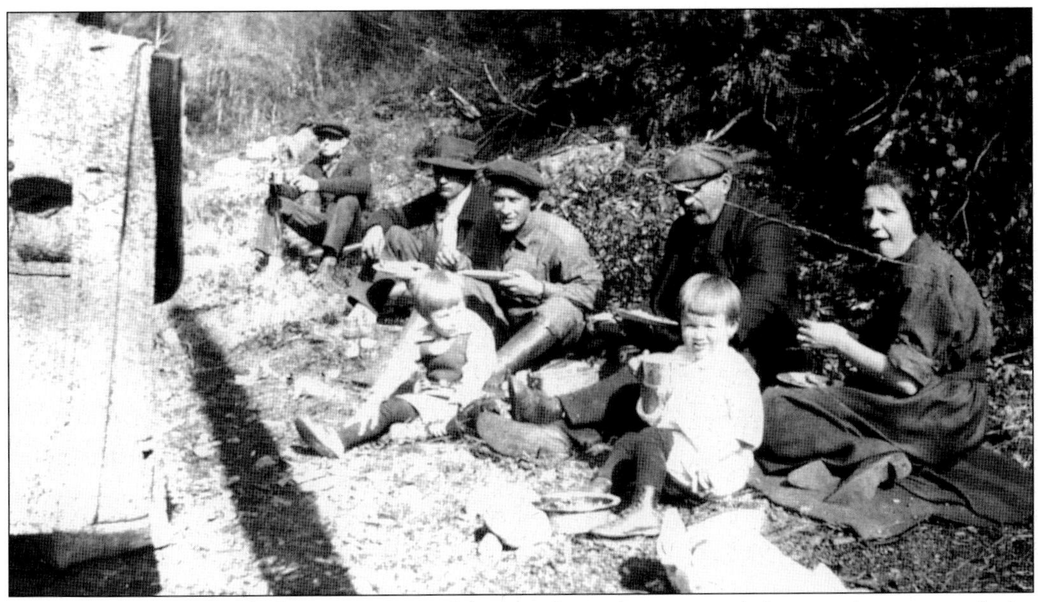

Americans discovered the great out-of-doors when the automobile got them out of the populated areas and into the countryside. Touring groups created a need for roadways such as the Adirondack Trail to open up the land of mountains and lakes. It was common practice to load up the family cars, pack picnic lunches, and drive into the mountains. Roadside picnics were social events that met the need for a lunch stop on the trail. Restaurants came later. State campsites and picnic grounds soon followed, and they are still open today.

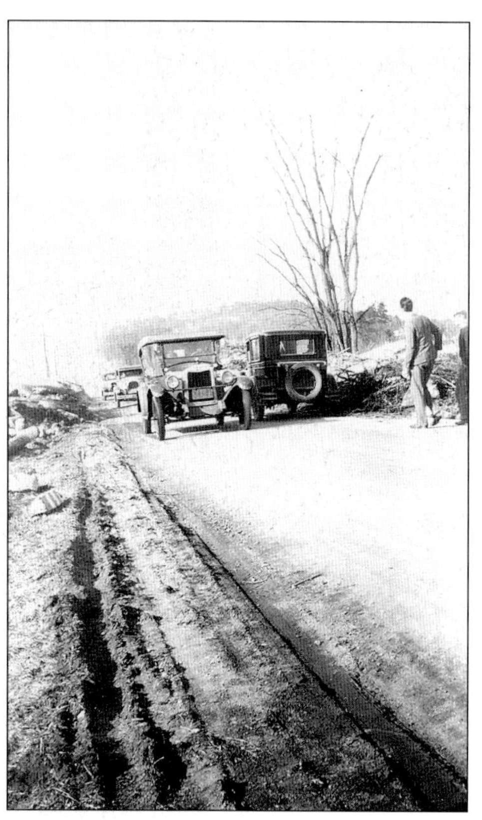

Before they were widened and paved, narrow roads caused problems for automobiles. Unpaved roads were bumpy, rutty, and often muddy. One report from an Adirondack tour told of using seven new tires on the trip. Spare car parts were often unavailable and had to be custom made by a local machinist.

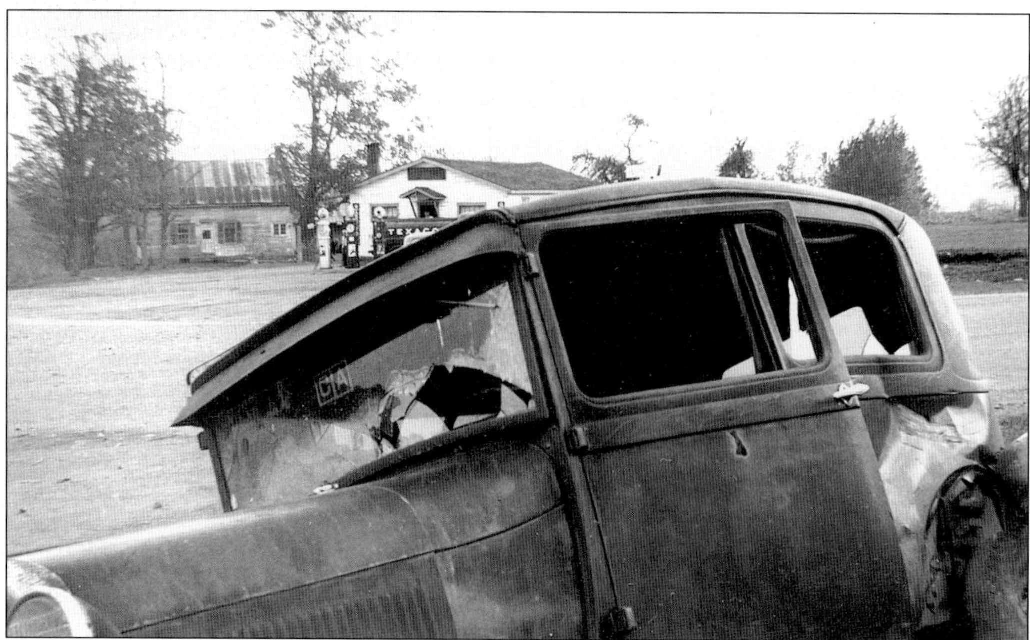

Accidents on the Adirondack Trail began with the influx of motor vehicles. Even though these cars were not able to reach a high speed, when they ran off the road, hit something, or rolled over, they did extensive damage.

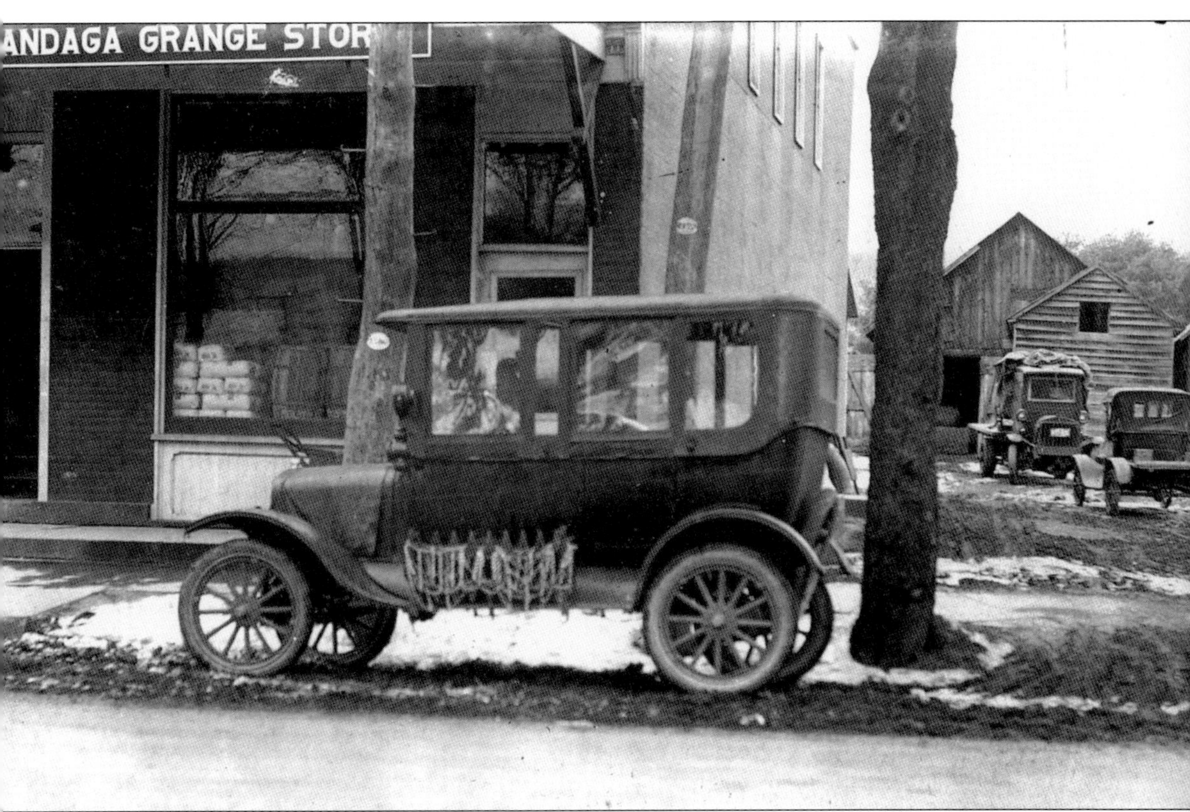

The development of the Adirondack Trail made it possible for the scattered settlers to drive their horseless carriages to and from the commercial centers to shop. General stores, banks, garages, feed stores, and drugstores became the lifeblood of the settlements. One of Henry Ford's famous Model T sedans is parked along the Adirondack Trail in Northville next to the Sacandaga Grange Store. The Grange is the nation's oldest general farm organization, founded in 1867. In 1934, cooperatives were formed to assist farmers with their needs, including grain and gasoline. In the background is a Model T pickup and a larger delivery truck, possibly a Mack, Sterling, or Autocar. When the stagecoaches stopped carrying the mail and turned the job over to one of the new trucks, the townspeople still said, "Here comes the stage" when they saw the mail arriving at the post office.

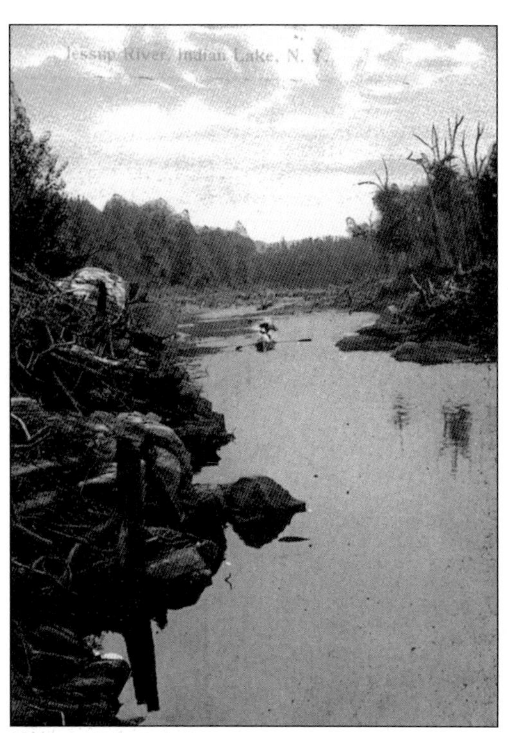

"Totten and Crossfield" appears on most of the land deeds in the southern and eastern Adirondacks. The Totten and Crossfield Purchase, one of the earliest and largest of the Adirondack purchases, took place in 1771. The truth was that Totten and Crossfield were New York shipwrights who loaned their names to the purchase. The real deal included the Jessup brothers, Edward and Ebenezer. Good friends of the English baronet Sir William Johnson, they were able to get the Crown's approval to buy Adirondack lands. In 1770, they had become Adirondack lumbermen. The Revolution took away their lands but left their name behind on Jessups River, Jessups Landing, and Jessups Falls. Jessups River, in the photograph, crosses the Adirondack Trail on its way to Indian Lake.

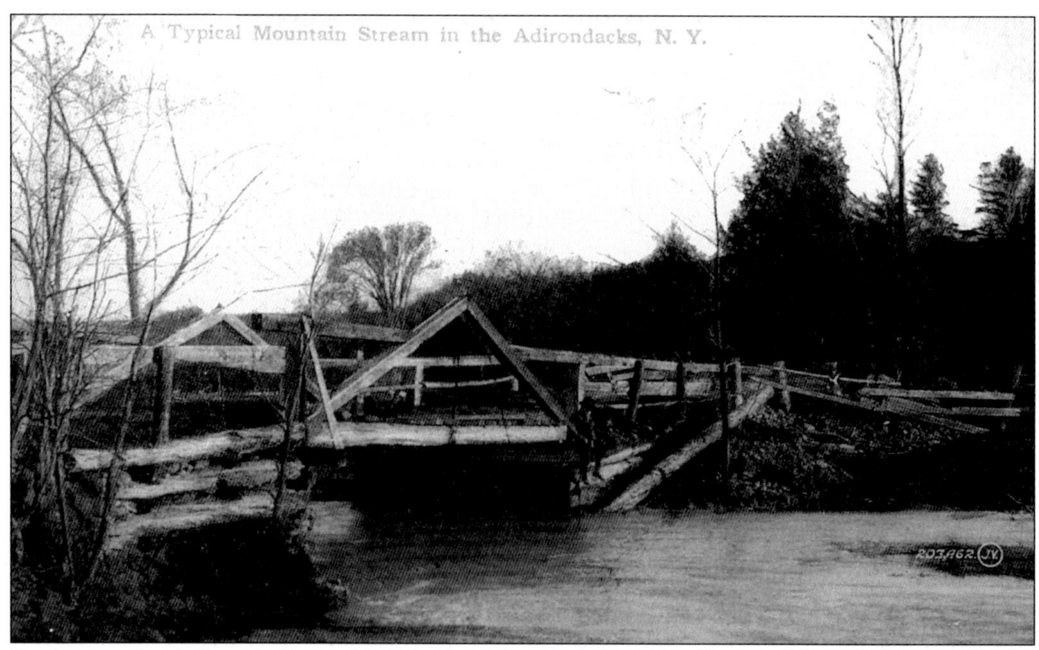

Bridges on the Adirondack Trail before the advent of the automobile were simple log structures that could hold horses and wagons. Barriers were placed along the roadside by the bridges to keep the cars on the road and away from the water.

Those who toured the Adirondacks in the first automobiles soon developed styles of clothing that were necessarily comfortable. Some of the open automobiles required heavy coats and hats. Goggles were a requirement in some vehicles. Boots were useful when a tire blew or the car got stuck in the mud. Here, Allie Handy and his mother are well dressed for a trip.

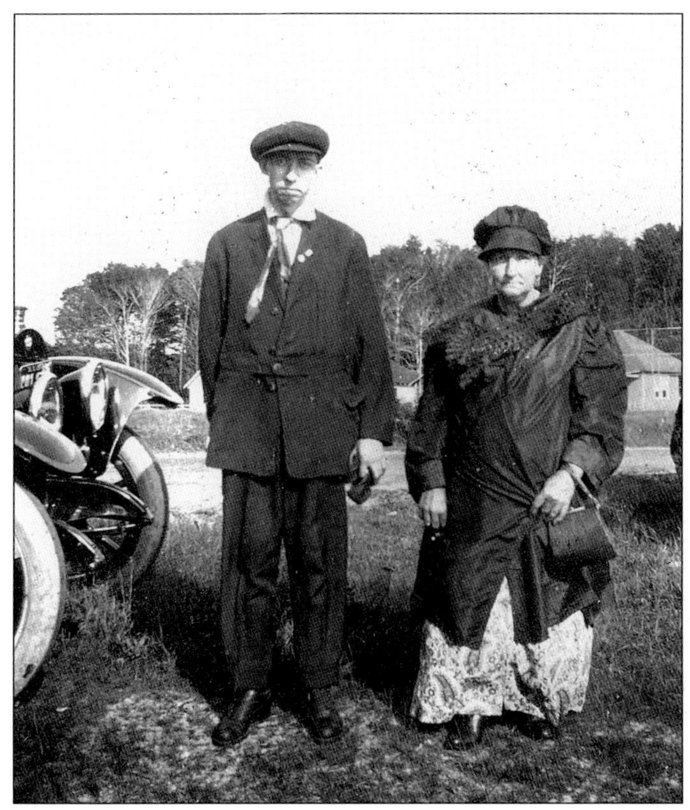

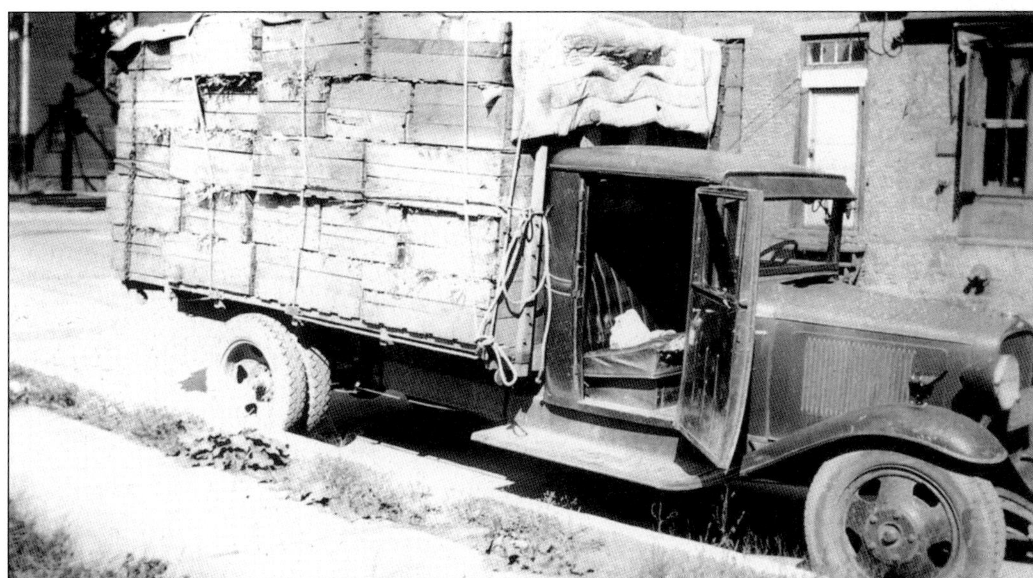

A little-known industry along the Adirondack Trail grew along with the coming of motorized vehicles. There was a day when ferns were a valuable crop from the woodlands. Crates of ferns were taken by truck to the big cities to meet the needs of florists, who used them in bouquets.

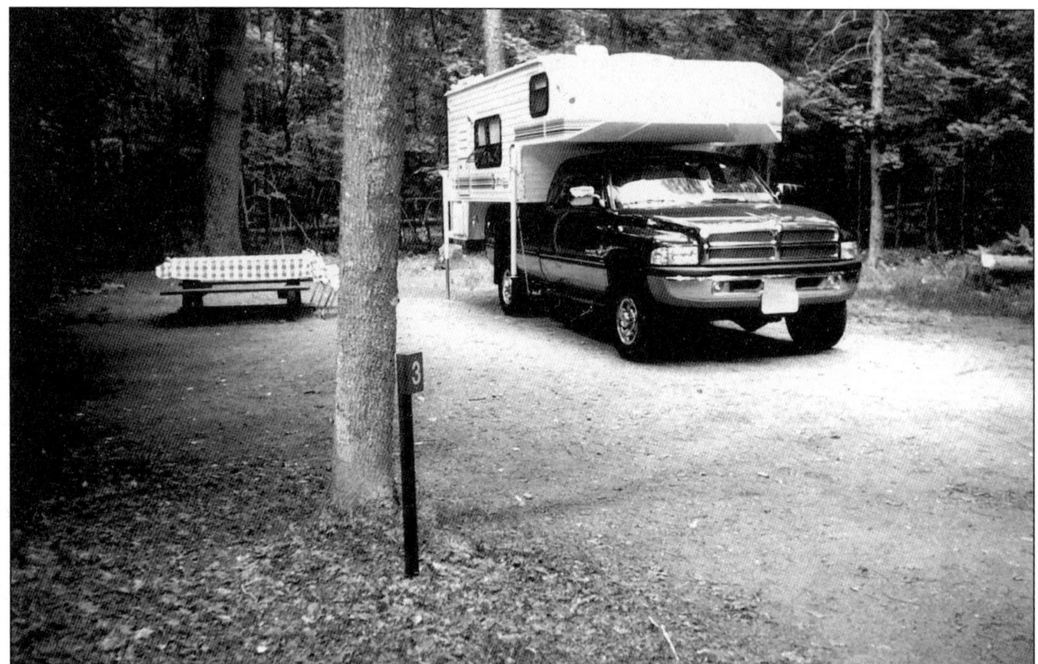

Nine state campsites are on the Adirondack Trail: Northampton, between Mayfield and Northville on the Great Sacandaga Lake; Sacandaga, three miles below Wells on the Sacandaga River; Lewey Lake beyond Speculator; Indian Lake Islands, beyond Speculator; Lake Durant, on Blue Mountain Lake; Lake Eaton, near Long Lake; Fish Creek, between Tupper Lake and Paul Smiths; Rollins Pond, between Tupper Lake and Paul Smiths; and Meacham Lake, above Paul Smiths.

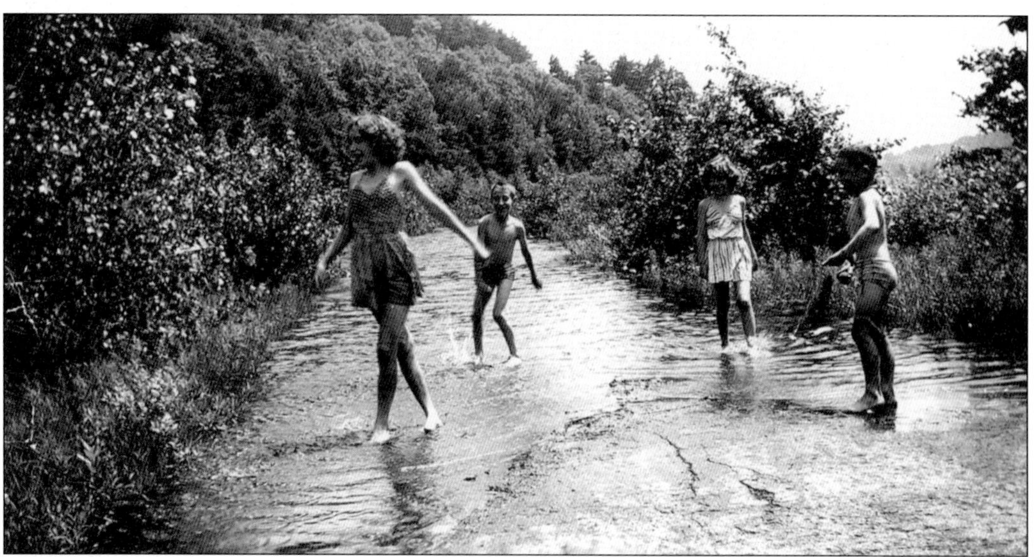

When the new roads were put in along the Adirondack Trail after the flooding for the Great Sacandaga Lake, the old roads were abandoned. The old roadbeds were great places for swimming, fishing, and washing the family car. These children have found a roadway a good place to cool off on a hot summer day in 1944.

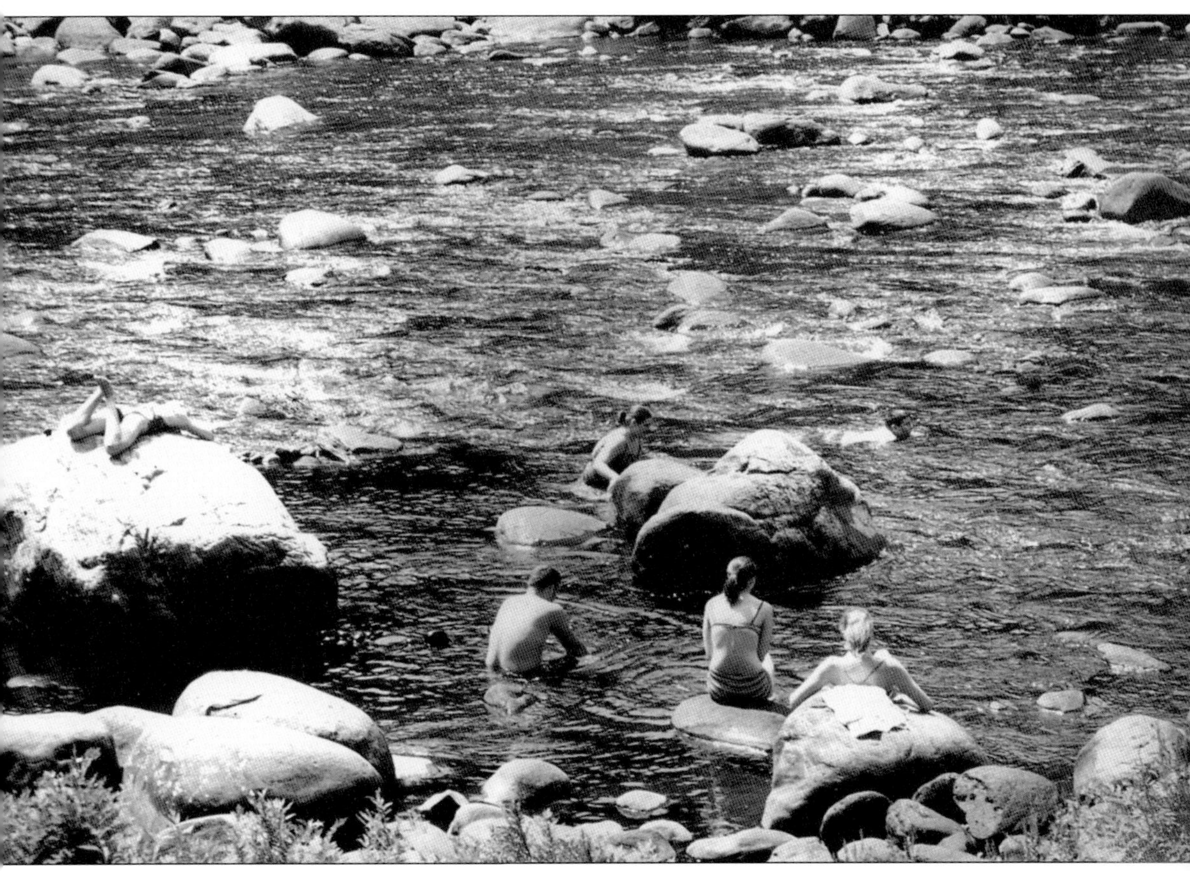

The rivers along the Adirondack Trail are popular with those who like to fish or seek relief from the summer heat. The rushing water reduces the stress of urban living, soothing aching muscles and renewing the connection between man and nature. Young and old alike enjoy soaking in the clean, pure waters. Rev. William Henry Harrison "Adirondack" Murray first told of the healing powers found in the Adirondacks' clean air and pure water in his 1869 *Adventures in the Wilderness*. He told of those who entered the mountains in a sickly condition and emerged a bundle of health. There was a time when all the waters along the Adirondack Trail were safe to drink, but with modern-day pollution, drinking the water is discouraged.

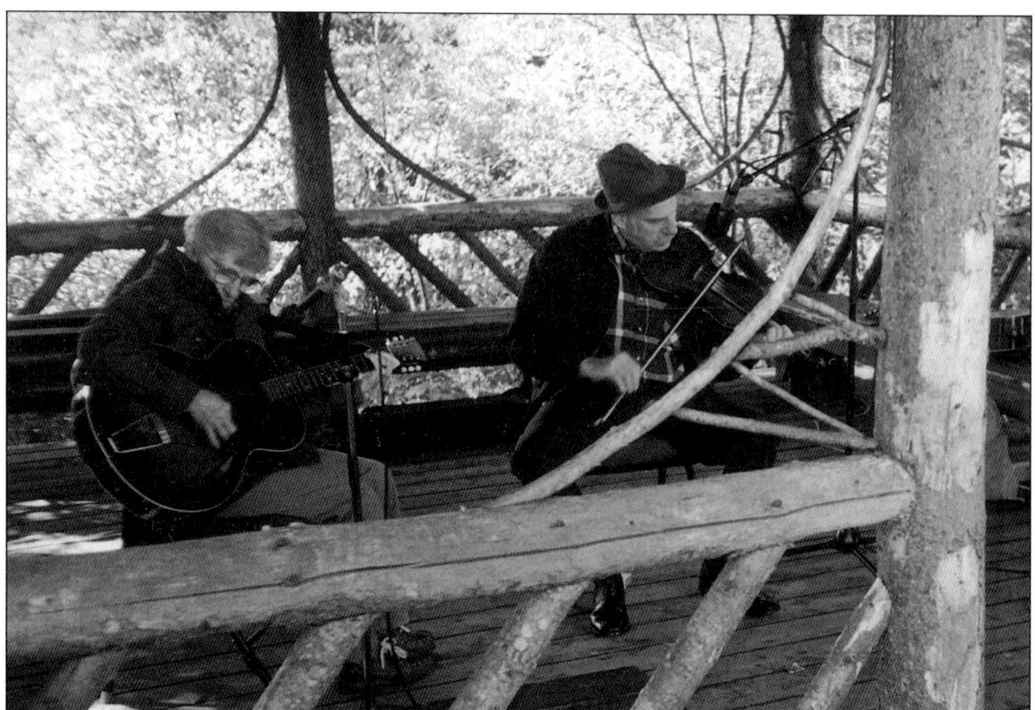

Nationally known Adirondack fiddler Vic Kibler has a vast collection of fiddle music. He knows some 400 or 500 songs and is the subject of a book of fiddle music. He is shown here playing at the Adirondack Museum summerhouse with guitarist Ermina Pincombe. Kibler was born in 1919 on the Adirondack Trail at Wells into a musical family. He picked up most of his Adirondack style from his grandfather. At one time, he played with the musical group the Adirondack Mountaineers.

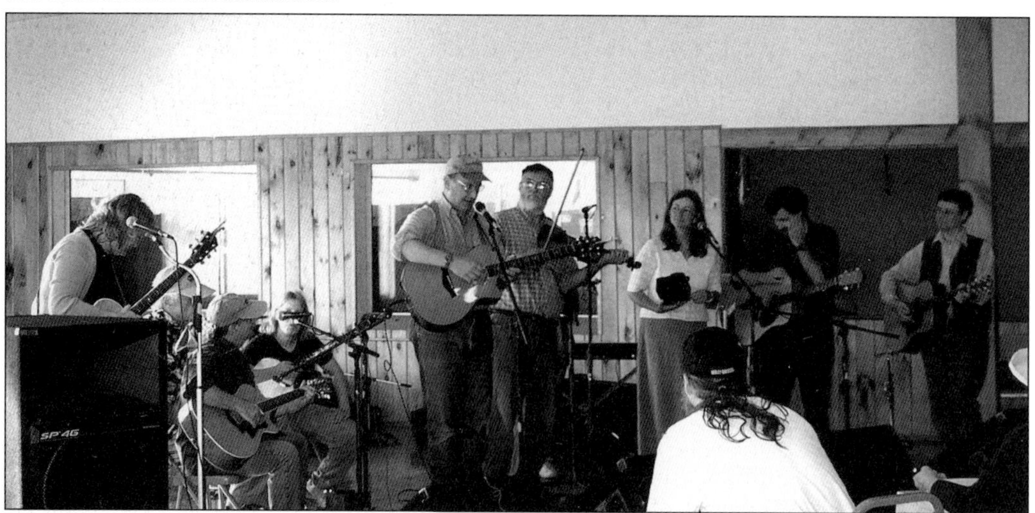

The Adirondack Trail has its own brand of music; songs of life in the lumber camps and hamlets have been written and sung since the first lumberman migrated into the mountains. Many families had members who could play fiddles and guitars. Gathering around the kitchen stove or on the stoop (porch) and jamming sometimes went on for hours. Adirondack folk singers and musicians, shown here, often perform at gatherings in the Adirondack hamlets.

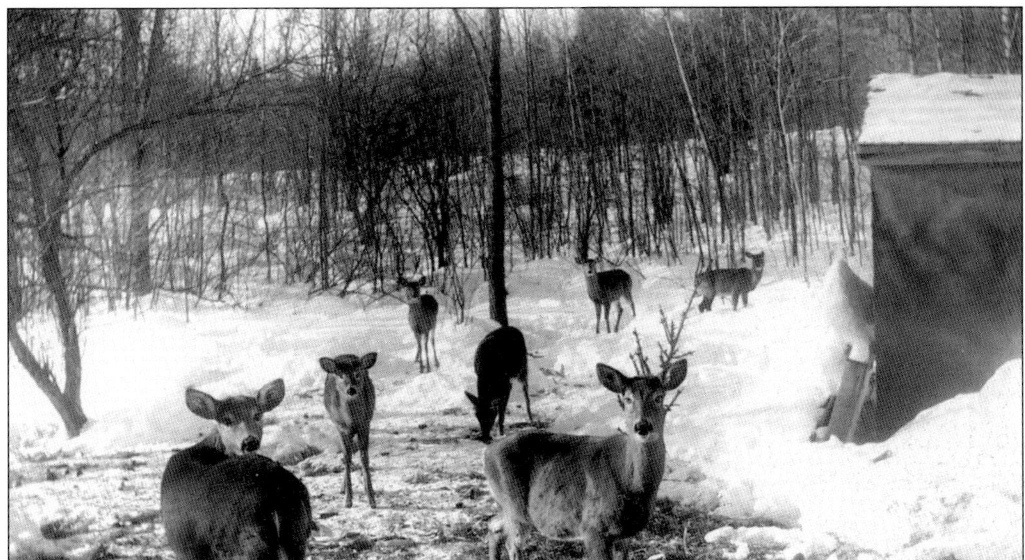

Adirondack white-tailed deer share the Adirondack Trail with tourists and residents, and often get into the roadway. Feeding the deer in the severe wintertime, especially near the highways, is discouraged in order to prevent them from crossing the road to eat. Deer yard up in the winter and often run out of good food. They have been hunted in the Adirondack wilderness since the first natives and settlers arrived. Much of the Adirondack economy has been connected to the hunting season over the years.

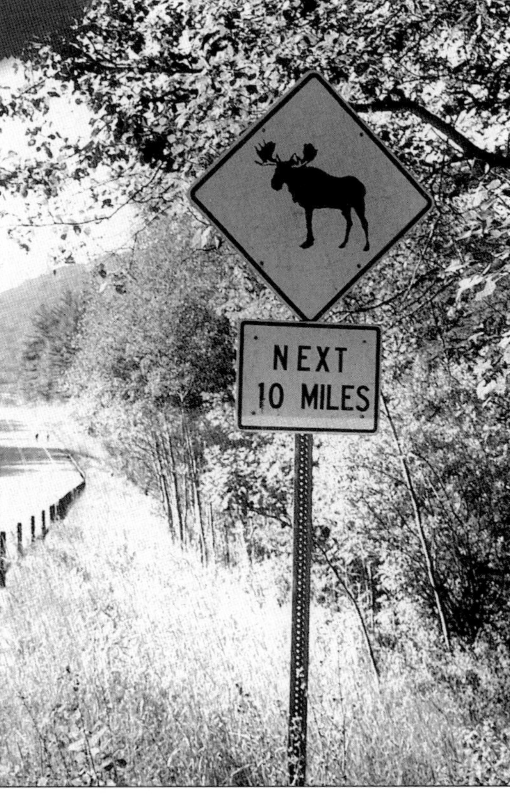

Moose have chosen to make their homes in the Adirondacks without any intervention from the New York State Conservation Department or animal groups. The population is growing, and warning signs for moose crossings have been placed along the Adirondack Trail to warn motorists about the danger of a collision with the large animals. Moose have populated the Adirondack Trail between Speculator and Indian Lake. Note the bikers in the distance riding on the bike trail along the highway.

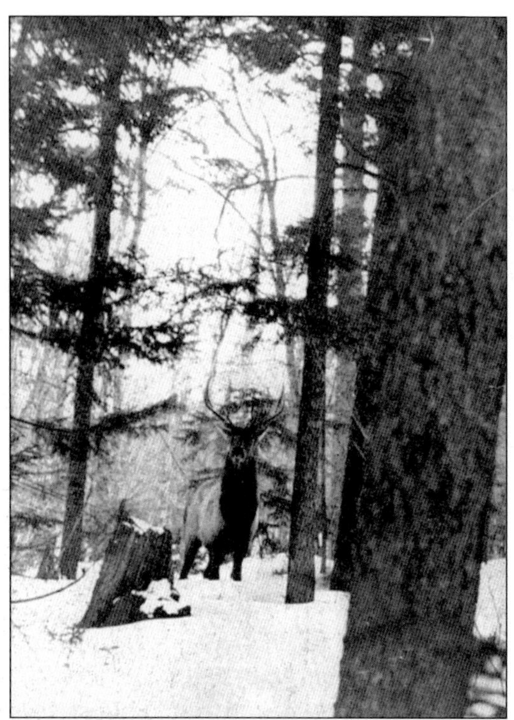

Oral history tells of herds of elk roaming the southern Adirondacks along the Adirondack Trail. A mid-1700s writer reported elk in the Adirondacks at that time. They apparently were here in the past but are gone today. The last known elk in the Adirondacks, possibly an escapee from a game farm, was shot in 1946. Several attempts were made from 1890 to 1916 to reintroduce elk in the Adirondacks, and they all failed. Maybe the elk will follow the moose and return on their own someday.

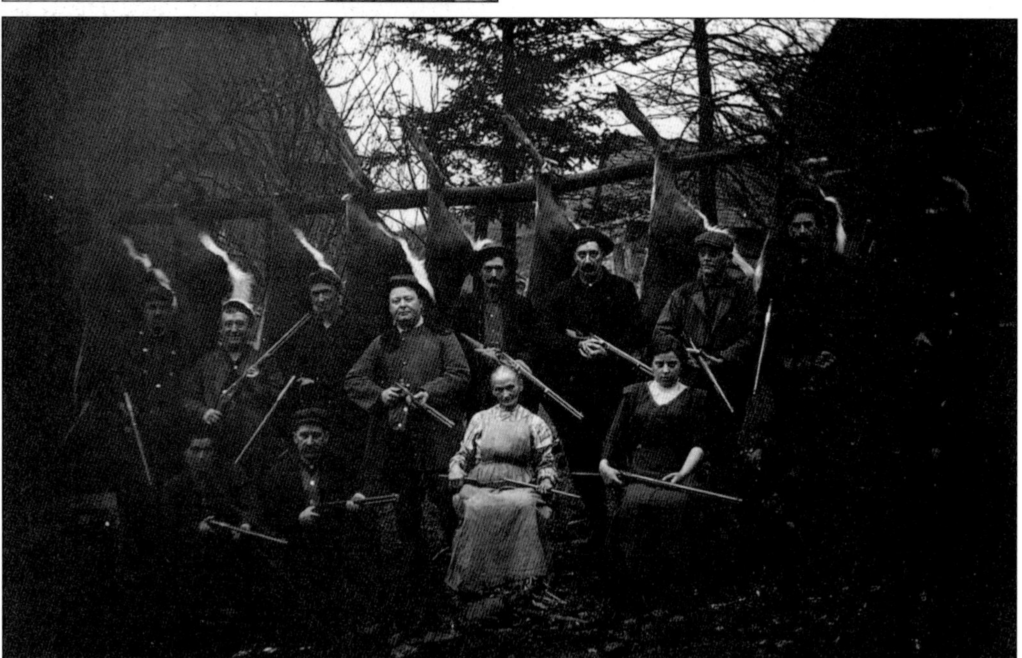

Those who lived along the Adirondack Trail in the late 1800s and early 1900s learned to live off the land. They needed the animals to feed their families in the remote mountains. It was not uncommon for the woman of the house to hunt along with the best of them. One young Adirondack girl, handy with a rifle, was known to keep the boys at bay by shooting at rocks and shattering them. Annie and Eve Whitman, shown with the hunting party, lived on West Hill above Wells.

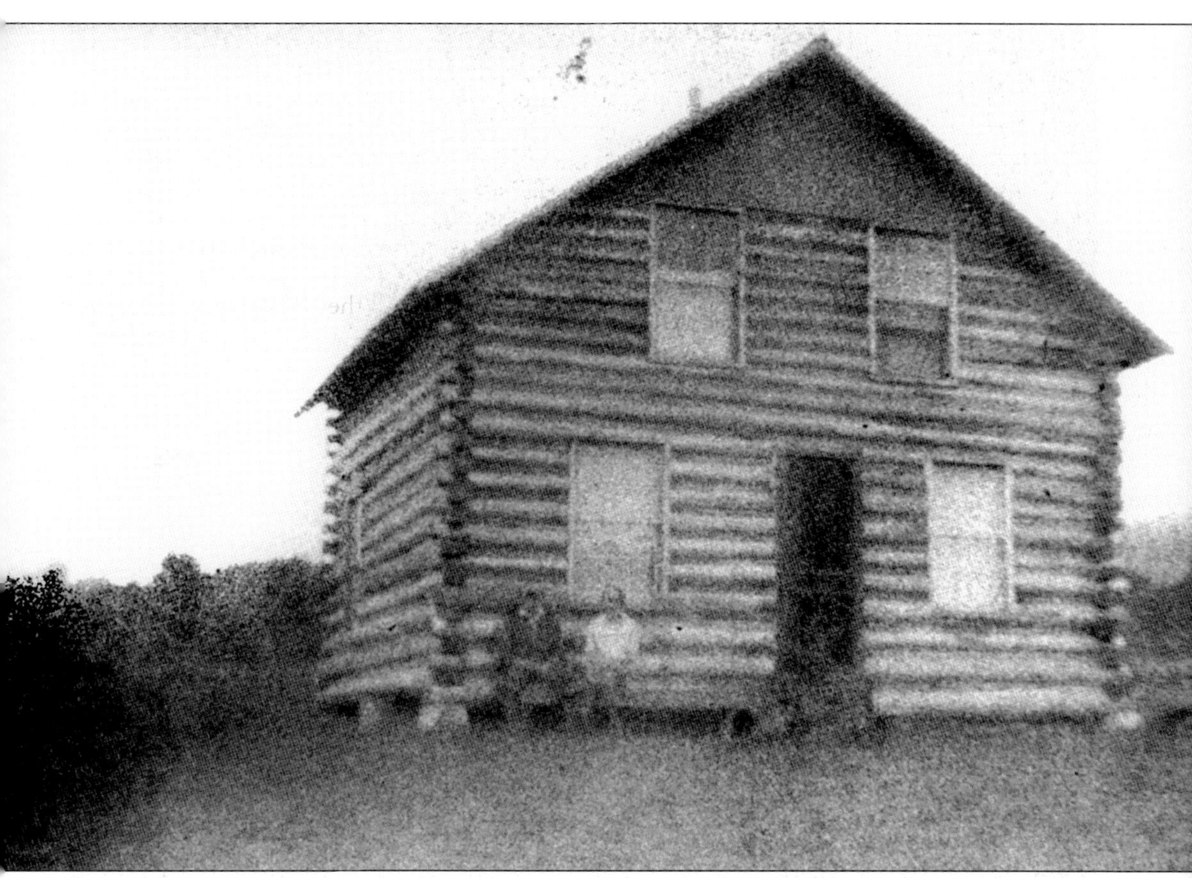

Ott and Lee Fountain were hotel keepers on the Adirondack Trail. During their career, they ran the Speculator Inn, Fountains Hotel, the Sturges House, and the Adirondack Inn at Wells. Their final hostelry was the well-known Whitehouse Resort in the hills above Wells, once operated by Ott's father. Ott knew her way in the woods and was known as "the Mighty Huntress." Ott and Lee are shown in this rare photograph in front of one of the Whitehouse hunting camps built by Lee.

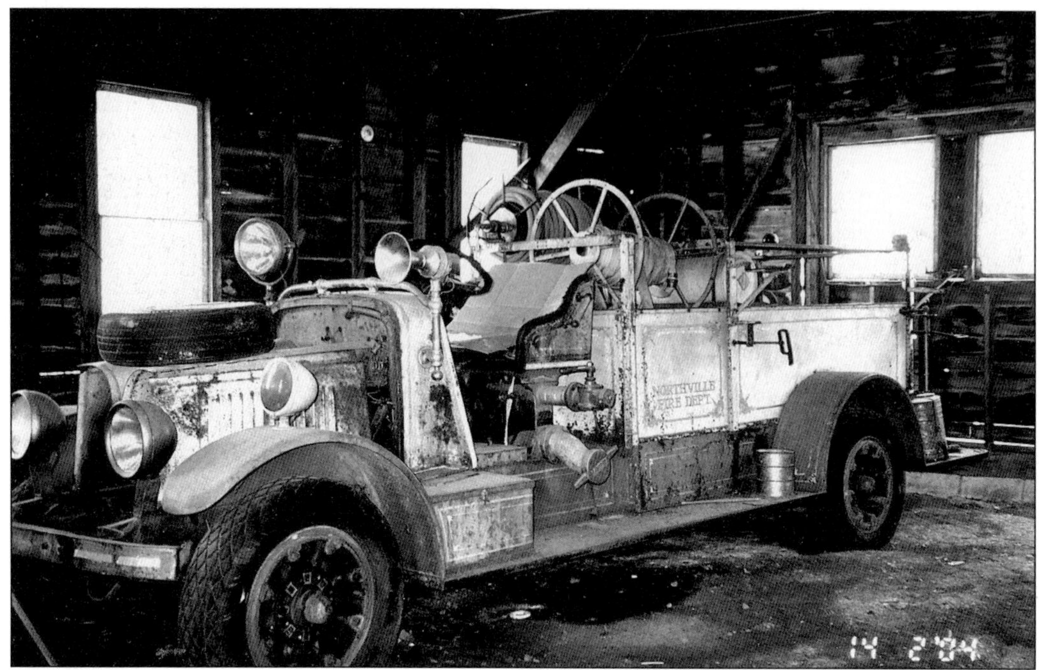

The Adirondack Trail settlements soon found that it was important to establish their own fire departments to fight one of humankind's worst enemies, fire. The history of the hamlets is a history of downtown buildings catching fire and burning up part of the town. Paul Smiths Hotel established its own fire department, and many other camp owners put in firefighting equipment. Paid and volunteer fire companies can be found in all the settlements, up and down the Adirondack Trail today. The antique fire truck shown here belonged to the Northville Fire Department and is slated for restoration.

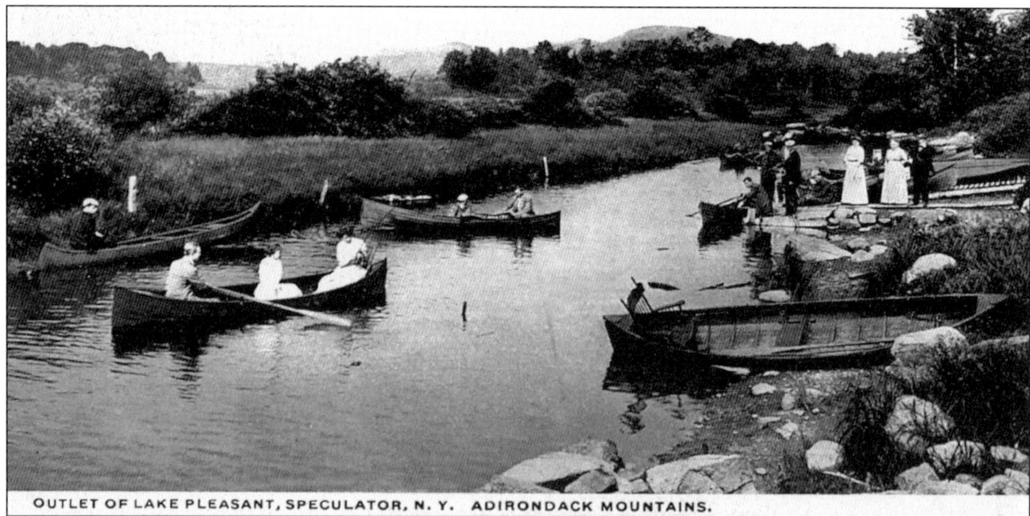

Guideboats became the boats of choice on the lakes along the Adirondack Trail. The strong boats originated in the Adirondacks and were built for use on the lakes and streams of the mountains. With a double set of oar locks and three seats, the boats could be rowed from the middle or the end. The long oars made for easy rowing with heavy loads, and a paddle could be used when going upriver or upstream. Vintage guideboats demand a high price today.

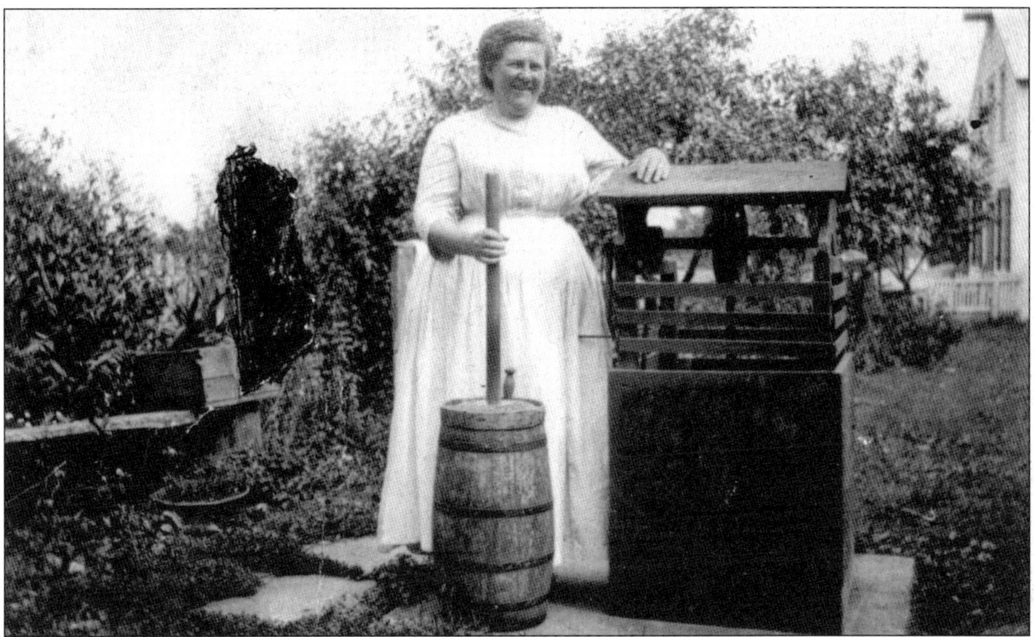

In the Adirondack lowlands, where farmers kept cows, the sale of cheese and butter became a major industry. Farm wives used hand-powered or dog-powered churns to turn the cream into butter that could be sold or bartered at the general store. Records show that the small hamlet of Wells was producing almost 18,000 pounds of butter per year from the Wells farms by 1845.

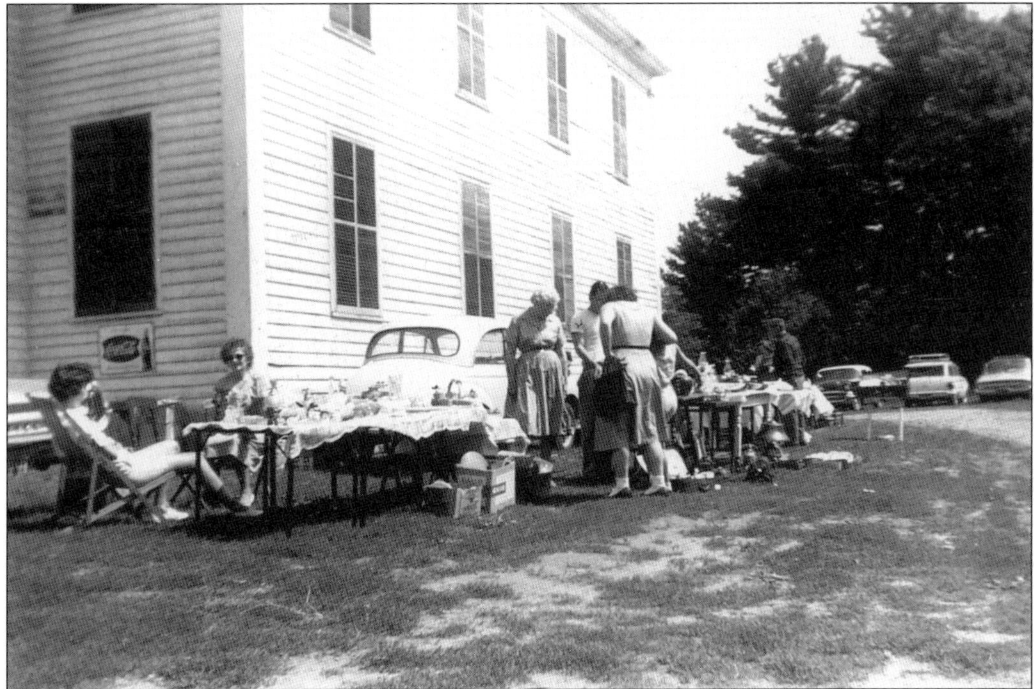

Flea markets and garage sales have become an American institution. It is not uncommon to see "garage sale" and "lawn sale" signs along the Adirondack Trail. Many of the Adirondack communities schedule annual townwide sales.

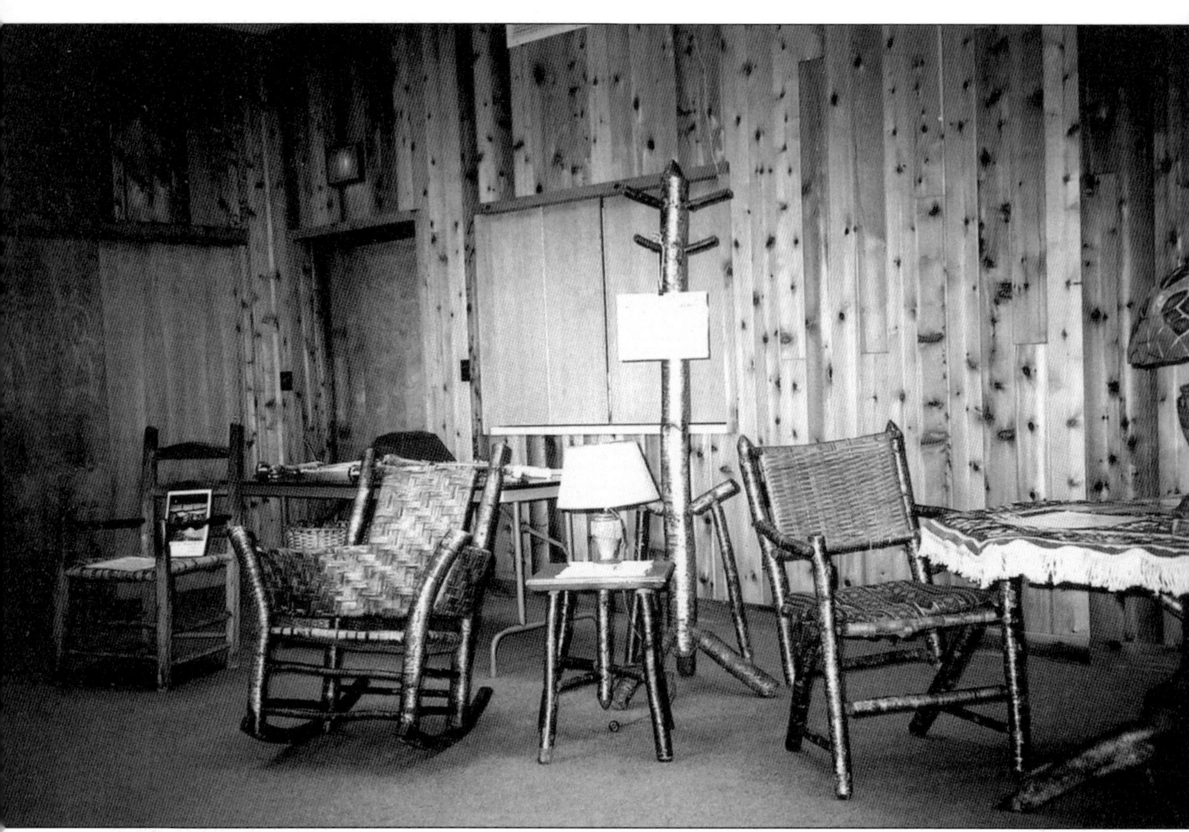

Lee Fountain, Adirondack hotel keeper, also made Adirondack birch furniture. He began making furniture *c.* 1910 behind his hotel near the four corners in Speculator and ended his years carrying on the furniture business at the Whitehouse Resort in Wells. He employed several local men for cutting splints, searching the mountainsides for the curved branches required for the rocking chairs, shaping the curved rockers, and delivering furniture to camps and homes in the Adirondacks. Shown are his giant stump table, a captain's chair, a rocking chair, a coat rack, a stand, and a special guide's chair, on the far left. At one time, he reportedly put out a catalog of his furniture. Unfortunately, much of his furniture has gone from the porches of the Adirondack camps to the dump, and his pieces are rare today. Jack Leadley of Speculator is carrying on the tradition of birch rocker making, and other high-quality Adirondack furniture is still being made by craftsmen and women along the Adirondack Trail today.

Native Americans once populated the southern portion of the Adirondack Trail and used the Adirondacks for their summer hunting and fishing grounds. They were the first to use the Adirondack Trail from the Mohawk Valley into the Adirondack Mountains. They were often seen in the 20th century, moving from settlement to settlement, making pack baskets for the residents. For several years in the mid-1900s, they sold Native American–made articles at the Pine Lake Flea Market. Today, a settlement of Native Americans has been established on Route 5.

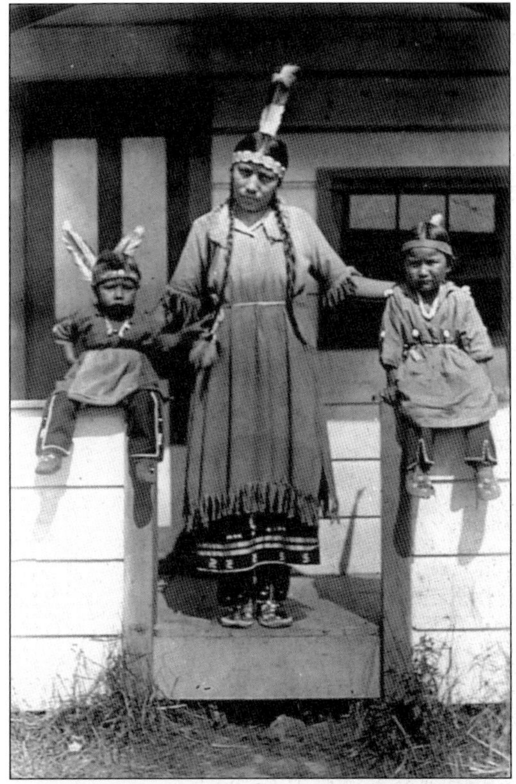

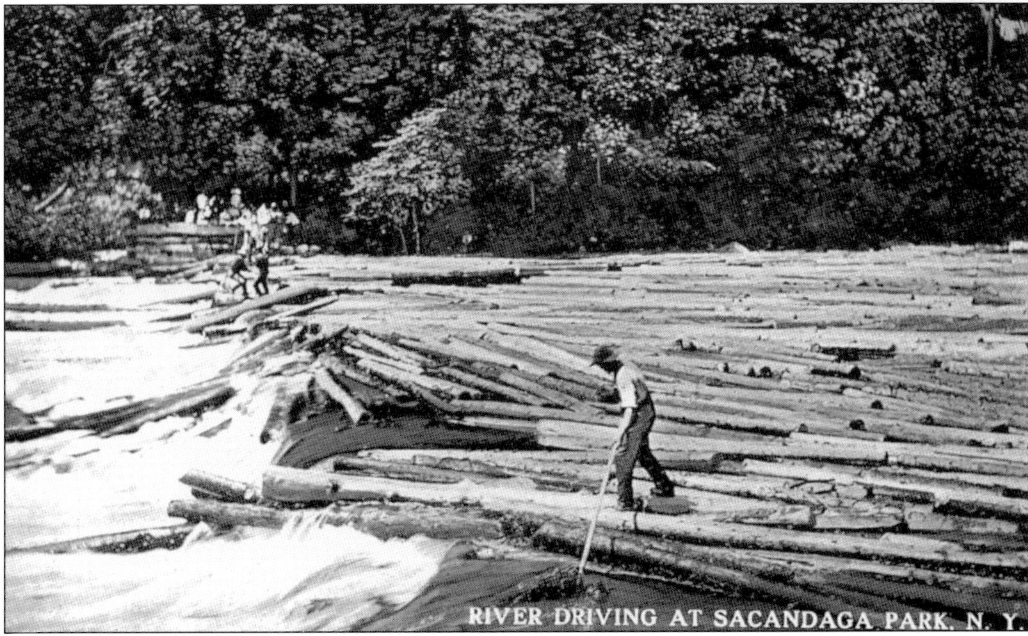

RIVER DRIVING AT SACANDAGA PARK, N. Y.

From the mid-1800s to the 1940s, logs traveled to the mills on Adirondack Trail waterways. It was the easiest, cheapest, and fastest way to transport the millions of logs to the market. River drivers risked their lives to move the logs on the fast-moving waters of springtime. They were a proud group and would do everything possible not to leave a stranded log along the riverbanks.

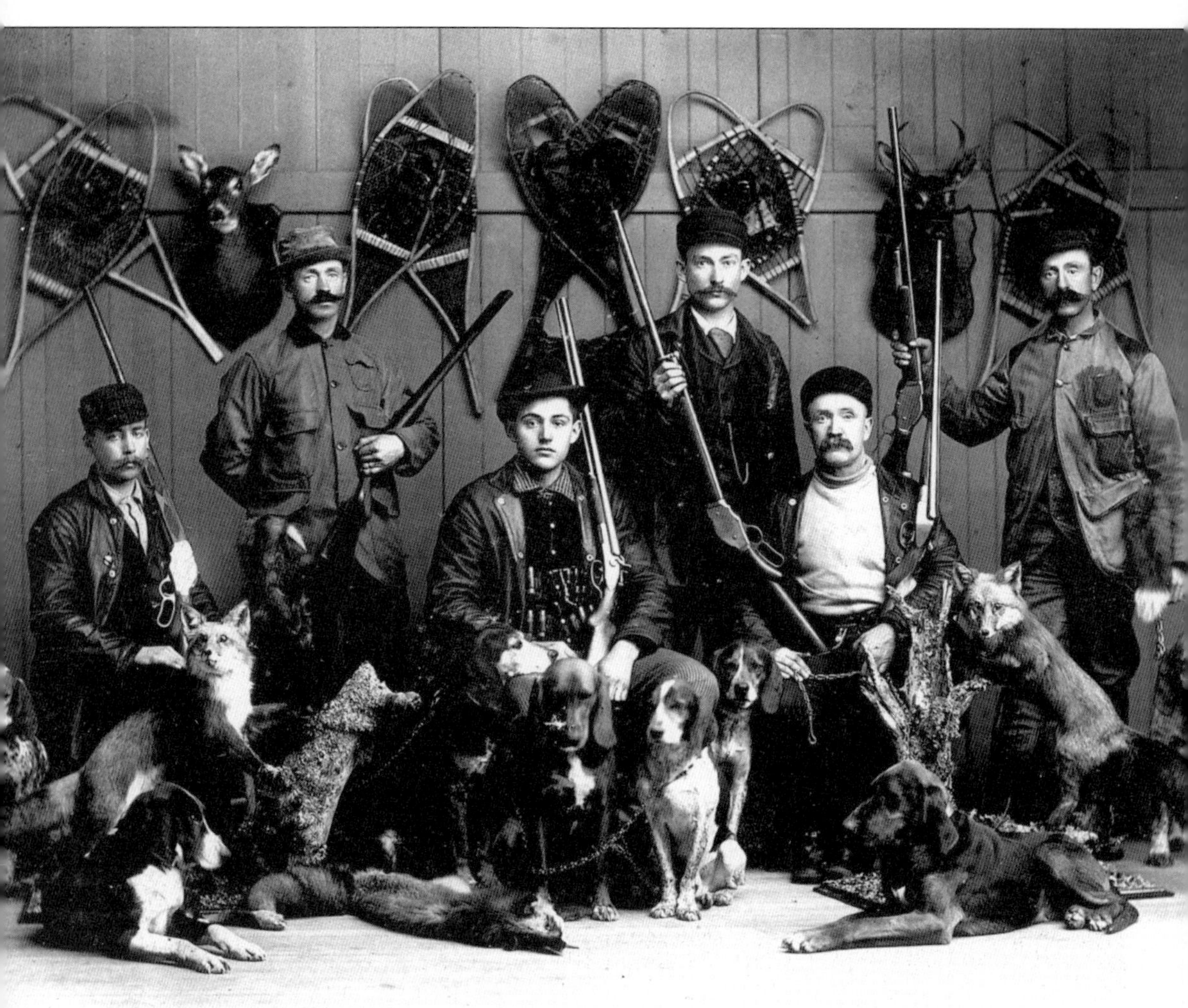

The Adirondack Trail has long served as the main route into the hunting country of the Adirondack Mountains. Hunting clubs from inside and outside Adirondack Park organized and claimed their favorite hunting territory to use, year after year. Some had their favorite guides and often would build a camp or use the guide's camp. Deer hunting is a tradition that has been passed down from father to son, along with the rules and techniques that have been learned over the years. The Gloversville Hunting Club, shown here, hunted fox and deer and made good use of hunting dogs in the day when it was legal. The snowshoes indicate that the members likely hunted year-round or hunted rabbits during the winter months.

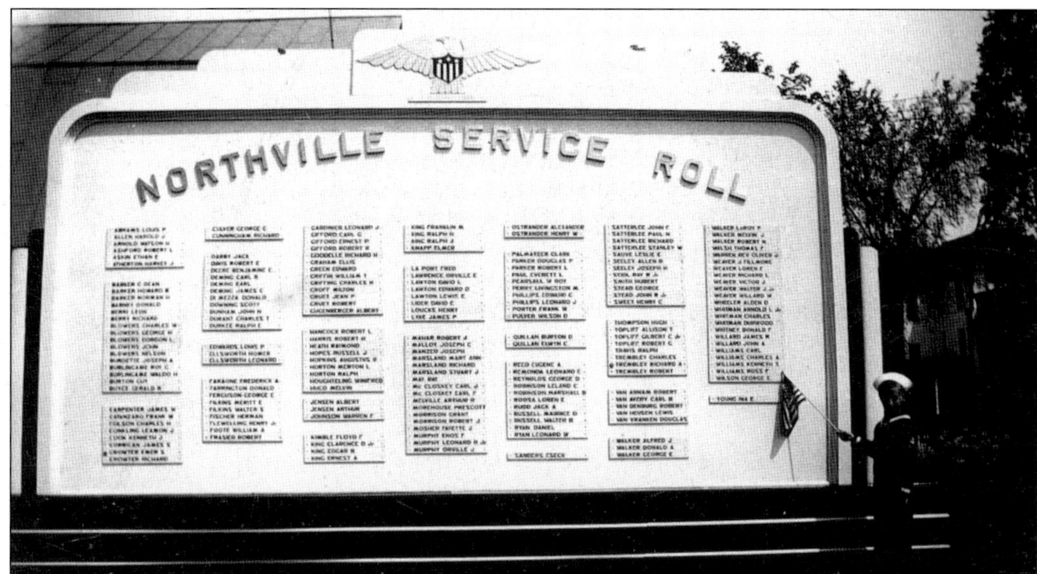

Over the years, Adirondack hamlets and towns have sent a good share of their people off to war. During World War II, communities erected honor rolls with the names of those in the service. Those who died in service had a star by their name. Adirondack youths who grew up in the mountains and spent their growing years in the out-of-doors were well prepared for the survival skills needed in the military service. Many of them were good marksmen, having grown up in hunting families. It became a matter of pride for the children of the servicemen and servicewomen to point out their parent's name on the monument in the village square. The honor rolls were taken down after the war was over.

WELLS HONOR ROLL

BABCOCK GEORGE Jr.
BAILEY JOSEPH
BERRY RICHARD
BRADT HENRY
BUYCE ROY
CLARK JAMES Jr.
COMI BENJAMIN
CURTIS LINCOLN. A.
CYMBALAK MICHAEL
DAMPIER ROBERT
DAMPIER WILLIAM
DAVIS WILLARD
DI CAPRIO LOUIS
DYE MERRILL
EARLEY CHESTER
EARLEY WILLIAM
EARLEY VINCENT
FISH TOWNSEND
FULLER GEORGE
GALLUP HAROLD
GALLUP DONALD
GALLUP NORMAN
GALLUP JOSEPH
GREYBECK CHARLES
HARRINGTON HAROLD
HOSLEY MORGAN
HOUGHTON HAROLD
KINNEY DONALD
LAWTON WILLIAM
LE VEILLE DONALD
MORRISON FRANK
MORRISON IRVING Jr.
MORRISON SANFORD
NORMAND LOUIS
PARKER FRANK
PARKER RAYMOND
PECK ROBERT Jr.
POTTER ARDEN Jr.
POTTER ARTHUR. W.
POTTER JOHN
REANDO ALEXANDER
REECE CARL
SCHUYLER CLAYTON
SCHUYLER ELLSWORTH
SCHUYLER GERALD
SHOTWELL SAMUEL
SIMONS EDWARD
STUART DELBERT
STUART EARL
STUART LLOYD
STUART MORGAN
STUART NELSON
SWEET LEONARD
WADSWORTH ROBERT
WHITMAN HARRY
YOUNG CALVIN
ZOLLER EUGENE

GOD BLESS OUR BOYS

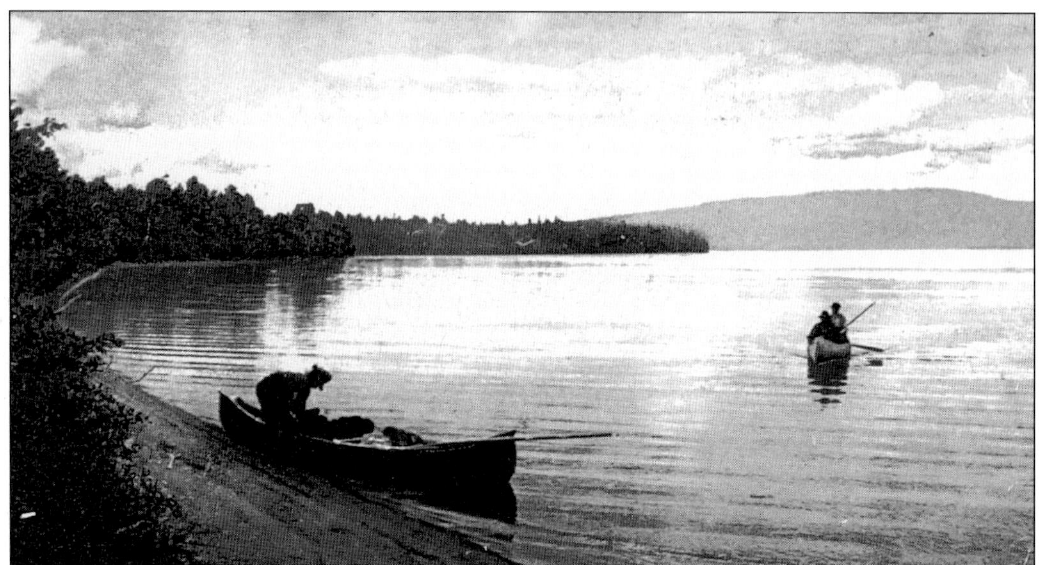

The lures of fishing brought many people up the Adirondack Trail. After a good day of fishing on a peaceful Adirondack lake, fishermen could return at sundown, free of the stress of the daily grind. Even without fishing, a day on one of the dozen lakes bordering the Adirondack Trail will do the same for those who seek it out.

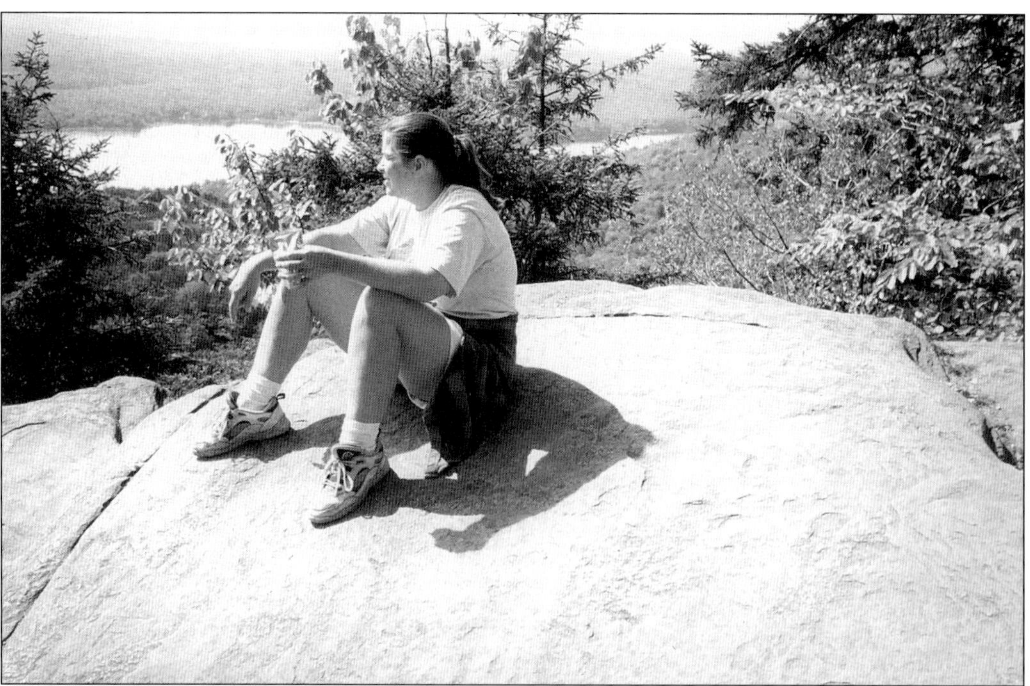

Several trailheads border the Adirondack Trail and provide hiking of all ratings. Hiking up to the fire towers or mountain ledges or to the top of a high peak provides the breathtaking view offered by the Adirondack vista. Most trails are clearly designated by colored markers on the trees, and there is no danger of getting lost if one stays on the trail. Find your way to the Adirondack Trail, and seek out your own Adirondack experience.